The Many

The Many Worlds of Circus

Edited by

Robert Sugarman

Cambridge Scholars Publishing

The Many Worlds of Circus, Edited by Robert Sugarman

This book first published 2007 by

Cambridge Scholars Publishing

15 Angerton Gardens, Newcastle, NE5 2JA, UK

British Library Cataloguing in Publication Data
A catalogue record for this book is available from the British Library

ISBN (10): 1-84718-566-5, ISBN (13): 9781847185662

TABLE OF CONTENTS

LIST OF ILLUSTRATIONS

INTRODUCTION

The elements of circus–acrobats, jugglers, trained animals, and clowns–have been with us for as long as we have records. And probably longer. In the eighteenth century, Philip Astley is reputed to have introduced the forty-two foot ring as the smallest space in which a horse could gallop, and the elements of circus acquired a defining shape. The ring was practical, but also metaphoric. It became a magic space in which things happened that were far more remarkable than what went on outside the ring. Buildings were built to enclose the rings and tents were erected to accommodate traveling rings.

As mighty industries arose in Gilded Age America, circuses followed the industrial model. Small mud shows that had traveled overland pulled by horses, expanded as they moved onto the new railroads that crisscrossed the land. The circuses added additional rings to accommodate the crowds that came to the enlarged Big Tops that were the centers of canvas cities erected in the early morning and dismantled late at night. With the change in scale, the voices of the clowns were silenced and giant spectacles became part of the performances. In the days before movies, radio, and television, circuses brought exotic performers, exotic animals, and exotic visions of the world to isolated communities.

With the rise of the media, circuses faced competition that showed more accurate visions of the world. As automobiles and then airplanes became accessible, the world itself opened up. The age of cheap labor had passed and Gilded Age circuses, like Gilded Age mansions, could no longer afford the personnel to maintain them. With the development of large entertainment venues in cities, many circuses, including the largest–Ringling Brothers and Barnum & Bailey-moved indoors. Without the need to raise tents, circuses required fewer people. With increasingly sophisticated technical equipment, indoor circuses and those in tents fought to hold their own against the media and the new amusement parks.

Out of the ferment of the counterculture in the 1970's, new[1] circuses appeared that employed a single ring to return a human scale to performance. Most replaced the random arrangement of acts with unifying themes. One of

---

[1] The term *new* circus has been used by the British circus activist Reg Bolton for programs devoted to improving the lot of young people. In the United States, the term was popularized by Ernest Albrecht to mean what is described here.

the *new* circuses, Cirque du Soleil, became the largest circus organization in the world as it developed a unique mixture of circus skills, exotic imagery, and new age music. It abandoned the ring and the use of animals. Like Big Apple and some of the other *new* circuses, it found its audience among the affluent. However, in keeping with its roots-Cirque du Soleil was founded by street performers-approximately one per cent of its income has been devoted to social circus programs that work with at-risk young people around the world. However, the day when entire communities closed down to welcome the circus is long past.

Whatever its permutations, circus has engaged the imagination of artists in many media. Alexander Calder's fascination with the Schoenhut Humpty Dumpty circus figures he knew as a boy led him to develop his own model circus and mobile sculptures that had the balance of circus performers. Toulouse-Lautrec and Degas found inspiration in the circuses of the belle epoque. American painters of the Ashcan School were fascinated by the physicality, color and exuberance of the circus. Motion pictures have used circus as an exotic milieu recalling the days when such exoticism was the basis of live circus' appeal. Charles Dickens, Mark Twain, and other authors have been fascinated by the circus, but in recent years most circus themed books have focused on nostalgic, rather than reportorial, images of the circus.

Since 1997, the Circus and Circus Culture Area of the Popular Culture Association has explored many aspects of circus, its impact on the arts, and its relationship to its social context. It has sought to define the continuing appeal of circus and explore its significance. This volume contains papers presented at the annual conferences of the Popular Culture Association.

Robert Sugarman, Chair
Circus and Circus Culture Panel

Bibliography

Albrecht, Ernest. *The New American Circus.* Gainesville, Florida: University Press of Florida, 1995

Bolton, Reg. *New Circus.* London: Calouste Gulbenkian Foundaton, 1987.

Part I

Spectacles

CHAPTER ONE

IMRE KIRALFY MEETS BARNUM & BAILEY – AND THE CIRCUS SPEC IS NEVER THE SAME AGAIN

MICHAEL H. MEANS

Of all the varieties of circus acts and performances, the Grand Entrance Spectacle—the spec—has probably received the least attention from circus historians. This lack is especially puzzling when one considers how important it is to circus proprietors and, clearly, to circus audiences. As Fred D. Pfening, Jr. says at the beginning of his major pair of articles on the subject, "The Spectacle as a pantomime, pageant, tournament or grand entry is as old as the circus in America;…the grand entry presented at the beginning of or during a circus performance is the most glamorous, eye-filling and impressive feature of the program."[1] In forty-some words, the doyen of American circus historians has captured the variety and significance of the circus spectacle in American circus history. He continues, "From the time of Rickett's Circus in 1793, which is credited with being the first circus in America, all circuses have included in their performances a grand entry, a pantomime, a tournament, or some kind of a spectacular feature and the abbreviation 'Spec' has come to be the common name for any pageant or spectacle presented in connection with a circus performance."[2] That these specs commonly had a thematic, often narrative, element is clear from the examples he cites from early- to mid-nineteenth century: "Harlen's Pantomime, or The Ship Wreck," "La Belle Dorothea or Maternal Affection," "Jack and the Giant Killer," "George Washington or Old Put and Anthony Wayne," "Cinderella," "Mother Goose and her Golden Egg,"

---

[1] Pfening, "Spec-ology of the Circus: Part One," 4.
[2] Ibid.

"Scipio's Triumphal Return to Rome," "The Field of the Cloth of Gold," "Blue Beard," and "Humpty Dumpty."[3]

It should come as no surprise then that P. T. Barnum, America's great pioneer of showmanship, bunkum, and public relations, should inevitably be on the quest for the biggest and best for his late-in-life triumph, The Barnum & Bailey Circus, The Greatest Show on Earth. In 1889 he found what he sought in Imre Kiralfy and Kiralfy's stage spectacle, *Nero; or, The Destruction of Rome*. It was being performed on Long Island in a specially constructed open air theater having a proscenium opening of 480 feet.[4] As Kiralfy tells it, "Although [Barnum] was then an old man, I suppose he thought I was beginning to invade his own particular domain."[5] Barnum "offered [him] a great sum of money" to produce *Nero* as part of the Barnum & Bailey Circus in London where it was playing a winter engagement at Olympia Hall.[6] It was such a great success there, in 1889, that Barnum quickly contracted for it as the spec for the circus's 1890 season in the United States. And thus the circus spec took a quantum leap forward.

A good way to begin to understand what Kiralfy did is to cite some facts and figures. For the 1890 tent show, there were seats on one side and the two ends of a six-pole tent, with the *Nero* stage and scenery taking up the entire fourth side, about 450 feet.[7] There were four complete changes of scenery for that long wall.[8] A musical score which included songs and hymns, all in Italian, was composed by Angelo Venanzi of Milan[9] and sung by three principles and a chorus of twenty-four women and thirty men.[10] This music was also danced by a corps de ballet of one hundred twenty-eight female and male dancers.[11] But the most striking fact to me is that the performance lasted ninety minutes, one-half of the entire show, whereas earlier specs we know about tended to be ten or twenty minutes long. In other words, *Nero* was important enough to replace over an hour's worth of clowns, acrobats, horses and elephants, and all the other wonders that sell tickets to parents and kids. The most striking figure is that

---

[3] Ibid. Pfening states that "[o]ver forty circuses from 1800 to 1875 presenting a spectacle have been identified." One can reasonably assume that newspaper and other records from that era are incomplete.

[4] Imre Kiralfy, "My Reminiscences," 2.

[5] Ibid, 4.

[6] Ibid.

[7] *New York Clipper*, 19 April 1890, 85.

[8] Conover, Give 'Em a John Robinson," 29.

[9] [Program] *Nero; or, The Destruction of Rome* 29-30. The numbers varied slightly in 1891.

[10] *The Barnum & Bailey Official Route Book, Season of 1890, 29.*

[11] Program, 30-32.

that year the show grossed $1,225,000, the first time it had made that kind of money since its last tour with Jumbo, in 1884.[12]

What Imre Kiralfy was best known for was his ability to fill a stage with several hundred actors all in motion, with a precision that would have impressed Busby Berkeley, forming elaborate patterns of action that moved the story along briskly. A brief summary of the three Tableaux into which *Nero* is divided will give some suggestion of what that stage must have been like.

The First Tableau, "Outside the Gates of Ancient Rome," opens with hundreds of Romans going about their business until Nero and a few cronies in disguise, steal a poor man's donkey, play some pranks on each other, and then beat their victim just for fun. The passersby instantly coalesce into an outraged crowd. When Nero throws aside his disguise, the crowd immediately falls to its knees in fear. As Nero leaves, the crowd again becomes unruly and Nero's Guards attack them, but are beaten back. By this time a full-scale riot erupts and hundreds of soldiers enter from all directions to route and disperse the mob, all on stage.[13] The Second Tableau, "An Imperial Fete Day in Rome," opens with an equally choreographed mob scene: laborers putting finishing touches on decorations, crowds of all classes strolling, ladies in litters and chariots, "a vivid, animated, realistic view of street life in ancient Rome." All of this serves as context for "NERO'S TRIUMPHAL PROCESSION," consisting of "Gallic Embassy and Suite; Procession of Priests, Vestals, Augurs, and Attendants; Egyptian Embassy and Suite; Agrippina, the Emperor's Mother and her magnificent cortege of Ladies and Household Attendants; Persian Princes and Suite; Acte, the Emperor's Favorite, and her Attendants, distinguished by the most luxurious evidences of Imperial partiality." All the while, the chorus is singing a hymn to Nero who thereupon appears in his triumphal car accompanied by his own mini-procession of a hundred or so dignitaries. The whole affair is, of course, to show off a dozen or so elegant chariots, three or four hundred gorgeous costumes, and every show horse, camel, and elephant carried by the circus. As the procession moves on and the crowd begins dispersing, another mob rushes in, in bloodthirsty pursuit of Thirza, a Christian maiden. Thirza is saved, mostly because of Nero's instant lust for her. The Tableau closes with crowds of Christians fleeing "savage pursuers" and begging Nero for protection. He refuses and the Tableau ends.

The Third Tableau, in two parts, begins with Circus Games, given by the Emperor to impress Thirza and placate the crowd. There are horse and chariot races, "heroic and classic sports," and finally the "Grand Gladiatorial Combat." All of these activities require, of course, new costumes and traps, and they fill

---

[12] Conover, 29.

[13] Program, 1890. This and ensuing descriptions of *Nero* are based on this program.

up the three rings and hippodrome track of the performance area. After some plot developments, the scene continues with a variety of horse races and other competitions reminiscent of the nature of the modern circus in its eighteenth- and early nineteenth-century rebirth.

The second half of the Tableau opens with an imperial banquet replete with carousing, music, and, needless to say, pagan depravity—augmented by the ballet dancers. But this implicitly lewd display very quickly leads into the burning of Rome, the approach of Galba and his victorious army, persecutions of the Christians whom Nero accused of burning Rome, and Nero's suicide, all with casts of hundreds. As he is dying, Nero looks up to see Galba's triumphal entry and "THE GLORIOUS APOTHEOSIS, CELESTIAL VISION OF THE DAWN OF CHRISTIANITY." In other words, what he sees is the Grand Entrance Procession of the Barnum & Bailey Circus, which is the excuse for being of the whole spec.

Needless to say, this procession means all of the previous performers—right down to potato peelers and stable mockers-out—will be in new costumes. All the horses, elephants, camels, and caged cats will parade. New chariots and cars will swell the procession. And new music will give the audience an unforgettable mood to carry them home.

As I indicated earlier, the cast expense of this spec and all the problems and effort of setting up and taking down, often for one-night stands, paid off handsomely for Barnum & Bailey both in profit and pelf. It should come as no surprise that James A. Bailey early on hired Kiralfy for the 1891 spec.[14] A comparison of the 1890 and 1891 Route books shows changes in the spec, but nearly all were minor tinkering. The size of the chorus and ballet changed slightly, but were still larger than those of any circuses before and few, if any, afterwards. On tour in 1890 the spec closed the afternoon production but opened the evening because of the amount of time needed for set up and take down, but in 1891 it routinely closed each performance.[15] Management's approach to the 1891 spec quite clearly was the time-honored principle "if it ain't broke, don't fix it."

For the 1892, and as it turned out 1893, seasons, Imre Kiralfy had anticipated Bailey. As early as 1890, Kiralfy had begun preparing a spec (or at least a spectacular stage presentation) for the four hundredth anniversary of Columbus's "discovery" of America.[16] He engaged Anatole Venanzi to begin

---

[14] P. T. Barnum was in failing health in 1890 and died on April 7, 1891. See A. H. Saxon. 326-27. For reactions of circus personnel, see *The Barnum & Bailey Official Route Book, Season of 189*, 45.

[15] Pfening, 7.

[16] Barbara Barker (1994), "Imre Kiralfy's Patriotic Spectacles: 'Columbus and the Discovery of Amerca' (1892-1893 and 'America' (1893), 153. For an early draft, see

work on a score for *Columbus and the Discovery of America*. The international (i.e., Western) significance of the occasion prompted him to also seek *Columbus* commissions in Chicago, New York, Paris, and Madrid. As it turned out, only in Chicago was Kiralfy able to mount a dramatic tribute as part of the 1893 Columbian Exposition. It was called *America*, in five acts and a prologue, and was a version of the *Columbus* spec that toured with Barnum & Bailey in the 1892 and 1893 seasons.[17]

For Barnum & Bailey, Kiralfy treats the discovery of America in five scenes. As with *Nero*, each fills up a huge stage—again, one long side of the circus tent—with hundreds of characters in striking costumes, all in motion, accompanied most of the time by music, song, and dance.

The first scene leads up to the meeting of Columbus with Ferdinand and Isabella by way of the defeat of the Moorish king Boabdil by Ferdinand's Christian forces. Boabdil's court depicts Islam as depraved as was the paganism of Nero. The scene opens at midnight with the cries of the starving people competing with courtly music: "female slaves begin the slow, sensuous movements of oriental dances, while songs by female slaves are heard accompanied by the wild, weird, mysterious music...and the scene gradually becomes one of splendor."[18] When Boabdil promises to lift the siege, all the able-bodied men rush off with him to fight the Spaniards. The stage is left to the old and infirm, and of course, the continued singing of the female slaves. But the music is quickly drowned out by the cries of the defeated Moorish soldiers as they rush back into the city. As Boabdil and his family leave, they meet Ferdinand and Isabella who treat them magnanimously. This ends the long reign of Moorish kings in Spain. Scene One ends with Columbus emerging from the crowds to entreat Ferdinand to support his project and Isabella's famous cry to underwrite the cost herself. All join in glad songs over the end of the war.

Scene Two shows the port of Palos with Columbus' three ships in the bay. As usual, the scene takes place among large crowds. The only real action is the

---

Imre Kiralfy. "Columbus and the Discovery of America, A Grand, Operatic, and Ballet Spectacle. Copyright 1890. Typescript. Library of Congress; The American Variety Stage: Vaudeville and Popular Entertainment, 1870-1920. The 1892 *Columbus* program for Barnum & Bailey appears to be a tighter, better focused show.

[17] Gregory, *The Spectacle Plays and Exhibitions of ImreKiralfy, 1887-1914*, 1988, 18082. The Chicago *America* was also enormously successful artistically and financially.

[18] [Program] *Columbus and the Discovery of America, For the First Time Now Produced in Connection with the Barnum & Bailey Greatest Show on Earth.* (Buffalo, NY: Courier Co., Show Printers, 1892), [12]. Again, my description of the spec is from this source.

blessing of Columbus and his crew, all of whom get into boats and are rowed out to their ships. Because this scene, like the rest of the spec, was played in a different town almost every day from March to October, its mechanics had to be simple and portable; because it was by Barnum & Bailey, it had to be breathtaking.

Scene Three depicts the ships at sea with sails flapping and hulls rolling and pitching in a storm, and Columbus sighting land.   In the next scene, the Spaniards land and are met with "wonder and awe.' The sailors give the natives "beads, bells, and trinkets" and in exchange are given food and gold. The scene closes with Columbus and his followers kneeling and "A VISION OF PROGRESS AND CIVILIZATION appears before [their] ecstatic eyes."[19] The fifth and last scene is, essentially, the Grand Entrance, here in the form of Columbus's triumphal entry into Barcelona.   Columbus, at the end of the procession, stops before the throne and presents the king and queen with Indians, ornaments, and gold. To the music of chorus and cathedral organ the city is brilliantly illuminated, and the scene becomes a "Grand Finale of Joy."

Given the differences of plot and setting, there are important similarities between the two specs. I have tried to point some of them up in my summaries. Most of them can unsurprisingly be categorized as spectacle. Both specs had, in nearly all scenes, literally hundreds of performers, all elaborately costumed and all busily going about their business in thoroughly choreographed patterns that never interfered with the principal action of the scene. Kiralfy and Bailey set a very high standard of verisimilitude: riots looked like riots, and panic like panic. Rome burned (offstage except for its flickering light) and caravels sailed the stage seas. The number of costume changes must have been staggering in order to turn a chorus of sixty singers into three hundred, seventy to a hundred dancers into another three hundred, and four or five hundred performers into the twelve hundred advertised. The sheer audacity is breathtaking.

The two specs are also alike in their moral purpose. In both, Christians were pitted against non-Christians. Nero and Boabdil presided over corrupt, self-indulgent courts swaying to sensual music and dancing girls.   Christian rulers were, of course, courageous, manly, and victorious; even the dancing girls cleaned up their act.[20] A modern audience would find the pagan sensuality mostly symbolic and merely hinted at, but an 1890's audience would have no difficulty taking the hint. Similarly, Columbus's treatment of the "Indians" he and his crew encountered is just as triumphalist as the Christianity in both specs. After all, the 1890's was the age of westward expansion and the Columbus spec

---

[19] Programs, 20-21.
[20] So did Kiralfy. For "Columbus" he "lengthened the ballet girls' skirts and added drapery on bosoms" so he could claim that his performances were "entirely free from coarseness and devoid of the faintest suggestion of vulgarity." Barker, 153.

and the Wild West show both saw native Americans as "inferior" and a "problem." The soul-searching that characterized much of the observance of the Columbus five-hundredth anniversary in 1992 was simply non-existent for the four-hundredth. Both specs mirrored the combination of militant Christianity and manifest destiny which drove the capitalist expansion of the late eighteen hundreds.

But one or two specs do not a summer make, at least not in the good old days. While no circus proprieters that I know of attempted specs that took up half the performance, the major and successful proprietors worked hard to create exciting and dramatic specs that pulled audiences into the big top to be awed by historical pageantry or fairy tales brought to life. The Ringling Brothers' specs of the early twentieth century almost always lasted thirty minutes, were based on an original book and music score, and typically carried a corps of forty-eight dancing girls and a large circus band. Scenery and costumes were lavish, and every cook and stake-pounder swelled the progress of the Grand Entrance Procession itself. The claims of three hundred dancers and a cast of a thousand at least *looked* believable.

Imre Kiralfy's specs could not be duplicated and, indeed, should not have been in the twentieth and twenty-first centuries. But the artistic and fiscal triumphs of *Nero* and *Columbus* challenged the movers and shakers of the circus world to incorporate elaborately theatrical and explicitly uplifting entertainments into the circus performance. The spec had now become a necessary, and major, ingredient—right along with the elephants, clowns aerialists, and horses—of the circus experience.

Bibliography

Barker, Barbara. "Imre Kiralfy's Patriotic Spectacles: 'Columbus, and the Discovery of   America' (1892-1893) and 'America' (1893)," *Dance Chronicle*, 17, No. 2 (1994).

The Barnum & Bailey Official Route Book, Season of 1890. Buffalo, NY: Courier Co., Show Printers, 1890.

The Barnum & Bailey Official Route Book, Season of 1891. Buffalo, New York: Courier Co., Show Printers, 1891.

Barnum & Bailey [Program] *Columbus and the Discovery of America, For the First Time Now Produced in Connection with the Barnum & Bailey Greatest Show on Earth.* Buffalo, NY: Courier Co., Show Printers, 1892.

Barnum & Bailey [Program] *Nero; or, The Destruction of Rome.* Buffalo, NY: Courier Co., Show Printers, 1890.

Conover, Richard E.. *Give 'Em a John Robinson.* (Xenia, OH: Richard Conover. 1965).

Gregory, Brendan Edward. *The Spectacle Plays and Exhibitions of Imre Kiralfy, 1887-1914.* Doctoral dissertation, University of Manchester, 1988.

Kiralfy, Imre. "My Reminiscences."
www.studygroup.org.uk/Journals/Content/MyReminiscences.htm
New York Clipper, 19 April 1890.

[Program] *Nero, or the Destruction of Rome.* Buffalo, New York: Courier Co., Show Printers, 1890.

Pfening, Jr., Fred D. "Spec-ology of the Circus: Part One," *Bandwagon,* November-December 2003.

Saxon, A.H. *P.T. Barnum: The Legend and the Man.* New York: Columbia University Press, 1989.

Chapter Two

The Savage East in the Wild West: Buffalo Bill's Boxing Uprising, 1900-1901

John R. Haddad

Introduction

In 1901, Buffalo Bill's Wild West concluded with a rather unusual final act, one set not in the American West, but in the Far East. In the late 1890s, the Boxer Movement emerged in China in response to the increasingly intrusive presence of foreigners. In Europe and the United States, the Boxers were viewed as backwards and barbaric because they sought the violent eradication of the very things that signified "progress" in the West–churches, telegraph systems, railroads, and mining projects. The movement culminated in the summer of 1900 when the Boxers laid siege to the foreign legations inside the walls of Peking (Beijing). Had they succeeded in breaching the walls, a bloody slaughter would have ensued. In response to the crisis, foreign nations with interests in China hastily assembled a relief force. This international army congregated in Tien tsin (Tianjin), marched to Peking, scaled the city walls, routed the Boxers, and rescued the legations.

Intrigued by this faraway event, William Cody immediately assembled an elaborate reenactment of this stirring military victory for the upcoming edition of the Wild West. Across the United States, "The Rescue at Pekin" inspired audiences to stomp their feet, shout at the top of their lungs, and shake their fists. On some occasions, the show even prompted impassioned crowds to storm the arena floor in a state of wild ecstasy. Yet despite the sensation caused by the reenactment, it has been largely overlooked by scholars, perhaps because many view it as a bizarre aberration from what was standard in the show: unlike most Wild West acts, this one was based not on the mythic past, but on a contemporary event, and it was set not in the American West, but in the Far East. However, William Cody certainly did not view his recreation of the

Chinese conflict as apart from the show's mainstream. And the audience's strong emotional reaction strongly suggests that the viewing experience held powerful meaning for them as well.

Along with providing a detailed description of the reenactment, this essay explains its significance both for Cody and for his audiences. Far from being on the periphery, "The Rescue at Pekin" occupied a central position in the Wild West's mission. Through this reenactment, Cody could explain to his audiences how and why the lessons from the frontier continued to be relevant in a new century, and in a newly industrialized country.

The Rise and Fall of the Boxers

In 1898, a violent anti-foreign movement began to brew in northwest Shandong Province, an agricultural region wracked by floods, drought, locust swarms, and banditry. The misery and discontent generated by these blights transformed the region into a fecund breeding ground for a popular movement. However, it was the increasing visibility of foreigners and their industrial projects that ultimately lit the fuse of this powder keg. For along with these age-old afflictions, Chinese peasants now contended with new phenomena—missions, railroads, mines, and telegraphs—which they could only understand using an interpretative framework rooted in Chinese religions, beliefs, practices, and superstitions.[1]

When missionaries erected churches, many local residents believed that these conflicted with the geomantic principles of *fengshui* and therefore brought bad luck to the community. In fact, a sign posted on street corners by the Boxers pointed directly to a causal relationship between the foreign presence and the unfavorable meteorological conditions that had brought about so much human suffering: "No rain comes from Heaven,/The earth is parched and dry./And all because the churches/Have bottled up the sky."[2] Along with Western religion, Western industrial projects also frightened many Chinese and inflamed their passions. Under foreign supervision, railroads were constructed and mines were dug without regard to cemeteries, causing many Chinese to believe that their dead ancestors had been rudely disturbed. And finally, few rural Chinese understood the purpose or scientific principles behind the telegraph lines crisscrossing the countryside. Since an eerie sound reverberated from the wires, some viewed the lines as demon highways conveying evil spirits[3]

---

[1] Preston, *Besieged in Peking: The Story of the 1900 Boxeruprising,* 21-29; Esherick, *The Origins of the Boxer Uprising,*xiii-xiv, 14-17; Spence,*The Search for Modern China,*231-235.

[2] Spence, 232.

[3] Preston, 21-29; Esherick, xiii-xiv, 14-17; Spence, 231-235.

It was out of this environment of flux, hardship, and volatility that the Boxers emerged. The movement was steeped in superstition, with members engaging in an occult practice called spirit possession. By using a ritual to enter into a trance-like state, Boxers believed they could induce a spirit to enter their bodies, thus rendering them invulnerable to bullets. In this way, they sought to counteract the material superiority of Western arms by invoking a higher spiritual power. And to the consternation of foreigners, in 1899 the Boxers began to focus their rage on them, with missionaries in outlying villages initially bearing the brunt of this hostility. The Boxers harassed the missionaries, destroyed their property, and killed their Chinese converts. Though missionaries repeatedly sent alarming reports to the diplomats who worked in the foreign legations in Peking, the latter were slow to respond. It was not until the Boxers began to converge on the capital that the diplomats realized their impending peril.[4]

Despite requests from foreign diplomats, the Qing Government did not act to protect the foreigners, in part because the Empress Dowager Cixi was relieved that this movement, unlike previous ones, was strongly anti-foreign in its orientation and not anti-dynastic. Indeed, the slogan around which the Boxers rallied summed up their position quite clearly: "support the Qing, destroy the foreign!" For this reason, if the Boxer movement were to be crushed, foreign armies would have to carry out the objective without Qing assistance.[5] Though this scenario did take place, the situation had to reach the level of a crisis before foreign governments acted to intervene militarily. On June 19, 1900, the Boxers laid siege to the foreign legations, trapping inside 473 foreign civilians, 400 military personnel, and some 3,000 Chinese converts. Since the Boxers also destroyed the railroad tracks and telegraph lines leading to Peking, the beleaguered foreigners could not contact the outside world. With limited quantities of food and ammunition, they waited behind their barricades for outside assistance to arrive.[6]

With the situation growing more dire by the day, the governments of the foreign powers finally dispatched military forces to Tien Tsin. On August 4, a foreign expeditionary column of about 20,000 soldiers from various nations, including 1,700 Americans sent over from the Philippines, commenced the long trek to Peking. Along the way, the multinational force engaged in numerous skirmishes that slowed, but never halted, its progress. When it arrived in the

---

[4] Preston, 29, 34-37. Boxers stoned and spat on Pearl Buck's father, Absalom Sydenstricker, as he preached the Gospel on the street. And in one chilling incident, they tied him to a post and forced him to watch as a mob tortured to death a Chinese woman who was one of his converts. Conn, 28-29.
[5] Preston, 23-24, 29-30; Spence, 234.
[6] Preston, 35, 148-151; Duiker, 124.

capital in mid-August, the column separated into individual national armies and a competition ensued: which country's troops could scale Peking's walls, push back the enemy, and reach the legations first? The Russian unit approached the city wall first, but there it stalled as it met with stiff Boxer opposition. Though the Americans easily scaled the wall, they promptly found themselves engaged in street combat inside the city. After several hours of fighting, they broke into the legations only to find the Union Jack fluttering in the breeze. The British, who had advanced almost without Boxer resistance, had beaten them by about two hours.[7]

In this fashion, the allies successfully lifted the siege on August 14, 1900. From the perspective of those trapped in the legations, the dreaded massacre had been forestalled and the crisis was now over. Yet for Chinese civilians living in Peking, the crisis had just begun. Bands of allied soldiers began to loot the city, brutalize defenseless people, and rape Chinese women. George Lynch, a journalist for the British *Daily Express*, was outraged by what he saw. "There are things that I must not write, and that may not be printed in England," he wrote, "which would seem to show that Western civilization...is merely a veneer over our savagery."[8]

The Wild West's Reenactment

In the summer of 1900, the protracted siege by the Boxers and the successful international relief effort seized Americans' attention and dominated the headlines until the Galveston hurricane replaced it. That autumn, William Cody broached an idea to Nate Salsbury, his business partner and the behind-the-scenes impresario of the Wild West. Why not include a reenactment of the allied victory over the Boxers in the edition of the show being planned for the coming spring and summer? The two men promptly set about making all the necessary arrangements for the "The Rescue at Pekin," a stunning extravaganza that would stir the hearts of spectators with patriotism, and overload their senses with colorful pageantry, thrilling action, incessant gun firing, and booming pyrotechnical explosions.

Since the Wild West was famed for its commitment to authenticity, organizers went to great lengths to achieve a convincing battle recreation. For the mammoth Chinese wall, Cody and Salsbury instructed their scenic artist to construct a replica using photographs taken at Peking.[9] In addition, they obtained the most sophisticated and up-to-date weaponry. The *Logansport Daily*

---

[7] Preston, 175-185; Skelly, 44.

[8] Preston, 215-217.

[9] *Reading Daily Times and Dispatch* (June 4, 1901).

Reporter remarked that spectators were for the first time seeing "the working of the machine guns...of modern warfare." And most importantly, Cody and Salsbury secured actual soldiers from several of the allied divisions that had served in China. In Buffalo, a reporter for the *Evening News* snooping around the camp ground at night, stepped behind the Chinese wall and beheld a maze of tents. He joined groups of performers and soon had them swapping war stories and showing discharge papers that proved they had fought in China against the Boxers.[10]

Yet in making preparations, Cody and Salsbury faced one challenge that surpassed all others: who would play the role of the Boxers? The most obvious answer, of course, was to locate and hire actual Boxer soldiers. However, the hiring of authentic Boxer soldiers was not cost effective. Whereas other members of the traveling troupe could appear in more than one segment of the show, the Chinese could only appear in the Grand Finale. Consequently, the Wild West could not afford to invest so much money, time, and effort in securing Chinese soldiers who would appear for under 30 minutes.[11] For these reasons, Cody elected to pursue an alternative. In an article he wrote for *Collier's Weekly* describing a rehearsal (Fig. 2-1), he explained who his Boxers were and what their function was:

> Now we rehearse the battle of Tien-Tsin, the advance of the allies upon Pekin, and the taking of the Celestial City. Our Indians act as our Boxers–for real Boxers were not obtainable–and allow themselves to be mowed down by machine guns. Just as the last Indian-Boxer falls dead on the Great Wall of China, twelve o'clock sounds, and, with it, the bugle calls all hands to the mess-tent for luncheon.[12]

The lot of playing the Chinese ultimately fell to the Indians already employed by the show, namely the Sioux. After robbing the Deadwood Stage Coach, the Sioux donned loose-fitting Chinese uniforms and attached long braids to the backs of their heads to serve as queues. Their role, according to Nate Salsbury, was rather simple: "they have to do nothing except fire blank cartridges and fall dead at the proper intervals."[13]

---

[10] *Logansport Daily Reporter* (August 20, 1901); *Buffalo Evening News* (August 30, 1901).

[11] Organizers had confronted a similar dilemma in attempting to recreate the taking of San Juan Hill in Cuba; "importing a hundred or more Spaniards" for one segment of the show was simply not economical. "Wild West Show No Fake," *New York Sun* (April 7, 1901).

[12] *Collier's Weekly* (April 13, 1901).

[13] Salsbury was interviewed by *The New York Sun* (April 7, 1901).

In early April of 1901, the latest edition of the Wild West premiered in New York. After a two week engagement in Madison Square Garden, the cast embarked on a barnstorming tour of the United States, a series of mostly one-night-stands that lasted well into October.[14] With its 500 performers, stable of about 100 horses, menagerie of animals, props, sets, costumes, technicians, stage hands, tents, the two portable electric light plants, and the extensive scenery, the Wild West could only move about the country by train. It made stops at almost any city or town large enough to boast of a railway station, and covered several large geographic swaths including the mid-Atlantic region, upstate New York, western Pennsylvania, the upper South, and the eastern parts of the Midwest.[15]

All across the country, audiences came out in droves to witness the latest edition of the Wild West and its sensational grand finale. Two scenes comprised "The Rescue at Pekin." In the first, the troops from the several allied nations arrive in the port city of Tien Tsin. As each army files into the arena, it marches to its national anthem and parades around the arena carrying its flag. The procession inspired a journalist in Reading, Pennsylvania to make the following observation: "It is indeed a superb sight to witness the assembling of the troops from the different countries, in one allied army, to release from the tortures of the Chinese the members of the legation, who, being imprisoned behind the massive walls, await with fear the verdict of death to be rendered against them."[16] Once the several armies finish displaying their plumage, the commanders take leave of their troops to plan the march to Peking. In the meantime, the men indulge in sports and pastimes, including a live pig chase. In Warsaw, Indiana, the pig stole the show by escaping his pursuers and heading straight for the V.I.P. box occupied by the Governor and his wife. Greatly

---

[14] The following summary of the tour makes use of the newspaper clippings collected in William Cody's scrapbook, McCracken Research Library, Buffalo Bill Historical Center. Specific dates and the names of newspapers are cited whenever it is possible to do so.

[15] By tracking the Wild West's progress in Cody's scrapbook, one can piece together most of the tour: Baltimore, Richmond, Cincinnati, Irontown, Louisville, Evansville, St. Louis, Terre Haute, Indianapolis, Dayton, Newark, Wheeling, Hartford, Pittsburgh, Altoona, Reading, Allentown, Utica, Elmira, Oil City, Youngstown, Erie, Cleveland, Toledo, Detroit, Auburn, Warsaw, Chicago, Milwaukee, Waterloo, Iowa, Logansport, Buffalo, Connellsville, Bedford, Pontiac, Paducah, and Nashville. For the 1902 season, the Wild West brought essentially the same show to Midwestern cities not reached in 1901, and to the West Coast. Walsh, 327.

[16] See the New York section of the scrapbook; *The Reading Daily Times and Dispatch* (June 4, 1901).

amused, the audience promptly "arose en masse" to applaud the courageous animal's exploits.[17]

Fig. 2-1. Scaling the Wall of Peking during Rehearsal.
Collier's Weekly (April 13, 1901), 18.

These games continue until the sounding of a bugle interrupts the levity and ushers in a tone of high seriousness, as "all are animated by the stir of war." At this point, the men head for the exits to prepare for the second scene. As the setting switches to Peking, the audience watches as Chinese soldiers man the towering wall of Peking, prepare a massive Gatling gun, and raise the Chinese flag, described by one New York reporter as "the royal standard of Paganism floating defiant of the Christian world." Other Chinese soldiers assume battle-ready positions in front of the fortifications. Hidden from the audience, the allied soldiers who had recently exited the arena, join hundreds more for the climactic final engagement: the storming of the walls of Peking. They silently congregate around the front and side entrances to the arena and await the signal.[18]

---

[17] See "Wild West Chases A Pig" and "Colonel Cody's Motley Cohorts Rush in Mad Pursuit" in the Indiana section of the scrapbook.

[18] See the program for the 1901 Wild West Show. McCracken Research Library, Buffalo Bill Historical Center. See also the Baltimore and New York sections of the scrapbook.

When that signal comes, calmness gives way to mayhem as the allied armies stream into the arena from several different points, whooping and hollering and discharging their weapons in the general direction of the massive wall. The mock battle has begun. For audiences, it must have been an exhilarating moment and, with the amount of gunpowder and explosives expended, a deafening one as well. A reporter with the *Allentown Chronicle* wrote that, "with the rattle of musketry and machine guns, the blazing of red fire and the display of pyrotechnics, the feature proved most interesting." The *New York Herald* reported that "Powder was burned with a reckless extravagance," and in Pittsburgh a headline read, "WE DEMAND NOISE, AND BUFFALO BILL SUPPLIES THE DEMAND."[19]

As the Chinese Gatling gun at the top of the wall appears to fire at the onrushing units, allied soldiers fall from gunshot wounds. As they are carried off the arena floor, genuine cries of sympathy can be heard from the emotionally involved audience. However, it is the Chinese who suffer the greatest casualties, and part of the audience's pleasure undoubtedly comes from seeing them overwhelmed by the better trained and better equipped allies. The Boxers, a reporter from Elmira wrote, "are duly slaughtered to the tuneful uproar of Gatling guns, cannons, and a host of small arms."[20]

As the mock battle approaches its climax, all eyes in the arena look to the thirty-foot wall of Peking. With the allied victory a foregone conclusion, the show now derives its suspense not from the possibility that the Chinese will turn back the allied advance, but rather from the allies' competition: which nation will be the first to scale the wall, enter the legations, and garner the glory of replacing the Chinese flag with its own colors? Units from England and the United States are the first to cross the moat, reach the towering structure, and commence the task of climbing it. And as was *not* the case in China, where the British reached the legations first, in the Wild West's version the honors go to the soldiers from the United States. The thrilling, albeit historically inaccurate, conclusion would typically elicit a roar of approval from the audience. "The spectators rose in delight," wrote the *New York Journal*, "when the Americans scaled the wall ahead of the allies." "As the stars and stripes ascend the wall," reported the *Waterloo Daily Courier,* "the band plays 'The Star Spangled Banner' and the enthusiasm of the audience is vented in mighty cheers."[21]

In some instances, the unfolding drama inspired more than just cheers from a patriotic and appreciative crowd. In New York, William Cody invited all of the city's orphans to attend a special charity performance. On April 16, 1901,

---

[19] *Allentown Chronicle* (June 6, 1901). See also the Pittsburgh section of the scrapbook.

[20] *Elmira Telegram* (June 16, 1901).

[21] *Waterloo Daily Courier* (August 1, 1901). See also the New York section of Cody's scrapbook.

the bleachers of Madison Square Garden were packed with 5,800 children. As the reenactment approached its climax, the allied soldiers stormed into the arena and rushed the Peking wall. Though the orphans had been expressing their excitement all day, at this point their level of arousal surged to a new high. As they watched an American unit begin to scale the wall in the face of heavy Chinese fire, their passions reached a feverish pitch. They became so enraptured by the display of heroism, that they could not bear to watch from afar and collectively decided to cross the line between spectator and participant. What one reporter described as a "mob of blood thirsty orphans" burst free of the stands and, like water from a broken dam, cascaded past the bewildered guards onto the dirt floor of the arena. The children then sprinted to the base of the wall where they shouted up at the incredulous American soldiers, begging for a chance to "plug a chink."[22]

New York's orphans were not the only ones to become consumed by the martial spirit. A show in Pittsburgh also erupted into a similar scene of pandemonium, only this time adults as well as children stampeded onto the arena floor. On this occasion, the cast of the Wild West should have seen the outburst coming since the entire crowd had risen to its feet and begun to applaud continuously from the moment the allied forces entered Tien Tsin. And as the fighting outside the walls of Peking reached its crescendo, the impassioned spectators finally gave into their emotions. "At the pitch of the battle," wrote a journalist for the *Pittsburgh Dispatch,* "the crowds surged from the benches into the arena to see the finish, being carried away by excitement." In an attempt to explain the scene of bedlam, the journalist could only conjecture that the "rapid-firing gun in action...slightly stirs the blood of anyone."[23]

A New West in the Far East?

"The Rescue at Pekin" differed from other acts in the Wild West that were set in the past, and in the American West. Yet, clearly, it could provoke an emotionally charged response in audiences. The question to consider, then, is twofold: what was William Cody's motive in selecting a conflict in China for his grand finale, and why did this particular recreation arouse spectators to such a high degree? One possibility is that "The Rescue at Pekin," unlike other acts, tapped into Americans' latent feelings of uncertainty as the United States coped with two large-scale transitions: the close of the frontier and the rise of modernity.

---

[22] "Orphans Fed Full of War," *New York Sun,* (April 17, 1901).
[23] *Pittsburgh Dispatch* (May 29, 1901).

In 1893, Major John Burke, the publicity agent for the Wild West, wrote in the show's program that the frontiersman is "rapidly disappearing from our country," and that the Wild West Show was presenting a "history almost passed away."[24] That same year in Chicago, the historian Frederick Jackson Turner delivered his now famous paper at the ninth meeting of the American Historical Association, "The Significance of the Frontier in American History," in which he announced the closing of the frontier, and tried to explain the significance of this finished chapter in American history. Turner's paper received little publicity at the time since it coincided with the Columbian Exposition. Through its architecture and exhibits, the Columbian Exposition offered a utopian vision for the coming century based on civil order, the wonders of the machine, continued industrial growth, agricultural abundance, and a dazzling array of consumer products.[25] With this glorious vision of modern civilization serving as his backdrop, Turner defined the frontier as "the meeting point between savagery and civilization," and argued that American civilization's continued friction with the "savage" (Indians and the wilderness) had fundamentally altered the American character. Out of the crucible of frontier conflict, a fresh American character had emerged that possessed "coarseness and strength," a "practical inventive turn of mind," "restless, nervous energy," and "dominant individualism."[26]

Though William Cody was present in Chicago (the Wild West played at a venue adjacent to the Exposition), he almost certainly did not hear Turner speak. Yet if he had, he would have agreed with Turner's theory that the frontier had altered the American character in a profound and, in Cody's view, beneficial way. Yet Cody would also have judged this theory to be exceedingly obvious, and lacking in novelty, given that he already regarded himself as the perfect embodiment of the traits Turner enumerated. In fact, the Wild West's program for 1886 had presented Cody as "the representative man of the frontiersman of the past...Young, sturdy, a remarkable specimen of manly beauty, with the brain to conceive and the nerve to execute, Buffalo Bill *par excellence* is the exemplar of the strong and unique traits that characterize *a true American frontiersman.*"[27] Yet questions Cody might have posed to himself in 1893 concerned the continued relevance of these traits in the dawning era. What good were expert horsemanship, deadeye marksmanship, rugged fighting skills, and manly valor in the ascendant civilization celebrated at the Exposition? Would the arrival of modernity consign Cody and his Wild West to obsolescence?

---

[24] Kasson, *Buffalo Bill's Wild West: Celebrity, Memory and Popular History,* 119-120.

[25] Muccigrosso, *Celebrating the New World,* 78-114.

[26] Faragher, ed.,. *Rereading Frederick Jackson Turner,* 32, 59.

[27] Slotkin in Kaplan and Pease, *Cultures of United States Imperialism,* 169.

Though Cody never fully articulated his predicament, Theodore Roosevelt did address in his philosophical writings the distressing problems attending America's transition. Roosevelt believed that the sorts of skills and traits possessed by Cody must never progress to extinction since they would always be vital to a nation seeking to preserve its supremacy. To combat the ill side-effects caused by a rapidly modernizing society, he developed and promoted what he called "the strenuous life"–a mode of living which prized extreme patriotism, self-reliance, rugged experiences in the natural world, dexterity with horses and firearms, and bravery in armed combat. Interestingly, Roosevelt believed not only that individuals needed to embrace his formula for their own good, but also that the overall health of the country was inextricably bound to their success or failure: "As it is with the individual, so it is with the nation." Indeed, if the wrong type of man were to proliferate–"The timid man, the lazy man...the over-civilized man, who has lost the great fighting, masterful virtues"–the United States would lose out in the high-stakes global contest to determine which nation would achieve "domination of the world."[28]

Though to lose this contest would, of course, be a shame in Roosevelt's view, a far worse fate awaited countries that failed to cultivate a salutary bellicosity in its citizens. In the essay, "Expansion and Peace" (1899), Roosevelt posited the theory that world peace paradoxically depended on the willingness of great civilizations to constantly wage effective war. "It is only the warlike power of a civilized people," he wrote, "that can give peace to the world." When civilized nations become "overpeaceful," they lose their "great fighting qualities" and become susceptible to attack by the "barbarian" peoples of the earth. Though a given civilization may exist as a shining embodiment of enlightened progress, if it failed to encourage martial prowess in its male subjects, it could still lose confrontations with inferior "savages." In Roosevelt's mind, the consequences of such a defeat could not be more dire: as advanced civilizations were overrun by "savage" peoples, the world would descend into a prolonged "period of chaotic barbarian warfare." To forestall this nightmare scenario, it was incumbent upon civilized peoples to maintain their "fighting instinct" by relentlessly advancing armies into "the red wastes where the barbarian peoples of the world hold sway."[29]

Near the end of the century, the United States entered into the exact sorts of conflicts that were in alignment with Roosevelt's prescription for national renewal. The Spanish-American War drew American forces to Cuba and Philippines, and the Boxer Uprising necessitated a military deployment to China. These wars also aided William Cody because they allowed him to do no

---

[28] Roosevelt, *The Strenuous Life: Essays and Addresses,* 1-21.
[29] Roosevelt, 25-38.

less than reorient the Wild West's mission after the frontier's closing. Without these wars, he could offer little more than a living museum of Western history that would appeal only to Americans' collective nostalgia; with them, he could demonstrate that the Western experience–the lessons it taught, the values it instilled, and the sort of man it produced–enjoyed continued relevance in the industrialized world. In particular, the Boxer conflict offered Cody the perfect vehicle for his new message, for here was a martial contest pitting the forces of "civilization" against those of "savagery," reminiscent of the Anglo-Indian confrontations of North America. In keeping with this idea, the Wild West's program portrayed the Chinese conflict as a clash between civilization and savagery: "The greatest historic event of 1900 was China's amazingly audacious affront to the civilized world, by her barbaric attack upon" the legations. And in Cody's eyes, these American soldiers were subduing the "savage" Boxers by applying the exact traits and skills that previously had won the West–and that were now showcased by the other acts in the Wild West's program.[30] Thus, "The Rescue at Pekin" not only succeeded as a stand-alone act, it enhanced the appeal of all other acts in the show by conferring relevance on their teachings for the new century.

This fact was not lost on those who attended the Wild West in 1901. Echoing Roosevelt, the *New York Evening Sun* dubbed those in the Wild West "exemplars of the strenuous life." A reporter for the *Chicago American* claimed that the reenactment "gives you an idea of a real war, as among real men." The *Allentown Chronicle* observed that the "capture of Pekin…aroused the fighting blood of the audience to the highest pitch." And the *Louisville Courier-Journal* praised Cody's "teachings in the art of war" for their practical rather than their entertainment value: "The stirring events of the past three years have shown that virility of martial manhood in its highest state of trained perfection is a necessity to the safety of the state, and that it plays a winning hand in the crisis of sudden and unexpected emergency."[31] More than just enjoying the sensory thrills provided by the action and explosives, many Americans apparently understood the cultural significance of Cody's mock battle with the Boxers.

Conclusion

Americans did not all embrace the meaning of the show. One notable individual who recoiled entirely from what he regarded as an ugly display of

---

[30] See the program for the 1901 Wild West Show. McCracken Research Library, Buffalo Bill Historical Center.
[31] *Chicago American* (July 16, 1901); *New York Evening Sun* (April 3, 1901); *Louisville Courier-Journal* (May 9, 1901); *Allentown Chronicle* (June 5, 1901); *Pittsburgh Dispatch* (May 29, 1901).

chauvinism was Mark Twain. Though a fan of Cody's brand of entertainment in general,[32] Twain felt strongly that the Boxer reenactment crossed a dangerous line.[33] In his mind, foreign imperialism, not Chinese savagery, had provoked the Boxers, and, therefore, the West bore the responsibility for the outbreak of violence. "[M]y sympathies are with the Chinese," he wrote a friend in 1900. "They have been villainously dealt with by the…thieves of Europe, and I hope they will drive all the foreigners out and keep them out for good. I only wish it; of course I don't really expect it"[34]

On the evening of April 2, the opening night of the 1901 season, Twain registered his protest. Sitting in a box seat in Madison Square Garden among other distinguished guests, he received a personal wave from Cody as the latter addressed spectators at the start of the show. And as one act followed another, Twain joined the crowd in applauding the performers. But when the time came for the grand finale, Twain rose from his seat and walked out.[35]

Bibliography

Allentown Chronicle, June 5,6, 1901.

Chicago American, June 5, 1901.

Collier's Weekly, April 13, 1901.

Conn, Peter. *Pearl S. Buck: A Cultural Biography.* Cambridge: Cambridge University Press, 1996.

Elmira Telegram, June 16, 1901.

Esherick, Joseph. *The Origins of the Boxer Uprising.* Berkeley: University of California Press. 1987.

Faragher, John Mack, ed., *Rereading Frederick Jackson Turner: "The Significance of the Frontier in American History" and other Essays.* New York: Henry Holt and Company, 1994.

Kaplan, Amy and Donald E.. Pease, editors. *Cultures of United States Imperialism.* Durham: Duke University Press, 1993.

Kasson, Joy. *Buffalo Bill's Wild West: Celebrity, Memory and Popular History.* New York: Hill and Wang, 2000.

Logansport Daily Reporter, Augsut 26, 1901.

Louisville Courier-Journal, May 9, 1901.

---

[32] Walsh, *The Making of Buffalo Bill,* 260-261.

[33] Zwick, ed., *Mark Twain's Weapons of Satire: Anti-Imperialist Writings on the Phillipine-American War,* xix-xxi.

[34] Twain to Reverend J.H. Twitchell (August 12, 1900). Albert Bigelow Paine, ed.., *Mark Twain's Letters,* Vol. 2, 699.

[35] *New York Evening Sun* (April 3, 1901); *New York World* (April 3, 1901).

Muccigrosso, Robert, *Celebrating the New World: Chicago's Columbian Exposition of 1893*. Chicago: Ivan R. Dee, 1993.

Paine, Albert Bigelow, editor. *Mark Twain's Letters, Volume 2*. New York: Harper and Brothers, 1917.

Pittsburgh Dispatch, May 29, 1901.

Preston, Diana, *Besieged in Peking: The Story of the 1900 Boxer Rising*. London: Constable and Co., 1999.

New York Evening Sun, April 3, 1901.

New York Sun, April 7, 17, 1901.

New York World, April 3, 1901.

Pittsburgh Dispatch. May 29, 1901.

Reading Daily Times and Dispatch, June 4, 1901.

Roosevelt, Theodore. *The Strenuous Life: Essays and Addresses*. New York: The Century Company, 1900.

Spence, Jopathan. *The Search for Modern China*. New York: W.W.Norton, 1991.

Twain, Mark. Albert Bigelow Paine, ed., *Mark Twain's Letters,* Vol. 2. New York: Harper & Brothers, 1917.

Walsh, Richard. *The Making of Buffalo Bill*. Indianapolis: Bobbs-Merrill Company, 1928.

Waterloo Daily Courier, August 1, 1901.

Zwick, Jim, editor. *Mark Twain's Weapons of Satire: Anti-Imperialist Writings on the Philippine-American War*. Syracuse: Syracuse University Press, 1992.

CHAPTER THREE

SPECTACULAR REPRESENTATION: RINGLING BROS. AND BARNUM & BAILEY'S *MARCO POLO* SPEC AS AN EXPLORATION OF CHANGE

JENNIFER LEMMER POSEY

"Ye Emperors, kings,…and all other people desirous of knowing the diversities of the races of mankind…read through this book and ye will find in it the greatest and marvelous characteristics of the peoples…."[1]

So begins the prologue to *The Travels of Marco Polo*, with language as enthralling and tantalizing as the midway call of "Step Right Up…," both filled with promises of entertaining spectacles and educational experiences. It is not surprising that over six centuries after the famed Venetian explorer's exotic travels, his story would become the subject of one of the grand circus spectacles presented by the Ringling Bros. and Barnum & Bailey Combined Shows. While *The Return of Marco Polo*, presented as the grand entry display for the 1940 season, must certainly have dazzled its audience, in retrospect, it also reflected a change in the nature of the circus spectacle and marked a transitional point in the history of the circus.

The Victorian concept of the spectacle was as a simulacrum of reality; an interpretation of the real used to educate and inform.[2] Ironically, as Joss Marsh observes in *The Victorians*, "the circus was unusual in Victorian spectacles in *really* delivering wonder."[3] In his work on Ringling spectacles, Michael Means has noted that actual risk taking is the heart of the circus performance and that the performance's primary goal is to "create a beautiful illusion," making the

---

[1] Polo, *The Travels of Marco Polo* trans. Ronald Latham, 1.
[2] Marsh, "Spectacle," in *A Companion to Victorian Literature and Culture,* 276-287.
[3] Ibid, 279.

risk look easy.[4] While the tremendous feats of the aerialists, animal trainers, and other performers were real, they appeared to be illusions. The spectacle, on the other hand, was the production of a fictionalized reality.

In circus vocabulary, the spectacle, or spec, is an extravagant production act within the show which incorporates as many of the circus' employees (both performers and roustabouts) and animals as possible in order to enthrall and entertain the audience with a colorful moving display (Fig. 2-1). Specs could be theatrical in nature, with narrative plots and dramatic scenes staged in the rings or on stages; they could be processional, parading around the tent or some combination of the two.[5] Costumed elaborately, the cast walked the hippodrome

Fig. 3-1 Marco Polo Spec, 1940. Courtesy of the John and Mable Ringling Museum of Art, Tibbals Digital Collection.

track while simultaneous acting, singing and/or dancing displays could take place in the rings or on a stage.[6]

---

[4] Means, *The Field of the Cloth of Gold.*
[5] Pfening, Jr., "Specology of the Circus," Pts 1 and 2. *Bandwagon,* 47, no. 1, 4-20; 48, no. 2, 3-21.
[6] Special stages were often constructed along one section of the sidewall to allow for theatrical performances.

Spectacles date back to the very beginnings of the circus in America with early precursors in English circuses and other European entertainments. By 1784, Philip Astley, generally acknowledged as the creator of the circus as we know it, was staging a theatrical tableau during his shows. In 1793, its first season in America, John Bill Ricketts' circus included a display entitled *The Grand Historical Pantomime*, a satire of Pennsylvania's Whiskey Rebellion.[7]

Whether referred to as a pantomime, a tournament, or a spectacle, early displays tended to share several common traits. First and foremost, they entertained and awed spectators with extravagances; rich and varied materials were used to create eye-catching props and magnificent costumes for the seeming multitudes of animals and performers. In spite of the massive displays of variety and opulence, these displays were produced as cohesive wholes, clearly conveying a story or idea. The early specs had lofty goals of educating the audience with presentations of Biblical, historical or literary stories that were energized by exotic or patriotic elements.[8] Like every aspect of the circus, the spec display was meant to transport the audience beyond the everyday. In early forms, the productions brought a form of high culture theatre to the masses. They also imparted edifying stories or messages that could be taken away when the audience emerged from the big top.[9]

Acting as a key point in the performance, the spec should also be understood as a framework that allowed the visitor to better appreciate the individual acts.[10] As the one moment of simulated reality in a show filled with actual dangerous and death-defying feats, the spec was a point of comparison. While the senses were overstimulated by the grandeur of the display, it did not create the tension and apprehension that other circus acts provoked. Rather than the personal involvement implicit in watching known personalities perform, the audience was provided with a reenactment. What took place during the individual performances was real, what happened during the spec was an act.

During the early nineteenth century, displays were relatively small theatrical productions, in scale with the small one-ring shows of the day. A dramatic change came in 1881 when Adam Forepaugh's show produced *Lalla Rookh and the Departure from Delhi*, a "larger and more spectacular pageant than had ever before been seen…"[11] This larger type of display was directly connected to the physical growth of the circus tent. As the performance area grew from one ring to two and finally three, processional specs became even more important. Most of the show's action took place in the rings, far from the audience. The

---

[7] Pfening, "Spec-ology of the Circus : Part Two," 4.
[8] Johnson, "The Old Time Spec," 8, 17-22. Also Stoddart, *Rings of Desire,* 103.
[9] Dahlinger. Email to the author.
[10] Stoddart, 80.
[11] Pfening, "Spec-ology of the Circus: Part One," 5. .

procession around the hippodrome track created a moment of intimacy in the performance.[12] By the end of the nineteenth century, grand spectacles became a means of showing up competitors for the larger traveling shows.

Even after the Ringling brothers purchased it in 1907, Barnum & Bailey's Greatest Show on Earth continued to produce awesome theatrical productions like 1912's *Cleopatra.* By the first years of the twentieth century, the Ringling Circus was also producing monumental specs that rivaled the pageantry of its competitors. *Jerusalem & the Crusades* (1903) and *Field of the Cloth of Gold* (1906) demonstrated the show's ability to produce lavish displays on a monumental scale. The next five seasons incorporated thematic processions rather than theatrical productions. In 1912 the Ringling Circus produced the grand opening display *Joan of Arc and the Coronation of King Charles VII.* This cycle of producing mammoth theatrical specs for several years (with each production running for two seasons), and then downsizing the production to processions in other years, became a pattern for the show.

When the two shows finally combined for the 1919 season, the procession had won out. Ringling Bros. and Barnum & Bailey Combined Shows traveled with so many people that even the walk-about productions could be long, visually and aurally overwhelming and thoroughly entertaining. Opulence and sheer numbers were now more important than narrative. Along with the growth of the performance area and the sheer cost of productions, this shift in attitudes might be attributed to the rising prominence of another entertainment: the cinema. Film's method of following a narrative might still have been silent, but it offered an intimacy that the Ringling show, with a seating capacity of as many as 15,000, could not match. Instead, the show offered immersion in a world of exotic sights, sounds and aromas and a storm of brilliant colors--something the cinema was not yet able to offer its audience.

It was not until the 50th anniversary of the Ringling Circus in 1933, that the extravagant titled specs reappeared. Even then, the *Durbar of Delhi* would be recycled for several seasons until 1937's *India.* When John Ringling North assumed control of the show in 1937, he realized that modernization of all aspects of the show, both behind the scenes and inside the big top was critical to its ongoing success. North recognized that American culture, and more specifically, entertainment, was rapidly evolving and if the show did not keep up, it would be obsolete.

By 1940 the circus was increasingly upstaged by the cinema, where Technicolor was bringing the movie closer to rivaling the visual richness of the circus performance. In her study of circus history, *Rings of Desire*, Stoddart likens the cinema of this period to the circuses of a decade or two before;

---

[12] Dahlinger.

pointing to each entertainment's interest in "the emergence of a generic form which presents variations on a similar show...."[13] If the danger of omni-present movie palaces were not enough, at the 1939 World's Fair in New York, the Radio Corporation of America (RCA) debuted the first commercial televisions.[14] The potential of having the world in one's living room was one of the final blows, bringing the heyday of the traveling circus to an end.

The Ringling Circus itself had changed significantly since the death of the last of the original brothers. In 1938 the show's management implemented changes to modernize the transport and set up of the show, instigating labor strikes that forever altered the nature of the traveling circus. The show drastically cut the number of employees from 1,400 performers and workers in 1937 to 1,000 in 1939.[15] This reduction changed the logistics of moving the show and foreshadowed the more drastic step of taking the circus out from under canvas less than twenty years later.

John Ringling North was intent on producing a show that was stimulating to a variety of senses. His productions would push the boundaries of American expectations through modern set and wardrobe designs and through contemporary musical compositions. Recognizing the revolutionary influences on popular culture, North and the circus management must have realized the importance of keeping the show fresh. The circus was no longer a primary source of entertainment; more than ever it was dependent on its novelty and its fleeting availability to attract crowds.

North brought in some of the day's finest talents to conceptualize and produce new and exciting shows. In 1941 North hired Norman Bel Geddes, the famous stage designer who had made a splash at the World's Fair in New York two years earlier. Under Bel Geddes, such influential creative minds as Miles White, John Murray Anderson and George Balanchine contributed to the production of the Ringling show. These creative geniuses would propel the circus into the modern world, creating a show, and more specifically, a spec, that would be attractive to Americans already mesmerized by the Technicolor brilliance of the cinema and the episodic narrative of radio and television. In the brief moment between the shows of the Golden Age and those that Bel Geddes and his colleagues would create, the 1940 season serves as the fulcrum point, produced from elements of the past and the future, of Western aesthetics and Eastern curiosities. That season, North invited Max Weldy, an American

---

[13] Stoddart, 57.

[14] Dunlap, 165. Interestingly, as early as 1940, television execs noted the marketability of the circus. The Ringling Circus was filmed at Madison Square Garden and televised with "behind the scenes footage."

[15] "Circus Signs Labor Pact," *New York Times*, May 30, 1937, 4.
"Circus, A.F.L. End Fight at Parley," *New York Times*, December 17, 1938, 10.

working in Paris, to produce a lavish spectacle. In Paris, Weldy had worked with the Moulin Rouge and the Folies Bergères, among others, to create shows during the 1920's. Weldy designed and, with his workshop, constructed costumes, props and scenery for stage productions.[16] *The Return of Marco Polo* was the only spec that Weldy would design for the circus although he remained involved in the production of the show for the next three decades.

Fig. 3-2 Ringling Bros. and Barnum & Bailey Combined Shows Poster, 1940. Courtesy of the John and Mable Ringling Museum of Art, Tibbals Digital Collection.

Marco Polo was billed as "the most magnificent opening spectacle in circus history."[17] As always, the length of history is just long enough to make circus advertising sound enticing (Fig. 3-2). The season's program goes on to explain that "every man, woman and child…knew the story of the world's greatest overland explorer from beginning to end…."[18] In fact, the circus' inspired press men turned the tale of Marco Polo into one of traveling showfolk, implying that the production was a metaphor of the show itself. The audience learns that some circus performers "amused themselves by checking over the 13th century explorer's wanderings to see how much of them they themselves had covered [while] foreign acts began to buzz with ideas for the 'spec.'"[19]

---

[16] "Sarasotan to Close Shop After 50 Years in Trade," *Sarasota Herald Tribune.*
[17] *Ringling Bros. and Barnum & Bailey Program*, 1941.
[18] Ibid., 22.
[19] Ibid., 22, 70.

Fig. 3-3 Max Weldy wardrobe designs for the Marco Polo Spec's China and India sections. Courtesy of the John and Mable Ringling Museum of Art, Tibbals Digital Collection.

Just like Marco Polo, the showfolk had traveled far, seen amazing sights, learned about other cultures and, most importantly, brought all of these splendid sights to their audience. The opening production, which ran for approximately ten minutes, functioned much like the narrative tales related by the adventurer. The procession was divided into six sections of varying length, with each section representing a distinct country and culture: Arabia, Persia, Tibet, China, India and Venice (Fig. 3-3). Much like the manuscript, the spec display offered the audience an experience of each culture filtered through one man's own creative process and Weldy's interpretation reflected the cultural climate of both the circus and the entire nation.

Stoddart has observed that the abundance of activity in the three rings made it "impossible to take in the whole performance at once and [so] appreciation of individual acts was replaced by an impression of the show as a whole."[20] This was exactly the intention of Weldy's spec. Unlike the theatrical productions of Imre Kiralfy, there was no specific action to behold and yet there was a narrative, unlike the old processional form. Instead, the audience, like the Venetian explorer and his own audience centuries earlier, was to be dazzled by the impressions of the exotic Orient. No single figure was intended to stand

---

[20] Stoddart, 41.

apart from the overall display, not even Marco Polo himself. Like the
performance, the Orient was something to be perceived rather than fully known.

Fig. 3-4 Max Weldy wardrobe designs for the Marco Polo Spec's India, Venice and Tibet
sections. Courtesy of the John and Mable Ringling Museum of Art, Tibbals Digital
Collection.

Even in the early designs for the costumes, Weldy appeared to perpetuate the
unknowable quality of his Orientalist display (Fig. 3-4). In the sketches that are
available, Weldy consistently avoided drawing faces on those figures that were
to be displayed as part of the Eastern cultures. In contrast, the majority of the
Venetians were given a defined identity. The only exceptions to this were the
few figures on which Weldy drew the stereotypical slanted eyes that were
intended to denote an ethnic, and therefore, cultural difference. Perhaps this
unwillingness to identify Eastern characters alludes more to the smoke and
mirrors of the show than to any racial bias; Weldy had to costume the
performers that were with the show, whatever their ethnicity. Thus the
characters become "intentional inaccuracies," portrayed by whoever fit the
costume.[21]

An inherent separateness has always been a defining quality of the traveling
show. The *Otherness* of the circus as a realm of the fantastic and freakish, of
the fascinating and fleeting has been addressed in part by Janet Davis in *The
Circus Age*.[22] Davis warns against descriptions of the circus and its performers
as voiceless, powerless *others*, choosing instead to focus on their control of the

[21] Stoddart, 102-103.
[22] Davis, *The Circus Age: Culture and Society Under the American Big Top,*.27-28.

spectacle of performance. Through their performance, the performers project a pre-defined image of themselves as individuals just as through the spec, the show projects an artificial image of itself.

The Return of Marco Polo represented the imagined homecoming of the explorer. In place of exalted tales of his exotic travels, the Venetian returned with the very men, women, animals and riches he would otherwise have described. This was no Victorian simulacrum of the story, this was a living recreation; the circus no longer imitated, it originated. By doing so, the performance escaped from its frame and invited a more active participation by its audience. *Marco Polo* displayed the living fantasy for the people seated in the stands, not for the Venetian court standing on the stage. Unlike earlier productions, *Marco Polo* was a self-conscious display of the spectacle. As a narrative and pseudo-educational story relating the explorer's travels it looked back on the early days of the circus spec, while through its sectionalized, linear narrative it suggested the fragmentation and thematic quality of the specs to come. Weldy's *Marco Polo* offered a new type of framework for the show, providing a unique perspective on the show by *re*-presenting the performers and animals to the audience as amazing and curious attractions.

Bibliography

Dahlinger, Fred. Email to author, August 15, 2006

Davis, Janet. *The Circus Age: Culture and Society Under the American Big Top.* Chapel Hill: The University of North Carolina Press, 2002.

Johnson, Robert Barbour. "The Old Time Spec, *The White Tops,* September-October, 1955.

Marsh, Joss. "Spectacle" in *A Companion to Victorian Literature and Culture,* . ed. Herbert F. Tucker. Malden, Massachusetts: Blackwell Publishers, 1999.

Means, Michael. *The Field of the Cloth of Gold.* Paper at Popular Culture Association, San Antonio, Texas, 1997.

New York Times. New York, May 15, 1940.

New York Times. New York, May 30, 1937.

Pfening, Jr., Fred. *"Spec-o-logy of the Circus,"* *Bandwagon* November-December, 2003, January-February 2004.

Polo, Marco. *The Travels of Marco Polo* trans. Ronald Latham. Hammondsworth, Middlesex: Penguin Books, 1958.

Ringling Bros. Barnum & Bailey Program, 1941.

Sarasota Herald-Tribune, January 30, 1972.

Stoddart, Helen. *Rings of Desire.* Manchester, UK: Manchester University Press, 2000.

Part II

Race, Gender, Difference

CHAPTER FOUR

CIRCUS PERFORMERS AS ACTION HERO: CODONA AND LEITZEL [1]

PETA TAIT

By the late 1920s, Alfredo Codona, from a Mexican family troupe, had established a reputation as the world's foremost flyer and successor to Ernie Clarke. For the first time, Alfredo's triple somersault was consistently caught by his catcher and brother, Lalo. In addition, Alfredo worked with revered lithe lightness, and a special 'lift' on letting go of the fly bar, and became a major artistic influence on aerial arts in the twentieth century. He was very good looking with an upright posture and a 'naturally classic' well-proportioned muscular body: 'Flying develops a muscled, lean, graceful torso'.[2] He had the body shape esteemed during the 1930s. His public persona, however, became caught up with contradictory attitudes to masculinity and aerialists, and the feminization of aerial performance in popular perception. These were prefigured by Alfredo's stunt work for two major films—*Variety* (1925)[3] and *Tarzan and His Mate* (1934). The two films depict extremes in male action hero identity; Artinelli, the suave sensual flyer as seductive lover in *Variety*; and Tarzan, the seminal muscular action hero swinging through the jungle.

---

[1] This paper was presented at Popular Culture/American Culture Conference, San Diego, March 26, 2005. It was subsequently published in *Circus Bodies: Cultural Identity in Aerial Performance*. London Routledge, 2005. pp. 85-6, 95-8, 98-100.

[2] Bradna, as told to Hartzell Spence. *The Big Top: My Forty Years with the Greatest Show on Earth*, 192.

[3] Information courtesy of Tim Tegge who has an extensive Alfredo Codona archive. Alfredo's work on *Variety* is not credited, and he also performed stunts, and with Vera Bruce, in *Tarzan and His Mate* and *Polly of the Circus* (1932), and as himself in *Swing High* (1932) and *Circus Clown* (1934). Alfredo and Vera probably initially did the stunt work for *Tarzan, The Ape-Man* (1932), doubling for Johnny Weissmuller and Maureen O'Sullivan.

Representations of male flyers in twentieth-century films reiterate a polarized tension between perceptions of aerial performance as a highly athletic male domain and one of feminine spectacle. Graceful flying transforms a muscular body's solid density and weight, which are apparent in sports with their aggressive competitiveness. The male flyer was certainly ripe for 1920s film narratives about a romantic seducer who could be both physically active and emotionally sensitive. Accordingly, this was received as atypical male behaviour.

The male flyer initially appears in cinema as a flawed hero. The prototypes are characters found in the silent film *Variety* (1925) (*Variété*), directed by Ewald Dupont and based on Felix Hollaender's novel, *The Oath of Stephen Huller*.[4] This is a semi-Expressionist film about a heavy-bodied, catcher-husband, Boss Huller (Emil Jannings), whose wife, Berthe-Marie (Lya de Putti), is seduced from domestic bliss by the trio's lighter-bodied star flyer, Artinelli (Warwick Ward). The catcher-husband imagines dropping his rival, the flyer, but murders him instead in a fight, and goes to prison. The seducing male flyer is the provocateur of extreme passion, a position subsumed by female aerialist characters in later films. But the male aerialist as a criminal, even murderer, intermittently reappears in representation because he epitomizes a capacity for extreme risk-taking, which is translated into socially risky immoral behavior.[5] But it is the male flyer who becomes especially vulnerable to depiction as a fallen hero, literally and for losing emotional control.

In analyzing the contrasts between 1920s male film stars and their roles, Gaylyn Studlar discerns '*transformative masculinity*' that can also be a performance, in a process of reaction against the threat of feminization.[6] Studlar finds cultural unease with the atypical masculinity of the numerous film characters created by John Barrymore and Rudolph Valentino; she specifies criticism of the depictions of a sensitive lover as a sportsman or gymnast who is not belligerent in his fighting, and especially towards the identity of the immigrant Latin-lover or dancer.[7] Moreover, the sexualizing of the male body, with his bared chest, was counterbalanced by a narrative of suffering, and emotional '*actions*' to avenge or protect.[8] Contradictorily, a male gymnast (flyer) overwhelmed by emotional pain is not heroic; excessive emotion counteracts masculinity.

---

[4] *Variety* was remade as a talkie called *Salto Mortale* (1931) (*Trapeze*), with a further remake in 1935.

[5] See, for example, *High Jump* (1958) about an ex-trapezist jewel thief.

[6] Studlar, *This Mad Masquerade*, 4, 7 (italics in original).

[7] Ibid., 16, 151, 185.

[8] Ibid., 138 (italics in original).

Alfredo's participation in *Variety* outlines some significant convergences and confusions: between early film stunt action and live aerial action; between a melodrama and his tragic personal life; and between a fictional character and a performer's public identity. Alfredo's reputation as a celebrity aerialist is comparable to that of a 1920s silent film star who acquired a textual identity from the merging of film roles with a media-created private life; this was a 'star persona as a marketable commodity'.[9] Alfredo, from a Mexican circus family, aspired to the flyer's dream and had mastered the triple by 1920.[10] In 1913, the Flying Codonas with Steve Outch and Ruth Farris, and with Victoria Codona on slack wire, started out at Wirth's Circus in Australia, with Alfredo practicing for the triple. They were working with the Siegrist-Silbon troupe for Ringling Bros. and Barnum & Bailey by 1916-17. The Codonas achieved star status in Europe in 1922, and in the USA during the mid-1920s. The troupe including Alfredo's first wife, Clara Gron (Curtin), were well established in Ringling's centre ring by 1927. By 1937 both Alfredo and Lalo had given up aerial performance; Alfredo snapped two shoulder muscles in a shoulder dislocation in 1933 doing the triple and could not return to flying, and Lalo developed muscle strain in 1936.[11]

Alfredo's tricks included a single somersault with a one-and-a-half pirouette on his return, and his triple somersault was followed by the double pirouette on the return. The Codonas worked 100 feet up with a net 25 feet from the ground and Alfredo describes split-second timing and how 'psychology and muscle are mingled in the triple'.[12] He makes his well-known claim that his body had been measured travelling 62 miles an hour turning three somersaults within 7 square feet.[13] Claims for the flyer's speed in a triple range from 40 to 60 miles an hour and depend on the height, weight and fly bar's length. Alfredo emphasizes the loss of mental control as the body in a second somersault turns faster and, he suggests, faster than the speed of thought in a 'momentary dream' space where vision and memory distort.[14] While acknowledging the trick's difficulty, other flyers dispute that the mind goes blank, and emphasize that achieving height and having muscles and a skilled catcher are crucial.

Alfredo did all his actions smoothly and seemingly effortlessly. Bradna describes his returning pirouette:

---

[9] Ibid., 2.

[10] Culhane, *The American Circus: An Illustrated History*, 186.

[11] Ibid., 195 (Codona's letter)).

[12] Codona, Alfredo, as told to Courtney Ryley Cooper, 'Split Seconds', *The Saturday Evening Post*, 76.

[13] Ibid., 12.

[14] Ibid., 79.

[t]he trick here is to propel the body, once it leaves the catcher, with a double motion: forward and upward toward the trapeze, and simultaneously around in a circle. To make the turn beautiful, the arms must be close to the body, the legs artistically posed, lest the whole effect be ungainly rather than romantic. All these muscular co-ordinations, exerted in precisely the proper order, within a space of one and a half seconds demand much more finesse than most flyers develop.[15]

The artistry is achieved by keeping the limbs and arms close to the body in a streamlined compactness and maintaining fluid, even movement.

In circus annals, Alfredo's personal story effectively upstages his work. He divorced his first wife, and married the star Lillian Leitzel in 1928. Both Alfredo and Leitzel had been child performers and became aerialist celebrities, but did not work in the same act. Leitzel's tragic death in 1931, and Alfredo's 1937 murder-suicide in which he shot his third wife and ex-Codonas flyer, Australian Vera Bruce, in a lawyer's office while she was negotiating their divorce settlement, ensured that their personal lives are retold.

Alfredo's and Leitzel's feats represented the outer limits of aerial physicality, and adoring audiences celebrated their off-stage union. While husband and wife partnerships are unremarkable in a field of constant touring and training, Leitzel and Alfredo's short marriage was played out as a public affair that exemplified celebrity romance. The popular diminutive, feminine Leitzel, became an ideal love match for flyer-hero Alfredo. An explanation for Alfredo's subsequent violence was more readily found in the emotional pain of losing an idealized lover like Leitzel rather than an aerial act through injury. The depiction of Alfredo as a victim of grief that leads to his subsequent scandalous behaviour confirms that, like Artinelli in *Variety*, the male flyer emotionally flouts the moral code by which stoic masculine heroism becomes imbued with honour. In all likelihood Alfredo's extreme violence four years after the loss of his aerial act was due to depression from compounded disappointment, and possibly also physical pain, a legacy of injury.

Leitzel used theatrical gestures and costuming for feminine effect to offset her muscularity as she executed an exceptional display of endurance and strength. As a child performer, Leitzel worked with her mother and aunts in the Leamy Sisters.[16] Leitzel's solo act on Roman rings was graceful and skilful. She climbed the ascent rope using one arm to turn her body three feet at a time in order to reach the suspended rings. Her hands and arms supported her weight on the rings in moves that included a legs split as the band played Gioacchino

---

[15] Bradna, Fred, as told to Hartzell Spence. *The Big Top: My Forty Years with the Greatest Show on Earth*, 169.

[16] Culhane *The American Circus: An Illustrated History*, 187-8. Lillian's biography, if not a full description of her act, is included in most comprehensive circus histories.

Rossini's 'William Tell Overture.' Leitzel dismounted, and for the act's second half, she was winched up to a web with a hand loop at the higher end. She began plange turns in which she swung her whole body up to shoulder level and over itself with increasing speed, from 60 to 100 times, accompanied by a snare drum and Rimsky-Korsakov's 'The Flight of the Bumblebee', and letting her hair out. The crowd chanted her turns; Leitzel's record was 249.[17] Even from a distance in the tent, spectators routinely describe the ugly jerkiness of this turning action.[18]

Alfredo Codona, explains how this act:

> requires muscle—a great deal of it. Of course it requires endurance, and a certain sense of fatalism, in as much as no bandage ever has been devised that can protect her arm from the constant danger of blood poisoning from rope burns. But more than this, it requires a knowledge of breathing as expert as that of any opera star. [19]

Leitzel's tricks were as dependent on muscular strength as Codona's flying tricks, but Leitzel deliberately gestured to a feminine identity with her costume, her movement and her routine. A perception of awkwardness may also have come from her performance of femininity set against strenuous muscular action. Billed as 'dainty' on her Ringling posters, to do her act she had the shoulders of a 'middle-weight boxer'.[20] But she was small-bodied, 4 feet 10 inches in height, and this was highlighted to enhance her act when she entered the ring in a white cape with a 6 foot 4 inch man at her side, sometimes even carrying her. In a gesture of frailness, and to the annoyance of the ring director, Fred Bradna, Leitzel used to fake a faint after her act on occasions. As a forerunner of the popular young Olympic gymnasts of today, who are perversely celebrated because they are small but extremely athletic,[21] the adult Leitzel achieved this impression through cuteness. She is described as 'looking like a little girl in her pink tights and short jacket bordered by silver beads', 'a fairy princess';[22] a 'little rag doll'[23].

Leitzel clearly controlled the composition of identity in her performance, and was independently minded about her personal life. While she cultivated a

---

[17] Culhane, *The American Circus: An Illustrated History*, 187.

[18] May, *The Circus From Rome to Ringling*, 271.

[19] Codona as told to Courtney Ryley Cooper, 'Split Seconds', 13.

[20] Verney, *Here Comes the Circus*, 205, 202.

[21] Chisholm, 'Acrobats, Contortionists, and Cute Children: The Promise and Perversity of US Women's Gymnastics', *Signs*, 415–50.

[22] Bradna, as told to Hartzell Spence. *The Big Top: My Forty Years with the Greatest Show on Earth*, 180, 182.

[23] Culhane, *The American Circus: An Illustrated History*, 185, quoting Taylor.

public impression of youthful frailty, this also made her muscular action seem more difficult, more exceptional, and less masculine. Leitzel was greatly mourned when she died.

All three of Alfredo's wives were leading aerialists and two worked in the Codonas act, although descriptions of Clara's work are difficult to locate. Ruth Manning-Sanders describes Vera's competent flying in a double passing trick:

> Lalo hangs from his trapeze, swinging Vera by the ankles.. Alfredo swings from his trapeze by the hands. The two trapezes swing towards each other; Lalo releases Vera's ankles and flings her forward; at the same moment Alfredo shoots over the top of his trapeze, and passes above Vera in mid-air. The next moment, Vera has caught the trapeze that Alfredo has just left, and Alfredo's wrists are gripped by Lalo's strong hands.[24]

The Alfredo described in circus annals is like a mythic Greek hero reaching physical perfection, but denied his 'true' love by fate; the flyer is the solitary Icarus who might fall. This story has assumed mythic dimensions because it suggests ideal love thwarted by death. Emotional pain dominates the Alfredo narrative when the aerialist and the aerial act converge into loss that merges melancholy about an unattainable love and mourning for a dead lover.

Aerial artistry generally masks any discomforting physical pain, especially in performances like those by Alfredo that appear effortless. A spectator, however, might perceive, for example, Leitzel's work having a painful effect with her staged femininity that heightens an impression of difficulty. Even though a spectator might fear the consequences if a male performer should fall, physical pain is not easily reconciled with the impression of lightness and ease in flying action.

Interestingly, Alfredo was also the stunt double for the first Johnny Weissmuller Tarzan films. Alfredo executed some of the aerial swinging of the prototypical masculine action hero, joining the elite ex-swimming and football champions who were cast as Tarzan.[25] Aaron Baker explains that American cinema's representation of sports asserted both masculinity and values of

---

[24] Manning-Sanders, *The English Circus,* 241. Also, see Beal, *Through the Back Door of the Circus,* 114-17. Vera was from a circus family, and was a rider like her mother, Anne. Born in Singapore, Vera lived in an Australian convent until 16, worked in vaudeville, and on a large web of female performers in a 'spider and fly' act at the New York Hippodrome, and then with the famous Australian May Wirth's Ringling riding act before joining the Codonas after 1928 to replace Clara, apparently at Leitzel's suggestion. It seems that Vera was asking for over $30,000 in marriage settlement at a time when neither she nor Alfredo was earning a top performer's wage.

[25] Essoe, *Tarzan of the Movies.*

individual heroism.[26] The numerous and popular Tarzan films made from 1918, based on Edgar Rice Burroughs' novel, *Lord of the Jungle* (1912), presented their hero living in wild jungle; that is, he was in untouched nature and fighting its corruption from an encroaching civilization. Tarzan is the 'gentleman' in a schismatic masculinity that maintains species and race hierarchies. On film his eroticized, albeit white body, delivers unsmiling monosyllabic responses.[27] But Tarzan becomes heroic only by rescuing Jane, who is emblematic of white womanhood faced with physical and social dangers from non-white villains in narratives with racist implications.[28] Maurizia Boscagli's astute psychoanalytical interpretation of the Tarzan character as a successor to nineteenth-century muscle man Eugen Sandow finds that while Tarzan does circus stunts, as a muscular Nietzschean superman his wounds are indicative of masochistic masculinity.[29]

Cinema carries on the nineteenth-century circus tradition of defining Africa.[30] When Tarzan and his chimpanzee (friend) do eventually venture to the centre of civilization, New York, to save Tarzan's adopted son in *Tarzan's New York Adventure* (1942), he ends up at the circus fighting the villainous kidnappers. Circus functions as culture's symbolic place of nature since it presents tamed wild animals who become intelligible through performances of human-like behaviour.[31] But a social space where the actions of animal and human bodies overlap also becomes one of depravity.

Tarzan personified culture's ongoing efforts after the 1880s to recoup a 'primitive masculinity'.[32] Gail Bederman discerns how the early twentieth century's white manhood in the USA was constructed in racist responses to boxing action, and through the reconciliation of identities that were 'civilized, manly and undervitalized' and 'primitive, masculine and passionate'.[33] Kristen Whissel argues convincingly that physically building up the male body in early American cinema also equated to building the national character through 'kinetic movement and circulation of the male body-in-motion'.[34] Later, the

---

[26] Baker, *Contesting Identities: Sports in American Film.*

[27] Morton, 'Tracking the Sign of Tarzan: Trans-Media Representation of a Pop-Culture Icon,' 112-3.

[28] Newsinger, 'Reader, He Rescued Her: Women in Tarzan Stories', Foundation: 44

[29] Boscagli, *Eye on the Flesh*, 121-2.

[30] Pollock, 'Empire, Identity and Place: Masculinities in Greystoke: The Legend of Tarzan,' 128.

[31] Carmeli, 'The Sight of Cruelty: The Case of Circus Animal Acts'; Kwint, 'The Circus and Nature in Late Georgian England'.

[32] Bederman, *Manliness and Civilization*, 157.

[33] Ibid., 102.

[34] Whissel, 'The Gender of Empire: American Modernity, Masculinity and Edison's War Actualities,' 147.

Tarzan character also featured in American nationalist, anti-Nazi films during WWII.[35]

Boscagli writes that by the 1930s the shape of the male body was changing in response to ongoing perceptions of a masculine identity crisis, and became visible as a tanned, muscular even unclothed 'spectacle of untamed natural strength' in places of leisure like the gym and the seaside.[36] Even in the late 1920s Tarzan still had to partially cover his chest with a leopard skin, as his undressed body merited comment.[37] His inarticulate aerial action of the rescue became prototypical of masculine action in cinema, and his bared chest set the precedent for the systematized look that became particularly accentuated in 1950s films.

If Tarzan's action initially mimics the flying action of an aerialist, the increasingly exposed chest of the male aerialist began to mimic Tarzan's body. The male 'body genre' came to involve 'sweat, muscles, shows of strength, tunics and loin cloths.'[38] But this foreshadowing of cinematic action hero identity highlighted ongoing contradictions in male aerial identity caught between the masculinized solidity of muscularity and feminized lightness of flying action. Nonetheless from this time and especially in the 1950s, cinema's doubling of body genres placed male aerialists in competition with cinematic action heroes without female equivalents.

Bibliography

Baker, Aaron, *Contesting Identities: Sports in American Film.* Urbana/Chicago: University of Illinois Press, 2003.

Beal, George B., *Through the Back Door of the Circus.* Springfield: McLoughlin, 1938.

Bederman, Gail, *Manliness and Civilization.* Chicago: University of Chicago Press, 1995.

Boscagli, Maurizia, *Eye on the Flesh.* Boulder: Westview Press, 1996.

Bradna, Fred, as told to Hartzell Spence, *The Big Top: My Forty Years with the Greatest Show on Earth.* NY: Simon and Schuster, 1952.

Carmeli, Yoram, 'The Sight of Cruelty: The Case of Circus Animal Acts', *Visual Anthropology* 10. 1997: 1–15.

Chisholm, Ann, 'Acrobats, Contortionists, and Cute Children: The Promise and Perversity of US Women's Gymnastics'. *Signs*, 27 no. 2. (2002).

---

[35] Essoe, *Tarzan of the Movies,* 115.

[36] Boscagli, *Eye on the Flesh,* 1, 4.

[37] Essoe, *Tarzan of the Movies*, 61, 70.

[38] Hunt, 'What are Big Boys Made Of? Spartacus, El Cidand the Male Epic', 66.

Codona, Alfredo, as told to Courtney Ryley Cooper, 'Split Seconds'. *The Saturday Evening Post*, 6 December 1930.

Culhane, John, *The American Circus*: An Illustrated History. NY: Henry Holt, 1990.

Essoe, Gabe, *Tarzan of the Movies*. Secaucus, NJ: The Citadel Press, 1972.

Hunt, Leon, 'What are Big Boys Made Of? Spartacus, El Cid and the Male Epic', in *You Tarzan: Masculinity, Movies and Men* edited by Pat Kirkham, Pat and Janet Thumim. London: Lawrence and Wishart, 1993.

Kwint, Marius, 'The Circus and Nature in Late Georgian England', in Rudy Koshar (ed.), *Histories of Leisure*. Oxford: Berg, 2002.

Manning-Sanders, Ruth, *The English Circus*. London: Werner Laurie, 1952.

May, Earl Chapin, *The Circus From Rome to Ringling*. NY: Dover Publications, 1963.

Morton, Walt. 'Tracking the Sign of Tarzan: Trans-Media Representation of a Pop-Culture Icon', in *You Tarzan: Masculinity, Movies and Men*, edited by Pat Kirkham, Pat and Janet Thumim. London: Lawrence and Wishart, 1993.

Newsinger, John, 'Reader, He Rescued Her: Women in Tarzan Stories', Foundation: *The Review of Science Fiction*. 39 Spring (1987).

Pollock, Griselda, 'Empire, Identity and Place: Masculinities in Greystoke: The Legend of Tarzan', in *Me Jane: Masculinity, Movies and Women*, edited by Pat Kirkham and Janet Thumim. NY: St Martin's Press 1995.

Studlar, Gaylyn, *This Mad Masquerade*. NY: Columbia University Press, 1996.

Verney, Peter. *Here Comes the Circus*. NY: Paddington Press, 1978.

Whissel, Kristen, 'The Gender of Empire: American Modernity, Masculinity and Edison's War Actualities', in *A Feminist Reader in Early Cinema*, edited by Jennifer M. Bean and Dianne Negra. Durham: Duke University Press, 2002.

Chapter Five

Playing in the Dark: Under the Big Top, the Africanist Presence

Jerrilyn McGregory

From its inception, the American amusement industry privileged its own esoteric vocabulary and work technology. Beyond utilizing terms such as freaks, geeks, and hype, it also engages its own set of racialized mythologies. Although spectacles such as circuses represent global productions, I interrogate how such performances in the United States mirror racialized tropes positioned in the popular imaginary.[1] From the era of U.S. slavery to the present-day multiculturalism, the American Big Top centers a constant for acting out race. Popular constructs such as melodrama, minstrelsy, human exhibitions, and multiculturalism dramatize race concept as a historical development. Much recent scholarship interrogates freakery as it relates to an Africanist presence.[2] However, these explorations fail to situate these embodiments as encoded performances, which—to use African American writer Toni Morrison's words—express a "playing in the dark."[3]

Morrison's text directs its gaze for a "close look at literary 'blackness'" in canonical U.S. fiction. I propose that just as her reading offers both peril and assurance as relates to white American fiction, likewise her exploration can be deployed to interrogate a similar Africanist presence under the Big Top. Morrison enlists Africanist to mean the denotative and connotative blackness

---

[1] In *Freakery: Cultural Spectacles of the Extraordinary Body,* 11, Rosemarie Thomson asserts, "It evidently was well worth the dime or quarter at a time when modernization rendered the meaning of bodily differences and vulnerabilities increasingly unstable and threatening."

[2] Other critics who explore an Africanist presence within the cultural domain of fakery include: Robert Brustein, Leslie Fiedler, and Barbara Lindfors.

[3] Toni Morrison, *Playing in the Dark: Whiteness and the Literary Imagination,* 9. Morrison's text is also the source for quotes related to "literary 'blackness.'"

that African peoples signify to a white population that contrasts itself as white in opposition to blackness. In U.S. circus vernacular, the "Big Top" translates to mean: "THE TENT IN WHICH A CIRCUS PERFORMANCE IS GIVEN, NEVER THE CIRCUS AS A WHOLE, NEVER A CARNIVAL [sic]."[4] Nonetheless, I utilize the term as a metaphor for all the sites within the American amusement industry—whether museums, ethnological exhibitions, world fairs, circuses as well as side shows—that routinely displayed human "oddities" in general, and people of African descent in particular.

For example, incidents in classic fugitive slave narratives pale beside the circumstances of the extraordinary birth of enslaved Africans, Millie-Christine McKoy, born Siamese twins. The intrigue revolving around their physical bodies and exploitation goes beyond the usual human slave trade. With the capacity to earn $600 a week, the twin sisters experienced multifaceted traumas of being constantly uprooted as well as a long perilous separation from their parents. As Frederick Drimmer writes, "Obviously their value as natural curiosities was recognized and it was high; in later years it was said that their final purchaser, J. P. Smith, paid thirty thousand dollars for them. They were still only infants."[5] The McKoy girls' lives bespeak the popularity of melodrama during the antebellum period. Susan Gillman's *Blood Talk: American Race Melodrama and the Culture of the Occult* coins "race melodrama" to define nominally and temporally a theory that "points to the irreducible historical identity of race itself as melodrama in the United States."[6]

As relates to melodrama, a binary opposition exists regarding victimization and escape. Compared to a fugitive slave narrative, the life of Millie-Christine contain all the melodrama and sentimentality without the physical escape. Fused together at the spine, their bodies locked them into a lifetime of exhibitionism. The slave auction is an abiding recursive motif in slave narratives; however, being sold at ten months to a showbusiness promoter for a flat fee and percentage of exhibition profits deviates from even this institutions' norm. Melodrama usually unfolds as a perilous existence, depending on excess and extremes. Typically, a fugitive slave took flight from an unscrupulous slaveowner, not disputing promoters. En route to being spirited across the

---

[4] In his *Circus Lingo,* 16, Joe McKennon capitalizes his definition.
[5] Frederick Drimmer, *Very Special People: The Struggles, Loves, and Triumphs of Human Oddities,* 86.
[6] Susan Gillman, *Blood Talk: American Race Melodrama and the Culture of the Occult,* 4. While Gillman situates "race melodrama" to interrogate "race literature," I locate its relevance within popular mass culture. Linda Williams, *Playing the Race Card: Melodramas of Black and White from Uncle Tom to O.J. Simpson,* xiv, too, situates melodrama "as the fundamental mode by which American mass culture has "talked to itself" about the enduring dilemma of race."

ocean to Britain, "The United African Twins," as they were often billed at three years old, stopped for a very public appearance at Barnum's Museum in New York City. Finally, J. P. Smith relocated the twins in England. Due to slavery being abolished in Britain, neither of the disputing parties could claim property rights; and although a trial actually restored the sisters to their birth mother, once back in the U.S., Millie-Christine continued touring under Smith's ownership.

Ironically, it is noteworthy that their status as freaks held hegemony over their race. Bogdan describes two presentation modes: exotic and the aggrandized statuses. The exotic defines presentations privileging difference, while the aggrandized defines representations with superiority.[7] As noted by their biographer Joann Martell, an eminent London doctor deemed them to be of above average intelligence compared to most European children of the same age; and their mistress, Mrs. Smith breached Southern laws by teaching them to read and write.[8] In his article, "Melodrama, Body, Revolution," Peter Brooks writes: "None of these melodramas can reach its denouement until the virtuous bodies have been freed, and explicitly recognized as bearing the sign of innocence."[9] Paradoxically, while attaining their quest for literacy, even after all slaves were emancipated in the U.S., Millie-Christine's virtual bondage continued. They elected to continue their career, melodramatically, supporting two families including their white mistress, who remained their guardian. As relates to feminist politics, the McKoys curtailed their victimization when they ended the invasive practice by voyeuristic doctors of examining them gynecologically. Their melodramatic embodiment ended in 1912 as Millie died and Christine succumbed soon after.

Like race melodramas, in principle, minstrelsy grants agency by propping up a racialized hierarchy. For instance, Zip, the What-is-it, was, in circus parlance, a pinhead. William Henry Johnson, today would possibly be diagnosed with microcephaly (born with an abnormally small cranium). The historical moment, which John Culhane labeled "The Golden Age" of the American circus, also coincided with what others variously called the Age of Darwin, the Age of Essentialism, and the Age of African Exploration. As African American psychologist, Robert Guthrie positions it, then, the impetus was to "question anew the relationship of man to the 'lower' animals."[10] Zip's public appearances speak to the racial profiling of his era. Barnum billed him

---

[7] Bogdan in Thomson, *Freakery,* 29.
[8] Martell, *Bandwagon*, 36-37.
[9] Brooks in Bratton, *Melodrama: Stage Picture Screen,* 16.
[10] Guthrie, *Even the Rat Was White*, 36.

"as the missing link between man and ape, and said he had been captured in Africa by a party in pursuit of gorillas."[11]

The 19th Century's adoption of colonialism and imperialism along with Darwinism was destined to lead to additional "curiosities."[12] It is Zip's longevity in this paradoxical role of demented, yet gentle, wild man that signifies the most. Early Barnum publications advertised him "as a most singular animal, which though it has many of the features and characteristics of both the human and brute, is not, apparently, either, but, in appearance, a mixture of both—the connecting link between humanity and brute creation." At a time when other African American men might be lynched for associating with white women, the circus proffered its own caste system which allowed Zip to transgress numerous boundaries for laughs.[13] Even his stage name embraces Zip Coon of minstrelsy fame. Contemporaneous with minstrelsy-about which much

---

[11] Culhane, *The American Circus:An Illustrated History,* 167, situates Zip within the context of his primary audience-"people who persuaded themselves they were higher on the evolutionary scale." Also, see Robert Bogden, *Freak Show: Presenting Human Oddities for Amusement and Profit,* 134-141; and Janet Davis *The Circus Age: Circus and Society under the American Big Top,* 181-183. Davis indicates: "In line with scientific constructions of racial differences, Johnson's race kept manlines, and all its association with whiteness and the respectable family, out of his 'developmental grasp.'"

[12] Philip Kunhardt, Jr, Philip Kunhardt III and Peter Kunhardt, *P.T. Barnum: America's Greatest Showman,* 149, indicate that Zip made his appearance within months of Darwin's publication of *The Origin of the Species.* James W. Cook, "Of Men, Missing Links and Nondescripts" in Thomson's *Freakery,* 149, recognizes the theatrical shifts in which Barnum, "never limited himself to permanently fixed or one-dimensional characters". Yet, I argue even within the grander schemes of evolutionary roles assumed by William Henry Johnson, he still ends up with a name associated with minstrelsy, Zip. Cook, however elects to contextualize Johnson solely within the discourse of American sectional controversies of the 1850's. I propose even greater fluidity is required in interpreting Johnson's shifting stereotypical role.

[13] Several photos in the Ringling Museum's photo collection present this shift. Zip is shown posing with white women, including teeing a golf ball off of the face of Mlle. Londy, the world's tallest woman. Photo accession number: P.G. 1-8-35, #364516. See James W. Cook, Jr., "Of Men, Missing Links, and Nondescripts: The Strange Career of P. T. Barnum's 'What is It?' Exhibition," in Thomson, 139-157. He, too, indicates a slippage in Zip's roles from a Darwinian theme to comic figure, belatedly adding the new name—Zip. Although Cook plays with staged hybridity as a construct to position Zip as tangential to the dehumanizing minstrel show's racial characterization, his interrogation situates a "different kind of racial categorization," 152. His query mainly historicizes Zip within the mid-nineteenth century sectionalist discourse. I attempt to recenter the difference as defamiliarizing yet a form of American-made minstrelsy, nonetheless. One cannot decenter the moniker "Zip" from its full context, Zip Coon of the minstrel stage. In essence, Barnum said it all by so renaming this curiosity, exhibiting him using more ludic and ludicrous displays, negating the African jungle imagery.

has been written of late-Zip's farcical career better positioned him "to act out in exaggerated stereotypic ways."[14] As Bernth Lindsfor surmises, "Zip was a new kind of freak—a happy, wholesome, harmless little monster."[15]

Concurrent with William Henry Johnson's performance, typically accompanying World Fairs, ethnological exhibitions also emerged as popular public display events. Zip's ethnological performance began on a lofty pseudoscientific note portraying him as "the missing link," but devolved into depicting him theatrically and predictably in the stale minstrel role of Zip Coon. Subsequently "[Zip] became a favorite object of press mockery and of circus publicity stunts."[16] Upon his death in 1926, he was reportedly almost 90 years old, having spent almost seven decades on stage. Quite the spectacle, according to reports, an estimated hundred million people ultimately observed him—more than any other phenomenon.

Ethnological exhibitions (also called human zoos) historicize the dreams, hopes, or frustrations of people during a particular era. As pertains to such exhibitions, Bogdan indicates:

> Display of non-Westerners in freak shows was not intended as a cross-cultural experience to provide patrons with real knowledge of the ways of life and thinking of a foreign group of people. Rather, it was a money-making activity that prospered by embellishing exhibits with exaggerated, bogus presentations emphasizing their strange customs and beliefs. Showmen took people who were culturally and ancestrally non-Western and made them freaks by casting them as bizarre and exotic: cannibals, savages, and barbarians.[17]

Their popularity speaks to colonialism as well as the broader construction of racial hierarchy, especially in relation to Africa—"the Dark Continent." Robert Rydell suggests that this exotic mode of exhibition gained legitimacy because "representations of Africa and Africans were prominent features."[18] Displays of African "Negroes" in the U.S. served to delimit a continuing fascination for the body of people of African descent.

---

[14] Bogdan, *Freakery: Cultural Spectacles of the Extraordinary Body*, 28. For more regarding minstrelsy, see Lhamon, Lott—also, Hoh & Rough mention that the first Black owned troupe, the Original Georgia Minstrels dates to 1865 founded by Charles B. Hicks, 67. For more details about minstrelsy as it relates to circus, see *Clowns* by John H. Towsen, 120-24, and *A History of the Circus in America* by George Chindahl, 193. Historian Sotiropoulos interrogates Jim Crow's blackface counterpart, Zip Coon, as "the minstrel invention meant to deride free blacks," 37. She further positions what she labels the "Coon Craze," 81-122.

[15] Lindfors, "Circus Africans," 12

[16] Bogdan, 137. Lindfors is the source of information about Zip's popularity, 13.

[17] Bogdan, x.

[18] Rydell, "Darkest Africa," 135.

In the 1930s, representatives of the African people, then erroneously and theatrically labeled as Ubangis, created quite a sensation. Bearing a distinctive physical feature, plate-sized lips, the Ubangis aroused condescending curiosity and much mirth. The commodification and enfreakment of cultural traits and the exhibition of ethnic groups outside their traditional context fit accepted ideology. As spectacles, the Ubangis' grotesque image of the body conformed to audience expectation of Africans. This brand of essentialism denotes the ways the human body manifests as a metaphor for society. According to Felipe Smith, "myths of race difference spawned mythic representations of the body in the cultural imaginary."[19] Toni Morrison's investigation into how American writers fabricated an Africanist presence in their works reveals a "powerful exploration of the fears and desires that reside in the writerly conscious."[20] The show stopping appearance of the five Ubangi men along with eight women similarly embodied a shrill, conscious response indicative of the anxieties as well as longings of white audiences.

In particular, the Ubangis fed a base need of a white American public during one of the U.S.'s dimmest hours: the Great Depression. During this era, "a dime [was] something you [didn't] throw away."[21] Therefore, to be persuasive, promotional ads for the Ubangis read: "Genuine Monster-mouthed Ubangi Savages World's Most Weird Living Human from Africa's Darkest Depths." This brand of imperial showmanship demonstrates how the amusement industry exploited the only functional aspect of racism: White Supremacy. Bogdan expresses that, by intentionality and design, these acts were promoted "to confirm African's inferiority and primitiveness."[22] The Ubangis' lipstretching rendered speech nearly impossible. Extant evidence indicates that, as Ringling's circus went into receivership, during its radio promotions, it capitalized on the Ubangi's exoticized speech patterns to enhance the circus' economy.[23]

---

[19] Smith, *American Body Politics,* xiii.

[20] Morrison, 17.

[21] Ronald Ostman, "Photography and Persuasion: Farm Security Administration Photographs of Circus and Carnival Sideshows, 1935-1942" in Thomson, 121-136. This article supplies the historical backdrop disclosing how the Ubangis kept Ringling Brothers and Barnum & Bailey's circus afloat. The details about their promotion occur in Bogdan, 193.

[22] Bogdan, 187. He also states: "what they saw merely confirmed old prejudices and beliefs regarding the separateness of the "enlightened" and "primitive" worlds; they left the freak show reassured of their own superiority by such proofs of the others' inferiority," 197.

[23] Joseph T. Bradbury, "Al G. Barnes Circus Seasons of 1931-1932," *The White Tops* 59 (1986) and Culhane discuss the Ubangi sensation, 218-221. Culhane is quoting Fred Bradna, 219. Also, see Bogdan, 193-7. He presents Bradna as saying "the Ringling paid

One of the most intriguing aspects of the Ubangis' visit is the supposed curse leveled against their promoter. Culhane recycles the legend that the Ubangis were miserably unhappy in America and used conjuration to rid them of their agent Dr. Bergonnier, who died mysteriously weeks after being "ordered to leave the show."[24] No doubt, as a caption in Lewis and Fish's book states: "The big attraction of Ringling's 1930 season, even to the circus people, was the Ubangis." Relying on personal experience, they go on to comment that fellow troupers were bemused by them, "trying to carry on conversations with them." Ethnocentric undertones gain clarity as they indicate: "The women smoked pipes, and one day I asked one of them to let me light my cigarette from her pipe. She began giggling, and all the rest of the girls giggled, too. Maybe they thought I was looking for a wife. I took a lot of ribbing from the other elephant men over it, and didn't visit the Ubangis after that."[25] Human zoos and freak shows, capitalizing on displays of the noble savage, represent the mode in which Americans engaged in racist discourse.

Although the freak show ran its course between the 1840s and 1940s, one must be just as vigilant about present-day "curiosities." Just as "Political change and profit maximization helped to bring dramatic changes in Hollywood's depictions of plantation life in the Old South,"[26] the present-day American circus industry lags slightly behind. In the name of diversity, the 1980s witnessed the return of Zulus under the Big Top, at the height of the divestment movement to protest South African apartheid. Earlier, Zulus captivated world audiences straight from the Anglo-Zulu wars where, by twice defeating the British, their prowess gained much renown and generated immense curiosity.[27] Equally problematic, Sampson Power, from Kenya, recently performed as a strong man in Ringling Bros. and Barnum & Bailey. Forming conga lines with audience members, he exhibited the ability to lift "awesome amounts of weight with his body," even hefting huge hunks of heaviness—with his teeth. The 126th edition of Ringling's program reveals an awareness of the present-day need for authenticity. The program states, "During his moments of verbal interplay with the audience, he uses Swahili words that bespeak his positive outlook on life. His favorites include "hula-hula" (I'm Happy), "Tunga tunga" (I'm one who

---

$1500 a week for the exhibit; Bergonnier took all and let the Congolese make what they could by selling souvenir postcards at 5 cents a piece," 194. The Ubangis also are credited with Ringling's downfall with it being no secret that this same year Ringling lost control of its empire and Samuel Gumpertz was placed in charge of all Ringling shows.

[24] Culhane, 220.

[25] George Lewis and Byron Fish, *I Loved Rogues,* 38.

[26] Robert Brent Toplin, (ed.), *Hollywood as Mirror: Changing Views of "Outsiders" and "Enemies" in American Movies,* xii.

[27] Lindsfor in Thomson, 214-17.

brings new ideas") and huga-huga ("I'm proud") (n.p., 1996).[28] He's portrayed attired in traditional "Zulu" regalia replete with a spear and decorative shield, while sporting dreadlocks. Actually, the language is agglutinative. The Kiswahili (coast people), in particular, are very proud of their language (sort of like Parisian French pride) and go out of their way to create long, poetical and mellifluous sentences. Even as the amusement industry reconstitutes itself, unfortunately, still the tendency is to exploit racial exoticism.

In 1999, the 129th edition of the Greatest Show on Earth premiered Ringling's first African American, and its youngest, ringmaster. Johnathan Lee Iverson speaks not only to social progress. but the possibility for transformative changes within the American circus itself. Iverson's appointment, however, reinscribes the multicultural and globalization themes. Circus performances have long been the domain of artists from elsewhere. He arrived under the Big Top at a time when the theme of racial diversity resonated. Yet multiculturalism is downplayed. Iverson has acknowledged: "You have Russian, Brazilian, and Hungarian performers. Race doesn't matter for them."[29]

Today, colorblind casting gains center stage as a means of including representations of people of color by casting actors of color in roles not written for them. Traditionally, within circus parlance, a "singing announcer and performance directors are not ringmasters"[30] Dating to 1951, Harold Ronk was the first singing ringmaster. He was classically trained. Iverson performed with the world-famous Boys Choir of Harlem and is a graduate from the University of Hartford's School of Music where he sang in the school's opera productions. His acclaim is as a songster in keeping with operatic vocal skills. While Ronk was a baritone, Iverson sings tenor and is described as having a "mellifluous, opera quality voice."[31] Moreover, when performing with the Boys Choir of Harlem the repertoire included a variety of styles including hip-hop. Nonetheless, known as the Lord of the Ring, Iverson's appointment, as a singer, perhaps can also be interpreted as overdue. In 1967, Irvin Feld purchased Ringling. Much of his fortune accrued from pioneering in the integration of the concert business by touring African American performers such as Chuck Berry,

---

[28] Program Book, 126th Ringling Bros.and Barnum & Bailey (1996).

[29] "Lord of the Rings,"
http://www.philly.com/packages/history/arts/stage/circus/CIRC14.asp
The article goes on to indicate that the "222 cast and crew members in this year's show represent 13 countries." Also, see "Circus Ringmaster Breaks New Ground," *Sarasota Herald Tribune*, January 3, 1999.

[30] Joe McKennon, *Circus Lingo* (Sarasota: Carnival Publishers, 1980), 78.

[31] "America's Youth Looks Up to the Wrong Iverson,"
http://www.robbywerner.com/iverson.htm.

Fats Domino, and Harry Belafonte. Yet it took Ringling many decades to integrate the position of ringmaster.

One concern with colorblind casting is that "Diversity for the sake of diversity is just a band-aid, a substitute for deeper considerations of culture, for actually committing to making a bigger world for ourselves."[32] Playwright Migdalia Cruz objects to the thrust toward diversity that conceals the inability to deal with cultural differences. In 2005, African American Tyron McFarlan became Ringling's thirty-fourth ringmaster, bringing a Broadway pedigree. As a cautionary warning, we must be adamant about contesting excessive universalism along with racial hierarchy. A cognate of essentialism, Grosz indicates: "universalism tends to suggest only the commonness of all [people] at all times and in all social contexts."[33] In conclusion, I raise the question: does the American circus industry now insist on a creating a utopian fantasy, without critiquing its historic role of playing in the dark to racial stereotype?

Bibliography

Ashcroft, Bill, et.al. *Key Concepts in Post-Colonial Studies*. New York: Routledge, 1998.

Bakhtin, Mikhail. *Rabelais and His World*. Translated by Helene Iswolsky. Bloomington: Indiana University Press., 1984.

Bogdan, Robert. *Freak Show: Presenting Human Oddities for Amusement and Profit*. Chicago: University of Chicago Press, 1988.

Bradbury, Joseph T. "Al G. Barnes Circus Seasons of 1931-1932," *The White Tops* 59 (1986).

Bratton, Jacky, Jim Cook, and Christine Gledhill (eds.). *Melodrama: Stage Picture Screen*. London: British Film Institute, 1994.

Brooks, Peter. *The Melodramatic Imagination*. New Haven: Yale University Press, 1976.

Chindahl, George. *A History of the Circus in America*. Caldwell, ID: Caxton, 1959.

Culhane, John. *The American Circus: An Illustrated History*. New York: Henry Holt, 1990.

Davis, Janet. *The Circus Age: Culture & Society Under the American Big Top*. Chapel Hill: University of North Carolina Press, 2002.

Drimmer, Frederick. *Very Special People: The Struggles, Loves, and Triumphs of Human Oddities*. New York: Amjon, 1973.

---

[32] "Migdalia Cruz" (1994) http://www.ntcp.org/compendium/artists/MIGDALIA.html.
[33] Grosz, *Space, Time, and Perversion*, 48-9.

Fiedler, Leslie. *Freaks: Myths and Images of the Secret Self.* New York: Simon & Schuster, 1978.

Freeman, Larry. *Big Top Circus Days.* New York: Century House, 1964.

Gillman, Susan. *Blood Talk: American Race Melodrama and the Culture of the Occult.* Chicago: University of Chicago Press, 2003.

Grosz, Elizabeth. *Space, Time, and Perversion: Essays on the Politics of Bodies.* New York: Routledge, 1995.

Guthrie, Robert. *Even the Rat Was White: A Historical View of Psychology.* Harper & Row, 1976.

Hoh, LaVahn and William Rough. *Step Right Up! The Adventure of Circus in America.* Whitehall, VA: Betterway, 1990.

Kunhardt, Jr. Philip, Philip Kunhardt III, and Peter Kunhardt. *P. T. Barnum: America's Greatest Showman.* New York: Knopf, 1995.

Kunzog, John. "Kicking Sawdust in the Center Ring of Memories: The Story of J. Augustus Jones and His Circuses." *Bandwagon*, Vol. 21.. March-April 1977.

Lewis, George and Byron Fish. *I Loved Rogues.* Seattle: Superior, 1978.

Lhamon, William. *Raising Cain: Blackface Performance from Jim Crow to Hip Hop.* Cambridge: Harvard, 1998.

Lindfors, Bernth, (ed.). *Africans on Stage.* Bloomington: Indiana University Press., 1999.

Lindfors, Bernth. "Circus Africans." *Journal of American Culture* 6 (1983).

Lott, Eric. *Love & Theft: Blackface Minstrelsy and the American Working Class.* New York: Oxford, 1993.

Mannix, Daniel. *Freaks: We Who Are Not As Others.* San Francisco: Search, 1990.

Martell, Joanne. "Fearfully and Wonderfully Made: Millie-Christine, the African Twins." *Bandwagon* (Jan-Feb, 1998), 35-38.

—. *Fearfully and Wonderfully Made: Millie-Christine, the African Twins.* Winston-Salem, NC: Blair, 2000.

McConachie, Bruce. *Melodramatic Formations: American Theatre and Society, 1820-1870.* Iowa City: University of Indiana Press, 1992.

McKennon, Joe. *Circus Lingo.* Sarasota: Carnival Publishers, 1980.

Morrison, Toni. *Playing in the Dark: Whiteness and the Literary Imagination.* New York: Vintage, 1992.

Plowden, Gene. *Those Amazing Ringlings and Their Circus.* Caldwell, ID: Caxton, 1967.

Ringling Bros. and Barnum & Bailey *Program,* 1996

Rydell, Robert. "'Darkest Africa': African Shows at America's World's Fairs" in *Africans on Stage* edited by Lindsfor.

Sarasota Herald Tribune. "Circus Ringmaster Breaks New Ground." January 3, 1999.

Smith, Felipe. *American Body Politics: Race, Gender, and Black Literary Renaissance.* Athens: University of Georgia Press, 1998.

Sotiropoulos, Karen. *Staging Race: Black Performers in Turn of the Century America.* Cambridge, MA: Harvard University Press, 2006.

Thomson, Rosemarie (ed.). *Freakery: Cultural Spectacles of the Extraordinary Body.* New York: New York University Press. 1996.

Toplin, Robert Brent (ed.). *Hollywood as Mirror: Changing Views of "Outsiders" and "Enemies" in American Movies.* Westport: CT: Greenwood Press, 1993.

Towsen, John H. *Clowns.* New York: Hawthorn, 1976.

Williams, Linda. *Playing the Race Card: Melodramas of Black and White From Uncle Tom to O. J .Simpson.* Princeton, NJ: Princeton University Press, 2001.

CHAPTER SIX

STRONG WOMEN AND CROSS-DRESSED MEN: REPRESENTATIONS OF GENDER BY PERFORMERS DURING THE GOLDEN AGE OF THE AMERICAN CIRCUS

MARCY WYNN MURRAY

"I don't want realism. I want magic! Yes, yes, magic! I try to give that to people. I misrepresent things to them. I don't tell the truth, I tell what ought to be the truth. And if that is sinful, then let me be damned for it—Don't turn the light on!"
—Tennessee Williams, *A Streetcar Named Desire* (1947)

The 'Golden Age' of the American circus (1860-1930) occurred during a time of rapid change and unrest in this nation. America during this time period was experiencing challenges to traditionally accepted norms long held to be innate and constant. These challenges included racial, social, and sexual transformations. The supremacy of the white, middle-upper class male was under attack from the immigrant, the working class, African-Americans, and the New Woman. In response to this change, the circus sought to establish itself as traditional and family entertainment. Janet Davis points out that, "the circus [was] an entertainment that had self-consciously defined itself as 'respectable' and 'moral' particularly since the late nineteenth century."[1] The performances presented in the circus during this time functioned as filters that aided society in coming to terms with the threats and challenges to the white middle-class, male hierarchy.

From the mid-1800s, America experienced a 'crisis of masculinity,' and in response the dominant male culture developed compensative strategies; "thinking about masculinity in this period meant thinking about sexual and

---

[1] Davis, "The Life of Tiny Kline," 4-8.

racial dominance as well."[2] Nineteenth-century pseudo-scientific theories were used to reaffirm the white, middle-upper class male's place at the apex of the social hierarchy while keeping women and non-white males in a separate and lower sphere. One example of this scientific reaffirmation is "the late nineteenth-century's popularized Darwinism [in which] one could identify advanced civilizations by the degree of their sexual differentiation...men and women of the civilized races had evolved pronounced sexual differences."[3] This theory supported the gender dichotomy on which the patriarchal hierarchy depended by encouraging middle-to-upper class women to embrace an ornamental role. Methods used to depict their ornamental status included cumbersome clothing and an insistence of their own physical frailty. These indicators announced their socio-economic position--a position in which they had the means to have others (usually members of the lower classes) move and do for them.

Another scientific voice that supported the gender dichotomy by discouraging women from entering into the 'male' sphere was that of Kraft-Ebing who published the first modern study on human sexual behavior. When defining the term lesbian, "Kraft-Ebing did not focus on the sexual behavior of the women he categorized as lesbian but rather on their social behavior and physical appearance. [He] linked lesbianism to the rejection of conventional female roles, cross-dressing, and to 'masculine' physiological traits."[4] The underlying warning to women (most notably to the New Woman) in Kraft-Ebing's categorization was that to deviate from the traditional female sphere by action or appearance was to be labeled as 'degenerate' and 'other'.

The gender dichotomies recommended by the scientific theories of the day were often reinforced in popular media. For example, in 1899, *The New York Times* ran a story that reported, "In every instance the children of the less muscular and less robust women carry off the palm...the children of the more robust mothers...are in every instance inferior...to those of the more womanly type."[5] This article and others like it implied that the health of future generations depended on females remaining in their appropriate social spheres. These articles did not take into account class differentiation. In other words, more robust women were likely to be found among a lower, working class. Lacking access to proper nutritional, medical, and educational advantages, they and their

---

[2] Kasson, *Houdini, Tarzan, and the Perfect Man*, 19.
[3] Bederman, *Manliness and Civilization: A Cultural History of Gender and Race in the United States, 1880-1917*, 25.
[4] Smith-Rosenberg, "Discourses on Sexuality and Subjectivity: The New Woman, 1870-1936," 269.
[5] "Muscular Parents," 19.

children would consequently be inferior to the children of middle-to-upper class (and less robust) women.

Men of the period were also assaulted by a media that advocated gender dichotomy. They were bombarded with images and stories of self-made men like President Roosevelt, Eugen Sandow, and Bernarr Mac Fadden; "these men emphasized how, by dint of determination and method, they had transformed themselves from puny boys to men of strength, confidence, and command."[6] The middle-to-upper class American males who had supposedly 'gone soft' from their years away from physical labor, were now required to build their bodies so that they could compete against the lower class, non-white males.

Despite the scientific theories and media attempts to confine men and women to separate spheres, a counterculture soon appeared that advocated less cumbersome clothing and more physical exercise for women. This counterculture gained a rapid popularity. Its proponents included Bernarr Mac Fadden whose publication *Physical Training* advocated physical health as a beauty aid; "there is not a sign denoting beauty which has not either its origin or its influencing power in the physical side of life…Health is the very foundation of all beauty-grand or simple."[7] Mac Fadden and his associates worked diligently to counteract the demands that the male-dominated American society placed upon its women.

It is in this environment that the strong woman and male cross-dressing performer existed. Although it may be argued that circus performers existed outside the boundaries of normative society, their existence and livelihood depended upon that society's acceptance. The balance that these performers attained indicates much about American society during the Golden Age of the American circus. Joanna Frueh points out that, "scholars now recognize that both the circus and the various forms of variety theater [in which circus acts performed during their 'off' season] in the late nineteenth-century were influential transmitters of ideals and images."[8] As mentioned above, the circus performer functioned as a filter through which the American society was able to come to terms with the threats and challenges to its male hierarchy.

The Strong Woman

"We are all monsters, if it comes to that,
We women who choose to be something more
And something less than women"
—May Sarton, *Mrs. Stevens Hears the Mermaids Singing* (1956)

---

[6] Kasson, 32.
[7] Ibid., 87-88.
[8] Frueh, *The Modern Amazon,* 50.

Circus acts often echoed and exaggerated the performance aspect that they perceived in the late nineteenth/early twentieth-century assigned gender roles. In the arena of the circus (and outside of the normative society's rules), the strong woman could safely challenge the stereotype of the innately frail female. Viewed as an anomaly or a freak of nature, the strong woman presented no direct threat to the male hierarchy though she stood as a reminder of female physical potential. Gail Bederman points out that mid-nineteenth century society conflated bodily strength with social authority and consequently "identified the powerful, large male body of the heavyweight prizefighter...as the epitome of manhood."[9] The strong woman, whose physical appearance and strength were closer to this ideal of manhood than many of the male members of her audience, might have been construed as threatening. The ever-vigilant circus press agents addressed this potential threat by coupling the strong woman's strength with her 'traditional' feminine qualities.

Fig. 6-1. Strobridge Lithographic Co., Barnum & Bailey: Katie Sandwina.
Courtesy of the John and Mable Ringling Museum of Art, Tibbals Digital Collection.

The billing of the strong woman truly illustrates the genius of the circus press. The advertisements simultaneously neutralized the strong woman's threat to the social hierarchy, negated the scientific theories of the day that would class her as 'primitive' and 'lesbian,' and promised a thrilling act! The strong woman

[9] Bederman, 8.

was billed as "a graceful athlete" and a "beautiful Herculean Venus (possessing) beauty and strength" (Fig. 6-1.) The lithographs used to advertise the strong woman indicates that they are anything but 'mannish'. For example, in figure 6-1, Kate Sandwina is depicted in a scanty costume, with a peaches and cream complexion, femininely posed amongst roses (one of which adorns her beautifully coiffed hair). Cecile Lindsay quotes advertisements of Sandwina that describe her as "the most beautiful...the most skillful...the strongest of the world's women."[10] It is the combination of beauty and brawn that made the circus strong woman a popular act.

Press releases about Sandwina were equally enticing; "Kate Carew, a reporter for a New York newspaper, described [her] as the 'most bewilderingly beautiful woman I have ever seen. She is as majestic as the Sphinx, as pretty as a valentine, and as wholesome as a great big slice of bread and butter."[11] and "William Ingliss...in a 1911 article for *Harper's Weekly* [reported] Sandwina had 'as pretty a face, as sweet a smile and as fine a head of silky brown curls as a man could ask to see...but she [also] had the muscles of Thor'."[12] Press releases such as these and circus bills indicate the circus' determination to balance the strong woman's physical might with more traditional feminine attributes, such as beauty, sweet disposition, and wholesomeness.

Fig. 6-2 and 6-3. Frederick Whitier Glasier, Charmion.
Courtesy of the John and Mable Ringling Museum of Art.

Charmion, another popular strong woman (and trapeze artist) of the period, paid homage to another side of the 'feminine' sphere in her act. During her

---

[10] Lindsay, "Body Building: A Postmodern Freak Show," 358.
[11] Frueh, 54.
[12] Ibid.

vaudeville months, she gained a great deal of fame and notoriety with her 'trapeze disrobing' act. Her act was unique; "unlike other strongwomen she didn't demonstrate her prowess by lifting things; instead she preferred to display her physique […] to the admiring throngs."[13] While she was with the Barnum & Bailey show (1904), Charmion was photographed by Frederick W. Glasier. These images capture her strength and femininity (Figs. 6-2 and 6-3.) Comparisons between Glasier's images of Charmion and Kate Sandwina (Figs. 6-4 and 6-5) and the photographs of Madame Yucca [another well-known strong woman of the period (Fig. 6-6) indicate the different aspects that each chose to display. Charmion's character is blatantly sexual-she looks directly at the camera and is often partially disrobed. Sandwina is coy and soft with no overt display of physical strength, almost cheesecake. Yucca appears strong and verges on the asexual-the gladiator-style costume that she wears is short, but not suggestive.

Though the feminine stereotypes that these strong women assumed were different, they all worked to ensure that the women remained unthreatening to the established gender hierarchy while their strength and physiques challenged and undermined the notions of theirs as the weaker, gentler sex.

Fig 6-4 and Fig 6-5.Frederick Whitier Glasier, Charmion and Katie Sandwina.
Fig. 6-6.Unknown artist, Madame Yucca.
Courtesy of the John and Mable Ringling Museum of Art.

The Cross-Dressed Male Performer

"This is a boy, sir. Not a girl. If you're baffled by the difference. It might be as well to approach both with caution"
—Joe Orton, *What the Butler Saw* (1969)

Male cross-dressing has traditionally been viewed as more threatening to the gender hierarchy than female cross-dressing. The female cross-dresser's

---

[13] Chapman.

desire to be male supports the hierarchy's claim of male superiority while the male's desire to be female challenges it. The dominant culture reduces the threat of the male cross-dresser by ridiculing him or labeling him a deviant or degenerate. For the most part however, male *circus performers* who cross-dressed from 1860 to 1930 escaped this treatment.

The male performer's cross-dressing was viewed (when detected or acknowledged) as his costume; it was a necessity of his act. The theory behind the necessity of the male cross-dressed circus performer was that the average male was stronger and more daring than the average female, but the audience craved the thrill and novelty of female circus acts. Laurence Senelick points out "there was more thrill in beholding a young girl carrying out perilous or difficult feats."[14] A 1902 *New York Times* article supports his assertion:

> The circusgoers [sic] were so much impressed with women who rode horses in ballroom gowns that this form of attraction has been amplified and all the circuses are trying to get riders who can jump through hoops [...] clad in cumbersome costumes [...] that an ordinary woman would find inconvenient even for a drawing room [...] the woman who essays to learn [this act] must be as strong as she is adept, and this is what makes it so hard for a manager to secure riders of the newly popular class.[15]

This article reiterates that it is not the act itself that is so thrilling, but the fact that a female performs it, and in evening dress no less, as the images here indicate (Fig. 6-7). The male cross-dressed performer who could perform these stunts and 'pass' as a woman was an asset to a circus.

In order to 'pass' the male performer used the gender stereotypes of the day to deceive the audience. The billings for these performers depict their 'womanly' qualities: Miss Daisy (Briton Albert Hodgini) was "billed as a graceful Italian rider;"[16] "*The Era* called Lulu (Eddie Rivers) 'a young and beautiful lady;'"[17] while "performing with Hengler's Cirque [...] Lulu was described as [...] 'young, good-looking and very modest in appearance, rejoicing in a profusion of light hair and [...] dressed tastefully;'"[18] The Bertram Mills Circus billed Barbette (Vander Clyde) as "gorgeous [and] indescribable";[19] and Berta (Herbert) Beeson was described as "that graceful chiffon-clad person."[20] These descriptions clearly indicate the male cross-

---

[14] Senelick, 296.

[15] "Latest Circs Wonders, The."

[16] Draper, "The Riding Hodgini Family," 5.

[17] Gossard, *A Reckless Era of Aerial Performance: The Evolution of the Trapeze,* 82.

[18] Ibid., 84.

[19] Jamiesen, *Bertram Mills: TheCircus that Traveled by Train,* 21.

[20] "Artist's Dance 'Floor" Fraction of an Inch Wide."

dressed performers' use of gender stereotypes to facilitate their disguise. They are young, beautiful, graceful, modest, and chiffon-clad.

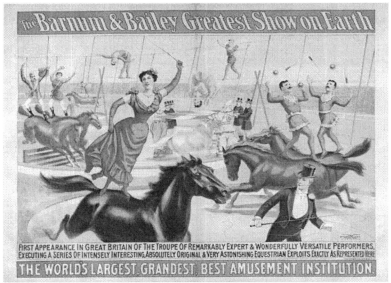

Fig. 6-7. Strobridge Lithographic Co., Barnum & Bailey: Performers.
Courtesy of the John and Mable Ringling Museum of Art, Tibbals Digital Collection.

This use of gender stereotype reinforced the existing gender hierarchy and, at the same time, indicated the constructed status of gender. As Rudolph Dekker points out, "one's sex is determined by physical characteristics; one's gender is determined by clothing, behavior, speech, and all the other external characteristics."[21] The male cross-dressed performers understood this constructed status of gender and incorporated the gender stereotypes (used to enforce the gender hierarchy) to deceive their audience.

The origins of several of these performers further indicate the learned status of gender. Most of them began their cross-dressing at an early age. Barbette, for example, was 14 when he began performing as a female. And Spencer Stokes, who 'created' Ella Zoyara from his seven year-old apprentice, Omar Kingsley, began the transformation by dressing the boy as a girl and providing him with female companions. Furthermore, he had the boy instructed in "sewing, embroidery, and other diversions of the female sex."[22] And when Farini began

---

[21] Decker and Van de Pol, *The Tradition of Female Transvestisim in Modern Europe*, 48.
[22] Kitchen, "Will the Real Zoyara Please Stand Up?"

dressing his adopted son, Eddie Rivers, as a girl and shooting him from his cannon, he created Lulu, "the eighth wonder of the world."[23] The early tutelage of these performers in the 'feminine arts' helped to create a more convincing illusion because they had no 'masculine' traits to unlearn.

Obviously the creation of a fictional person had some drawbacks; for the deception to be effective this female performer had to exist outside the ring as well as inside. The life that their female personae took on varied. For example, Zoyara seemed to exist as a female in and out of the ring. This is indicated by the fact that some of his fellow performers were unaware of his 'true' sex: "Richard Hemmings [...] stated that he performed with Ella [...] and then traveled through England with [her] and never had the slightest suspicion that Ella was not a girl."[24] Beeson created the illusion of a feminine existence via reports in the press such as: "a maid dressed in a Frenchy [sic] frock accompanies the wire artist to and from the rings [...] and seven trunks of wardrobe are carried on tour."[25] The deceptive nature of the cross-dressers' act complicated their lives outside of the ring. The public's discovery of the deception would destroy the illusion that they created.

It is interesting that Barbette's act, which ended in the revelation of his 'true' sex, was not affected by this disclosure. His 'true' identity as a male seemed, instead, to create a supernatural reality to his female alter ego: "it is only when he puts on his blonde wig [...] that he assumes all the gestures of a woman doing her hair. He gets up, walks about and puts on his rings. The metamorphosis is complete. Jekyll is Hyde. Yes, Hyde. For I'm frightened. I turn away."[26] While the fear that Barbette's transformation creates in his male observer could be read as the observer's fear of his own attraction to another male, it might also indicate his realization that masculinity and the idea of gender is an ambiguous and constructed category. In either case, Barbette's cross-dressing is depicted as being too successful for the observer's comfort.

This success is indicated in descriptions of his 'unveiling' during which he must convince the duped audience of his masculinity: "Cocteau describes the [...] many embarrassed, disbelieving faces [...] Barbette had introduced his act by miming the essence of femininity, he ended it by playing an extremely masculine role."[27] Barbette knew that a public deception as large as a female alter ego could not stay secret for long and, therefore, he refused to hide his masculinity and instead, made it the climax of his act.

---

[23] Gossard, 82.

[24] Kitchen, 24.

[25] "Artist's Dance Floor."

[26] Crossland, *Cocteau's World,* 222.

[27] Crowson, *The Esthetic of Jean Coctaeu,* 103

Other male cross-dressed performers also realized that their deception could not go on indefinitely. Lulu's cross-dressing stint for example was "played up as a novel publicity stunt: 'the illusion of LU LU's sex is now dispelled. The beautiful LU LU of 1871 is the same as the wondrous of 1879; but the

Fig. 6-8. Strobridge Lithographic Co., The Original and Only LuLu.
Courtesy of the Cincinnati Museum of Art.

performance of the LU LU of 1879 is *entirely distinct* from that of the LU LU of the former period."[28] (Fig 6-8.) When Beeson's deception was made public, he began to bill himself as "Berta Beeson, the Julian Eltinge of the tight wire."[29] This comparison between himself and the respected Eltinge who cross-dressed onstage, but maintained a 'he-man' persona off-stage, allowed Beeson to confirm the performance aspect of his cross-dressing and proclaim his masculinity. And "when [his] maleness was eventually 'discovered' by the circus press [...] Hodgini's publicity photographs confirmed his identity as a decent family man with a wife and two children."[30]

---

[28] Gossard, 86.
[29] Spiegel.
[30] Davis. *The Circus Age: Culture and Society Under the American Big Top.* 116.

Only Zoyara refused to 'act the man' off-stage. Though he married twice and fathered four children, Zoyara continued to cross-dress both in and out of the ring. He refused to conform to the dominant culture's gender assignments and, as a result, received both profits and threats from the public. The question of Zoyara's 'true' sex and the publicity that it generated was profitable for the circus. Audiences flocked to the show to see if they could determine Zoyara's sex. At the same time, there was element of anger at the deception. This is indicated in an excerpt from the February 11, 1860 issue of the *New York Clipper* which seems to threaten Zoyara with the potential consequences of his continued masquerade: "If the imposition is not soon stopped, we fear there will be a public manifestation and examination [of Zoyara's person] not set down on the program."[31] This implied threat, however, did not deter Zoyara who continued to perform as a woman until 1867 and "even after giving up the charade it is said that he continued to do needlework and would sit in his dressing tent wearing a female's wrapper."[32] Zoyara's attachment to the feminine aspect of his person, along with his pre-pubescent tutelage in that aspect, indicates that gender is a learned (rather than innate) behavior.

Although Zoyara refused to kneel to the dominant society's insistence of male behavior, other male cross-dressed performers felt the necessity to do so. The adoption of 'manly' behavior by Beeson and Hodgini reflects society's conflation of gender and sex, and its insistence on innate differences between male and female. But it is Barbette's performance that indicates that he not only understood the constructed status of gender and its power, but openly ridiculed it: "Only at the end of the performance, when he removed his wig, did he dispel the illusion, at which time he mugged and flexed in a masculine manner to emphasize the success of his earlier deception."[33] This display of masculinity that was used to 'prove' Barbette's maleness mocked that same masculinity as performance--the show that Barbette recognized it to be.

The strong women and the cross-dressed men of the American circus between 1860 and 1930 contributed to the nation's changing perceptions of gender. They contradicted the gender stereotypes of their day from the safety of the fringe in which they lived. As social outsiders and performers, their actions reflected and challenged the dominant culture's values without posing a discernable threat to them. Their influence was subtle. They planted the seed of possibility in the circus audience's mind; the seeds that would take root and create new attitudes about gender roles and the hierarchy that they supported.

---

[31] Kitchen, 26.
[32] Ibid., 28.
[33] Curlee, "Clyde Vander," 1.

Bibliography

"Artist's Dance 'Floor' Fraction of Inch Wide." *Mansfield News*. 18 Jun. 1926.

"Barbette in Amazing Feats at the Palace." *New York Times*. 8 Feb. 1927.

Bederman, Gail. *Manliness and Civilization: A Cultural History of Gender and Race in the United States, 1880-1917*. Chicago: University of Chicago Press, 1995.

Chapman, David. "Gallery of Ironman: Squeezable Charmion." Ironman Magazine. <http://www.ironmanmagazine.com/detail.php?pid=721>. 29 Jan. 2004.

Cline, Milonga. "Barbette." *Circus Report* 25 Dec. 2000.

"Condition of Women, The." *New York Times*. 1 June 1879.

Crosland, Margaret, ed. *Cocteau's World*. New York: Dodd, Mead, and Co., 1972.

Crowson, Lydia. *The Esthetic of Jean Cocteau*. Hanover: University Press of New England, 1978.

Curlee, Kendall. "Clyde Vander." The Handbook of Texas Online. 4 Dec. 2002. 22 Oct. 2003. <http://www.tsha.utexas.edu/handbook/online/articles/view/CC/fcl54.html>.

Davis, Janet M. *The Circus Age: Culture and Society Under the American Big Top*. North Carolina: The University of North Carolina Press, 2002.

—."The Life of Tiny Kline." *Bandwagon*. May-Jun. 2001.

D'Emilio, John and Estelle B. Friedman. *Intimate Matters: A History of Sexuality in America*. New York: Harper and Row, 1988.

Dekker, Rudolph M. and Lotte C. Van de Pol. *The Tradition of Female Transvestism in Modern Europe*. New York: St. Martin's Press, 1989.

Dolin, Anton. *Ballet Go Round*. London: Michael Joseph, Ltd., 1938.

Dowling, Colette. *The Frailty Myth*. New York: Random House, 2000.

Draper, John Daniel. "The Riding Hodgini Family." *Bandwagon*. May-Jun. 1993.

"Dress for Women." *New York Times*. 4 Dec. 1892.

Dubuque, Berry L. "The Original Miss Daisy." *Bandwagon*. Nov.-Dec. 1979.

Flugel, J.C. *The Psychology of Clothes*.1930. New York: International UP, Inc., 1971.

Frueh, Joanna, et al, eds. *The Modern Amazon*. New York: Rizzoli International Pub., Inc., 2000.

Gilbert, O.P. *Men in Women's Guises*. Trans. Robert B. Douglas. London: Jane Lane the Bodley Head, Ltd., 1926.

Goldbarth, Albert. *Different Fleshes*. Geneva: Hobart & William Smith Colleges Press, 1979.

Gossard, Steve. *A Reckless Era of Aerial Performance: The Evolution of the Trapeze*. 2nd ed. Normal: Self-Published, 1994.

Jamieson, David. *Bertram-Mills: The Circus that Traveled by Train*. England: Aardvark Pub., 1998.

Kasson, John F.. *Houdini, Tarzan, and the Perfect Man*. New York: Hill and Wang, 2001.

Kitchen, Robert. "Will the Real Zoyara Please Stand Up?" *Bandwagon*. May-Jun. 1993

"Latest Circus Wonders, The." *New York Times*. 23 Mar. 1902.

Lindsay, Cecile. "Bodybuilding: A Postmodern Freak Show." *Freakery: Cultural Spectacles of the Extraordinary Body*. Ed. Rosemarie Garland Thompson. New York: New York University Press, 1996.

Lorber, Judith. *Paradoxes of Gender*. New Haven: Yale University Press, 1985.

Mac Fadden, Bernarr A. *Mac Fadden's Physical Training: An Illustrated System of Exercise for the Development of Health, Strength, and Beauty*. New York: The Mac Fadden Co., Inc., 1900.

Mars, Vivienne. "Richard Hemmings, 1834-1919." *The White Tops*. Mar.-Apr. 1955.

"Muscular Parents." *New York Times*. 9 July 1899.

Musser, Charles. *Before the Nickelodeon*. Berkley: U of California Press, 1991.

O'Dell, George C. D. *Annals of the New York Stage*, Vol. 9, (1870-1875). New York: Columbia, University Press, 1937.

—. *Annals of the New York Stage*, Vol. 11, (1879-1882). New York: Columbia, University Press, 1937.

Ogden, Tom. *200 Years of the American Circus*. New York: Facts on File, 1993.

Peters, Arthur King. *Jean Cocteau and his World*. New York: The Vendome Press, 1986.

Senelick, Laurence. *The Changing Room*. London: Routledge, 2000.

—. "Lady and the Tramp: Drag Differentials in the Progressive Era." *Gender in Performance*. Ed. Laurence Senelick. Hanover: University Press of New England, 1992.

Short, Ernest. *Fifty Years of Vaudeville*. London: Eyre and Spottiswoode, 1946.

Smith, Gene and Jayne Barry Smith, eds. *The Police Gazette*. New York: Simon and Schuster, 1972.

Smith-Rosenberg, Carol. "Discourses of Sexuality and Subjectivity: The New Woman, 1870- 1936." *Hidden from History: Reclaiming the Gay and Lesbian Past*. Eds. Duberman, Martin, et al. New York: Meridian, 1989.

Speigel, Irving. "Ex-Star of Circus Advance Man Now." *New York Times*. 3 May 1954.

Steegmuller, Francis. *Cocteau: A Biography*. Boston: Little, Brown, & Co., 1970.

"Ways of Jaguarina, The." *New York Times*. 11 Apr. 1897.
"What a Woman Should Be." *New York Times*. 24 Jun. 1897.
"Vander Barbette is dead at 68." *New York Times*. 10 Aug. 1973.

CHAPTER SEVEN

THE FREAKS ENTER THE BIG TOP:
THE COUNTERCULTURE STRIKES AGAIN

ROBERT SUGARMAN

During most of the twentieth century, Americans knew what a circus was and what a sideshow was. A circus presented unconnected acts by acrobats, jugglers, trained animals and clowns in, or above, forty-two foot circus rings. Specs–parades, often based on fairy tale themes-sometimes interrupted the action to circle the rings. A circus was for kids, or the kid in all of us; it provided family entertainment. Circus acrobats were costumed to show off the trim, disciplined bodies of professional athletes. A circus was built around recognizable norms. Performers demonstrated what those in the audience might achieve if they had such skills and training. A sideshow, presented in a special tent outside the circus Big Top, challenged norms and showed what life could be if we were distorted or developed skills that ran counter to what bodies normally do. A sideshow held human oddities–tall, fat, short, armless, legless, bearded ladies, those presented as missing links or representatives of primitive societies. There were also those with eccentric skills–fire eaters, swords swallowers. African-American musical performers, representing an outsider group at variance with the white norm, sometimes presented a minstrel show. And there were Punch and Judy show operators and instant sculptors. An annex, for an additional fee, held a "blow off" which was often a dancing girl who, to some degree, disrobed. If circuses were for kids, sideshows were for adults, or at least adolescents.

Unlike a circus that presented consecutive acts, a sideshow was a "ten-in-one." Each performer stayed on a platform throughout the show while members of the audience moved from one platform to the next. In a circus, except for the Ringmaster who announced the acts, the show was largely non-verbal. There was virtually no direct contact between performers and audience. Performers performed, audiences watched.   Earlier, talking clowns like Dan Rice[1], interacted with audiences, but that was gone by the 20th century. In a side show, although a Talker might introduce the performers, the performers interacted with members of the audience, if only to sell souvenir pictures of themselves.

Audiences came to the show grounds to see what went on in the circus Big Top. A sideshow talker enticed audience members on their way to the Big Top to enter the side show tent. "There's still plenty of time before the big show starts!"

In the later part of the twentieth century things changed. Side shows were downsized and then eliminated in response to objections to the display of those who came to be seen not as unusual, but as deformed or hopelessly bizarre in an increasingly homogenized society. Costumed African-Americans no longer were able to pass as aborigines. Minstrelsy evaporated in the wake of the civil rights movement. Side shows were reduced to presentations of unusual skills. Big top performers sometimes learned such skills to be able to double in the side show. Then sideshows were eliminated. Another reason was the increasing cost of labor that affected all aspects of circuses. In earlier days circuses were as profligate of cheap labor as the Robber Barons' mansions.

In response to the Vietnam War, a dynamic counterculture emerged that reacted to the dominant culture that was held to have produced the war. This changed the circus along with other aspects of American life. The traditional circus had been built around families who passed their skills from generation to generation. Outsiders now entered the circus as middle class youngsters, often college educated, saw circus performance as a creative activity that had a physical authenticity absent from their middle class upbringing. At the same time, Russian circus performers became available as the restrictions of the Soviet Union loosened.   Russian circus *artists*, for that is how they saw themselves, performed here and passed their skills on to the newcomers. A Russian circus couple taught the first Big Apple Circus company their skills and brought to the company a sense of circus as an artistic discipline.   Today, the Big Apple Circus is extremely successful. It has a permanent training center in Walden, New York and an annual tour highlighted by a stand at New York's Lincoln Center.

At the time Big Apple began, Canadian street performers Guy Caron and Guy Laliberté reinvented circus by integrating it with other arts. The result was Cirque du Soleil which became the largest circus organization in the world with "five resident circuses, one touring show playing across North America, two

---

[1] An authoritative account of Rice is found in David *Carlyon's Dan Rice, The Most Famous Man You've Never Heard Of.* New York: Public Affairs, 2001.

being presented in the Asia-Pacific and two performing throughout Europe"[2] and a vast training base in Montreal.

The point for this paper is that as Big Apple and Cirque du Soleil succeeded, they abandoned their counterculture roots and became part of the establishment if only because their prices restricted their audiences to members of the carriage trade.

And what of the side show? It has been resurrected by another generation of, often well educated, middle class performers that has adopted the counterculture identification--Freaks. Many participants master side show and circus skills and revel in their outsider status to create anti-establishment messages that challenge traditional gender roles and middle class propriety. In addition to side show, they have drawn inspiration from burlesque, cabaret and the experiments of Performance Art. They have then created their own circuses. Some of the freaks have moved into Big Tops where they present their often raunchy and outrageous performances. Or, having established their credentials in the counterculture, they soften their anti-establishment edges, and join the dominant circus hegemony. Others, with less emphasis on skills, develop ritualistic gatherings based on drugs, extreme body scarification and grotesque behavior. These groups stay far out of the Big Top in gatherings with the like minded.[3]

We shall look at two skills-based groups in New York City, Circus Amok and the Bindlestiff Family Cirkus, that have moved towards the mainstream in different ways. The key person in Circus Amok is Jennifer Miller, a delightful, bearded lady whose shows begin as she, dressed in a tight fitting evening gown greets her audience, "Ladies, Gentlemen, Boys, Girls, *and the rest of us*, welcome to Circus Amok." In recent years the show has given free performances in New York City parks each fall. The politically outspoken, cross gendered group's audiences are the blue collar and middle class folks who had seen announcements in the neighborhood as well as those who happen to be in the park at the time. A hat is passed at the end of the free performances.

The seven performers, seven musicians, and two or three roustabouts, arrive several hours before the performance to unload costumes and equipment from a large rental van. They lay out a circus ring filled with gym mats, erect a scaffold to which they fix the Circus Amok façade that contains the performers' entrance. Meanwhile musicians practice a combination of Klezmer, Mariachi, Neopolitan, and various kinds of ethnic music as well as traditional and contemporary American melodies that will be used in the show.

---

[2] "The journey never ends."
[3] Hill, *Freaks and Fire.*

During the set up and after the show, Miller and other company members readily answer questions from onlookers. While traditional freak shows and the new tribal groups exploit the otherness of the performers, Circus Amok performers assert their community with the largely family and straight audiences they encounter. After the equipment is in place, the performers warm up and practice juggling and acrobatics in the ring before whomever cares to watch.

When Circus Amok started in 1989, it performed indoors at venues familiar to gay and other outsider performance groups. Circus Amok moved outdoors in 1994 to play to the world at large. The 2004 show opened with a dynamic demonstration of stilt dancing by the company that was followed by the band leader having the first of a series of encounters with a pretend elephant that continued through the show. Before the elephant was "disappeared," it had become a symbol of the Republican Party, and was subjected to considerable verbal abuse.

The show's theme was Back to School. There were frequent references to overcrowded class rooms, cuts in school budgets and problems generated by the No Child Left Behind Act. The least effective act was the most didactic, and the most joyless. A series of overlifesized Bread and Puppet-style puppets represented educational reformers while a litany of how their achievements were being compromised was read.

An act that has become a favorite with the show was "Rodney's Rope of Death." While other members of the troupe held a rope, a performer got on it and did a slack wire presentation. Part way through, he cast off his derby, jacket and slacks under which he wore a tutu. While on the rope he completed the act by putting on stiletto heels as he maintained his balance. No explanation was necessary for the point to be made about the arbitrary nature of gender roles.

For Circus Amok, sexuality is a political issue. Miller could remove her beard and pass as a non-freak, but she has explained that doing so would be as dishonest as a person denying a racial identity to win mainstream acceptance.[4] Instead, Miller wears her beard proudly as a rebuke to those who think of gender simplistically. In the old days, bearded ladies were seen as anomalies to be pitied. Miller has reversed that. She is secure with her beard and turns the table on her audiences who are forced to reconsider their ideas about gender.

The show contained expert tumbling and juggling.   At one point a supposed USO troupe, The Liberty Sisters, was introduced. They wore silver wigs and flashy red, white, and blue dresses. Miller and two bearded men were the sisters. Miller introduced herself as Cybil Liberty. After saying how happy they were to be in Iraq, they performed a fast paced juggling routine which they interrupted with political comments.

---

[4] Smith, "Step Right Up, See the Bearded Person."

"I hear we're going to cut Iraq into three parts. Regular, High Test and Super."

"The President is afraid Iraq will end up run by religious Fundamentalists. I say, if it's good enough for the Republican Party, it's good enough for Iraq."

As with any Agitprop presentation, there is no way to determine what political impact the shows have, but the Circus Amok audiences have a good time as they are exposed to ideas seldom seen in the mainstream media.

Just as Jennifer Miller sets the tone for Circus Amok, Stephanie Monseu and Keith Nelson are the principal forces in the ten year old Bindlestiff Family Cirkus. In the past, the group, which varies in size, toured for about half the year with the Auntonomadic bookmobile with Anarchist and other books, Nelson graduated from Hampshire College with a major in Anarchist studies. After the tour, the group presented a cabaret and a show in New York City for three months and used the rest of the year for booking, practice and research.

Monseu, who appears for the most part in high boots, hot pants and a top hat as Ringmaster Philomena, does whip cracking, stilt walking, fire, juggling, character comedy, songs and sideshow stunts. She is perhaps best known for lying "buck naked on the ground while a clown (Nelson) inserts one end of a dildo tipped four foot pole into her vagina and spins plates on the other end."[5]

The 2005 Bindlestiff show, "From the Gutter to the Glitter: A Night Out With the Bindlestiffs," consisted of Monseu, Nelson who performs as Mr. Pennygaffe a sword swallowing con man, and a pianist. After a two week tour it opened on the Lower East Side in New York City alternating with a Bindlestiff Cabaret.

At the first performance of the Cabaret, Nelson appeared as Kinko, a hobo clown, in the first half and did sometimes erotic balloon manipulation. In the second half he did sword swallowing as Mr. Pennygaffe. Monseu was the Mistress of Ceremonies, and did an act in which she inserted a condom in her mouth and pulled it out her nose. Other acts included a contortionist, an eccentric magician, a more eccentric Yo-Yo performer, a New York cowboy who did rope tricks, then faced upstage, took off his clothes and faced downstage with his hat supported by, and hiding, his erect penis. There was also a group of young Boston musicians doing Edith Piaf songs.

The next night, "From the Gutter to the Glitter," was more genteel. Aside from a few, easily excised risque asides, the performance would have fit comfortably on the old Ed Sulllivan variety show. Nelson repeated the sword swallowing act, Monseu did whip cracking, and the two did fire eating. Joined by their pianist, they did partner juggling. Monseau's high spirits, excellent singing voice demonstrated in a number of period songs, and mastery of

---

[5] Steven Kotler, 'The Strangest Show on Earth," *Details* January 2000: 58.

traditional skills made for a pleasant, nonconfrontational show.   Monseu, still presenting herself in the dominatrix persona she has developed over the years, morphed in the new show into an attractive woman with a high spirited stage presence.   For Monseu, sexuality is just that and can be toned down as the occasion demands. Unlike Jennifer Miller, there is no political dimension to her sexuality. By retaining the beard, Miller is always making a political statement. She can not, and does not want to, move into mainstream showbiz.

Not surprisingly, Monseu and Nelson spent five weeks before presenting their shows in New York performing on a cruise ship.[6] They hope to hone their hour and a half show to a half hour that could earn them top billing on a cruise ship.[7] It is a long way from where they started with "an erotic fire performance act called Fireplay that they worked in the city's adult cabarets, S&M clubs and fetish balls."[8].

Some of the self created Freaks are moving into the Big Top of traditional family-oriented entertainment with its larger financial rewards.   Some have created their own small Big Tops in which they present circus skills shaped by their outsider orientation. Others, like Todd Robbins' Coney Island Side Show, recreate the Side Shows of the past. Still others, like The End of the World Cirkus and the Yard Dog Circus, have established counter cultural tribal units that invite those who share their orientation into their version of sideshows.

An analogy can be drawn to the changing ways immigrant groups exist in this country.   In the past, it was traditional for them to merge into the mainstream. Today, however, many immigrants, connected by the internet and easy travel to other identities, are not rushing into the melting pot.   Some Americans take pride in their outsider status. So it is with the some of the freaks inside and outside the Big Top of general acceptance.

Bibliography

Adams. Rachel, *Sideshow U.S.A.:Freaks and the American Cultural Imagination.* Chicago: University of Chicago Press, 2001.

Hill, J. Dee, *Freaks and Fire: The Underground Reinvention of Circus.* Brooklyn: Soft Skull Press, 2004.

"journey never ends, the." Cirque du Soleil advertisement. *Spectacle*, Winter 2005, back cover.

Kotler, Steven 'The Strangest Show on Earth." *Details* January 2000.

---

[6] Stephanie Monseu, Keith Nelson, "From the Performers' Perspective: Krooze Komics Take to the Sea," 34.

[7] Interview with Stephanie Monseu.

[8] *Freaks and Fire*, p. 129.

Monseu, Stephanie. Interview with the author, Theatre for the New City, New York City.

Monseu, Stephanie and Keith Nelson. "From the Performers' Perspective: Krooze Komics Take to the Sea." *Spectacle.* Winter, 2005.

Smith, Dinita. "Step Right Up and See the bearded Person." *New York Times Weekend Section,* 9 June 1995. Cited in: http://www.circusamok.org/smithreview.html. July 24, 2004.

Stencell, A.W. *Seeing is Believing: America's Sideshows.* Georgetown, Ontario. 2002.

Part III
History

CHAPTER EIGHT

RECONSTRUCTING CIRCUS HISTORY THROUGH MINIATURIZATION: THE HOWARD BROS. CIRCUIT EXHIBIT AT THE RINGLING CIRCUS MUSEUM

RODNEY A. HUEY

Introduction

After two years of construction and installing the largest miniature circus in the world, the Tibbals Learning Center at The John and Mable Ringling Museum of Art opened to the public at precisely 10:00 am on Saturday, January 14, 2006. Three evenings of VIP openings had already accounted for almost 2000 pre-public-opening guests, so approximately 100 adults and children gathered under the tented canvas entrance to hear former Ringling Bros. and Barnum & Bailey Circus Singing Ringmaster Johnathan Lee Iverson blow his ringmaster's whistle to signal Howard C. Tibbals, his wife Janice, and several Tibbals grandchildren to simultaneously cut a 20-foot red ribbon that temporarily blocked the entrance. Against an acoustical background of circus music, the small crowd spilled into the new 30,600-square foot steel, marble and glass facility, and straight into the 3,800-square foot exhibit of the Howard Bros. Circus, which had been dubbed "the largest miniature circus in the world." The opening of the Tibbals Learning Center, which features the Howard Bros. Circus and a new interactive display entitled *Circus in America*, not only launched a new era in the history of the Ringling museum complex by being the first new building to be added to the facility since 1948, but also sparked a renewed interest in the bygone days of the tented American circus when it was at its largest.

The Man Behind the Model

Fig. 8-1, Courtesy of the John and Mable Ringling Museum of Art,
Tibbals Digital Collection.

In order to fully appreciate the Howard Bros. Circus, it is important to try to understand the man behind the model. Howard C. Tibbals, age 69, is a successful businessman and a generous philanthropist with an impressive record of donating to needy causes, primarily the school system in his hometown of Oneida, Tennessee; as well as reputed anonymous gifts to needy friends in the larger circus community. He is a master model builder who set a new standard for accuracy and authenticity in circus model building; and he is a self-taught circus historian whose philanthropic efforts also reflects his desire to re-tell the history of the America circus in fine detail. However, unlike many circus fans, enthusiasts, and schooled circus historians, Tibbals' interest in the circus is focused on its physical attributes and characteristics--its train, equipment, and tents; and how it moved from town to town on a daily basis during the "golden age of the American circus." Also, unlike most circus fans, he has little interest in the people of the circus, as noted in his more than one million photos of circus equipment, with practically no photographs of circus performers (unless there was a wagon or piece of rigging in the background).

Tibbals' worldview of the circus was firmly cemented in his psyche between the ages of three and five. His father would not allow him to wander around the circus backlot alone, so the young Tibbals was forced to watch the circus from afar–more specifically, through an antique pair of binoculars while standing in a chair in the home of his grandparents' neighbor. Tibbals has retold the story time and again in various media interviews of how he would look down at the circus as it was being erected on a nearby vacant lot, then would focus his binoculars on some small detail of operation: the pounding of tent stakes in the ground; raising the Big Top; setting up the dining tent to feed 1500 people three meals a day; or watering the animals. He watched as the working men horsed around with one another, and interacted with performers on the back lot. What Tibbals did not see, contrary to the many fabled tales from youngsters who supposedly crawled beneath the tent flaps to catch a glimpse of an acrobat, trapeze artist, or bumbling clown, was the actual performance of the circus–one of the primary focal points in the memory of most circus fans. To Tibbals, the circus was not about peanuts, cotton candy, Midway barkers, or exotic human performers; it was about wagons and tents unloading and reloading equipment, and the constant blur of activity that goes on behind the scenes at any tented circus. By the age of five, Tibbals had already established his vision of the American circus through its behind-the-scenes activity, which in a sense became his own version of Citizen Kane's "Rosebud" sled–a mental scenario from his childhood that he spent a half century trying to re-create.

As a 14-year-old teenager, Tibbals built his first circus wagon (which he still has today), and pitched makeshift tents made from his mother's old bed sheets in his backyard. In 1952 he saw an article in *Popular Mechanics* entitled "Here Comes the Circus" which detailed the logistics of moving Ringling Bros. and Barnum & Bailey Circus. The article contained a schematic of the 79-car train; a cut-away layout of the circus grounds; and a diagram illustrating the rigging and set up of the Big Top tent. Tibbals was hooked, and by 1956 he started sewing and constructing his own Big Top tent, a mammoth task that would eventually take 18 years to complete and fill with 7,000 folding chairs, 1500 audience members, and more than 35 acts on the floor, around the hippodrome track, and above the four stages and three circus rings.

But it wasn't until 1958 that he began his journey into serious model building. As a student at North Carolina State University, Tibbals visited a downtown department store in Raleigh, where he met noted circus model builder Harold Dunn. Tibbals often recalls how he timidly approached Dunn to ask "dumb college student questions," but fondly remembers how Dunn, encouraged by the young man's interest in model building, spent a lot of time explaining his model and sharing his enthusiasm. That first meeting grew into a lifelong friendship and partnership, and when Dunn died in 1992, Tibbals acquired Dunn's extensive circus memorabilia collection along with his models, which included a 250-foot circus street parade with more than 725 hand-carved animals that, incidentally, is also on display in the Tibbals Learning Center.

While most college students engaged in an active campus life, Tibbals turned his energies toward his newly acquired hobby–circus model building. After college, he returned to his hometown, got married, started a family, and joined the family flooring business that his father had acquired in 1946. When the FHA began financing new homes with wall-to-wall carpeting instead of requiring substantial wood flooring in the 1970s, the bottom fell out of most wood flooring businesses. Howard convinced his father to allow him to develop a line of parquet flooring, an innovation that most likely saved the family business. All during his working career, in addition to providing for his family and building the flooring business, Tibbals worked incessantly on his model. Earlier he had written a letter to the management of Ringling Bros. and Barnum & Bailey Circus asking permission to use the famed circus' name and logo on his circus equipment. The request was denied, and following in the practice of adopting family names for circuses, he simply called his model the Howard Bros. Circus, a name that now has taken on new meaning for museum-goers.

Tibbals' life changed dramatically in 1989, and those changes have reverberated down to 2006. His father died and he inherited the family business, and immediately sold it to the Hartco Company, which later became part of the Armstrong flooring company. For the first time since he was a young college graduate, Tibbals was out of the flooring business and had accumulated enough wealth to pursue his hobby fulltime. Often traveling with Harold Dunn, Tibbals visited circuses across the country, looking for old circus equipment and collecting historical circus photographs and posters. He eventually amassed more than one million photographs as well as 4500 antique circus posters, which is believed to be one of the finest personal collections of American circus posters anywhere.

The Howard Bros. Circus and the Dunn model circus were displayed in several venues from the 1980s through the early 2000s, including the National Geographic Society in Washington, DC; the Ford Museum in Detroit, Michigan; the 1982 Worlds Fair in Knoxville, Tennessee; and Circus World Museum in Baraboo, Wisconsin. But as his model continued to grow, it became impossible to display it in its entirety at any one venue. Tibbals began to ponder about his legacy, and searched for a permanent home for his miniature circus. After talking with various museums, he decided on The John and Mable Ringling Museum of Art in Sarasota, Florida. Tibbals made a $3 million donation as seed money to erect a new building for his model, plus another $3.5 million as an endowment for maintenance and the study of the American circus. The new

Tibbals Center is the result of his philanthropic efforts, and is the permanent home of the complete (at least to date) Howard Bros. Circus.

The Model

The Howard Bros. Circus is difficult to describe to someone who hasn't seen it, and photographic images do not do it justice. It is simply the largest miniature circus in the world, covering 3,800 square feet (larger than the average American home), and is the relative equivalent of a 20-acre lot. The walkway around the model's perimeter measures 450 feet in length, or one-and-a-half football fields. The sky above the model, with puffy clouds hand-painted by a local Sarasota artist, covers 6,500 square feet; and the entire enclosure behind hermetically sealed glass that remains dust-free due to a positive air filtration system consumes 75,000 cubic feet. In other words, the entire first floor of the Tibbals Learning Center, of which Tibbals had significant input, was designed around his model. The lighting for the exhibit alternates between six minutes of daylight and two minutes of darkness.

The model itself consists of eight large tents, including the cook tent, dining tent, two baggage horse tents, menagerie tent, large dressing tent, a number of small individual working and dressing tents. The six-pole Big Top tent measures 16' x 32' x 4', and provides a footprint large enough to park nine Mini Cooper automobiles. Like the tented circus in real life, the entire show, minus the Big Top muslin tent and most of the performers and townspeople, fits neatly into 152 hand-made circus wagons that can be loaded onto the 55-car circus train. In fact, when Tibbals began to set up his model, he unloaded each wagon in sequence, and erected the tents in the order that the actual circus was erected in the mid-1930s.

Tibbals' attention to detail borders on obsession, and his dedication to proportional accuracy is unprecedented in model building. His miniature circus is built on a ¾-inch-to-the-foot scale, as opposed to the more popular ½-inch-to-the-foot scale. Tibbals chose the larger scale to allow him to pay attention to the smallest detail, and to reproduce those details down to ¼-inch nails that hold together the sides of many circus wagons. Paradoxically, Tibbals' model was built big enough so that it could be detailed to the smallest degree.

The Howard Bros. Circus is set up in the typical layout of Ringling Bros. and Barnum & Bailey Circus circa 1938, the last year that Ringling utilized a six-pole tent. Empty wagons stand idle around the lot; the spec parade is lining up at the back tent portal; the working staff is attending to myriad daily details of operating the circus from shoeing horses and repairing machinery to cooking pancakes; and performers are practicing their acts. Townspeople fill the Midway to buy their tickets and concession items, while the barker beckons crowds into the Sideshow. Hundreds of audience members are seated in the arena watching 35 troupes performing their various acts simultaneously.

Outside the circus grounds is a small mountain with a radio tower, a townscape roughly resembling a warehouse district of Knoxville, Tennessee, complete with a mockup on the Tibbals Floor Company. There are approximately 900 feet of custom-made rails affixed to 15,000 six-inch railroad ties by 30,000 ¼-inch hand-driven spikes, including one ceremonial golden spike given to Tibbals by circus fans who volunteered their time to assist in laying the track.

The authenticity of each piece of equipment is mind-boggling. There are real working hinges on the dog train car; working pulleys to hoist the Big Top tent; actual individual tickets in the ticket wagon with coins in the cash drawers; bottles of mustard and ketchup, as well as miniature bananas, apples and oranges in crates; sliced food on the table with 900 place settings; tubes of lipstick and bars of soap; and tiny rolls of toilet paper in the restroom areas. All items were reconstructed from actual historical photographs, and personal trunks and performer figures were taken from actual route books in the mid-1930s. No detail from any piece of equipment has been overlooked, and no physical historical fact has been ignored. Quite simply, Tibbals wanted to re-create the circus of his childhood imagination in three dimensions as accurately as humanly possible.

Reconstructing Circus History

Stepping into the darkened walkway that surrounds the *Howard Bros. Circus* becomes a virtual experience of the sights and sounds of a golden age Circus Day. One feels as if he, or she, is actually stepping through a time portal, where the present-day world is exchanged for a glimpse into one magical day in circus history.

The *Howard Bros. Circus* presents a three dimensional history lesson. For those familiar with the circus history, as well as first-timers, the presentation of Tibbals' model almost demands a suspension of belief. The miniaturized 20-acre circus grounds is a flurry of back lot activity, Midway excitement, and multiple thrills under the Big Top. What is hard to believe is the fact that in real life, this mammoth circus was erected, dismantled, and moved up to 100 miles *every day*–a feat that would be impossible to duplicate today. That is Tibbals' desire–to tell the story of how the circus moved daily to bring new thrills to townspeople in cities and villages across the country. The sheer size of the operation is overwhelming to viewers as they walk around the 3,800 square feet of miniature circus.

However, oddly enough Tibbals' circus is not historically accurate in time sequences. He requires viewers to also subliminally suspend time when they tour the exhibit. For example, he has constructed every wagon he could research from the Ringling circus in the early 20th century, but at no time did all of these wagons appear on the show at the same time. Tibbals also took liberties with various famous circus acts from the early 1900s through the mid-1950s. Famed clowns Emmett Kelly and Lou Jacobs perform alongside Unus (who did not perform with Ringling until the 1950s); and Jacobs appears in at least two different areas of the model. May Wirth is shown washing her hair outside her individual tent, and John Ringling himself is found strolling the back lot. The giant sea lion Goliath is also in this show, along with other exotic animals.

Tibbals also reproduced several historical circus graphic tableaus in 3-D, including a re-enactment of a Norman Rockwell's *Saturday Evening Post* cover; the graphic from a Ringling program book entitled *The Children's Clown*; Harold Alzana's regular warm-up walks on the guy lines of the Big Top; and the Midway barker with one of the Doll midgets. All these are recreations of famous circus photographs or prints. In one way, this is Tibbals' attempt to play with the uninformed viewer, as well as a substantiation of popular circus icons for circus enthusiasts. In another way, however, Tibbals is actually reconstructing history through duplication of graphic circus narratives; and by condensing time sequences, Tibbals is presenting an "idealized" view of the tented American circus during its golden age, because in reality, the real life version of the Howard Bros. Circus never actually occurred at any one time in any one place.

Conclusions

The Howard Bros. Circus is a wonder to behold. But there is no denying that this physically correct model represents an "idealized" and "romanticized" version of the Big Top era of the American circus. Time and space must be ignored if one is to fully appreciate, and indeed, understand the working of this historical mobile city that, according to historian Janet Davis,[1] played a key role in nation-building in the late 19th and early 20th centuries. The Howard Bros. Circus does not really present a slice in time as viewers suspect, but rather is a collection of historical realities and fantasies . . .a glimpse of what could be possible in the "dream circus" if all equipment could be gathered in one place, if

---

[1] Davis, *The Circus Age: Culture & Society Under the American Big Top.*

all acts could perform at once, and if all performers could be everywhere at the same time.

But the fact that Tibbals' circus is physically authentic, yet historically imaged, does not diminish the powerful historic presentation of this half-century labor of love. The viewer is uncertain whether the Howard Bros. Circus is Tibbals' *magnum opus*, Tibbals' "folly," or Tibbals' joke on the unsuspecting, because one gets the feeling that the creator of this masterpiece possesses a marvelous "secret" about the circus that he is willing to share with the public through miniaturization. But it is up to each individual viewer to uncover this secret, and to immerse himself or herself into a idealized and romanticized world that perhaps did exist at one time in one place–in the mind of a five-year-old child standing in a chair looking through a spyglass!

Bibliography

Davis, Janet M.. *The Circus Age: Culture and Society Under the American Big Top*. Chapel Hill: The University of North Carolina Press, 2002.

CHAPTER NINE

CIRCUS KIRK: A MUD SHOW BACK TO THE FUTURE
(*WHAT THE CIRCUS DID FOR US*)

MORT GAMBLE

Thirty-three years have passed since Circus Kirk first toured, twenty-five since the final performance. During its nine seasons, the all-student, 3-ring traveling tented circus inspired over 400 young people in their teens and twenties to step inside a beloved tradition during the most nontraditional of eras, the Sixties and Seventies. As performers, riggers, musicians, front-end, and advance personnel, Circus Kirk's cast helped to preserve, and to foster, the circus arts. For most of the troupers, the experience proved to be much more than the most unusual and memorable of summer jobs.

Circus Kirk was not just any show-it was a celebration of the exuberance and creativity of youth coming of age, circus style, under the guidance of a seasoned big top veteran, Dr. Charles W. "Doc" Boas, a professor of geography at York College in Pennsylvania. Playing dates from New England through the mid-Atlantic region, into the South during its heyday in the mid-seventies, Kirk drew its energy from the traditional one-day stand. From the show's "Biggest Brass Band" and a strong front end, showcasing a sideshow of skill and illusion, to flamboyant billposting and inspired marketing, Kirk owed much to circus history and custom. Also, in part, it took the successful formula of other student shows-the Wenatchee, Washington, Youth Circus; the Florida State University Flying High Circus; the Sarasota High School Sailor Circus-and put the academy under canvas and on the road, competing successfully with other truck circuses of the era.

It can also be said that Circus Kirk was ahead of its time. Emphasizing human-not exotic animal-feats and narrative themes, the ever-youthful troupe was constantly experimenting, changing, and growing, while promoting a kind of under-canvas total quality management in which cast and crew shared responsibility for running the operation. As in any "mud show," however, personnel had several jobs, honoring the code of the big top and building a lore unique to Circus Kirk.

Fig. 9-1. From the Circus Kirk website.

This is the story of a college professor's vision for what would become the "All-American, All-Student" traveling tented circus, a show I was privileged to serve for two seasons under the leadership of Doc Boas. It is also a story still in progress. Those of us who came of age under the big top make up to this day an extended family of the original troupe, consisting of spouses and partners, children, grandchildren, and friends. For us, the Circus Kirk celebration continues.

Circus Kirk, playing from May or June to September, from 1969 through 1977, offered a different kind of circus experience, yet one that drew heavily from established circus tradition. The audience saw a well-produced show, to the accompaniment of traditional circus marches and contemporary tunes from the biggest brass band on the road. The audience thrilled to the student aerialists and gymnasts, and laughed at classic clown bits like the Clown Band and the washerwoman routine. Here was the old-fashioned, family-friendly circus under a tent, playing smaller towns mostly, but often venturing as well into the more populated suburbs of the East. Urban audiences, especially, seemed to appreciate the novelty of a student show. Doc was proud of the show's classic elements. "I wanted a simple old-fashioned show," he told an interviewer in 1973. "If someone from 1850 were spirited into the tent he'd recognize everything but the electric lights."[1]

This was not a circus for those expecting splashy production numbers or a lot of wild animals. Circus Kirk featured for a while Baby Lisa, later a star elephant on Roberts Bros.. Amazonian monsters were coiled in the pit show. But dogs, ponies, and llamas made up most of the menagerie. For the '74 season, we offered the "Miniature Animal Exhibit" on the midway. "Strange but True! Can It Be Possible?" proclaimed the walk-through banner in front of our petting zoo of baby farmyard favorites.

Doc, the founder of the show, had assembled more than a student circus performance. He had created a *circus*. Some of the oldest and best traditions he wanted to preserve were to be found out on the midway where the audience heard the legendary sideshow talkers living again through the rich tones of Doc himself. He had mastered the technique of turning a crowd into a tent faster than most people could say "sword swallower." His oratory was a performance in itself. Standing on an orange platform in front of the "Museum of Curiosities and Annex of Wonders," Doc testified to the mysteries of the torture chamber, the Houdini straitjacket escape, the electric woman, and "that funny old magician," of late, a student at Penn State. He announced that "now's the time to go if you're going, do as these folks are doing, hurry *just* a little. Boys, tear those tickets." He warned that after the show moved on early the next morning, only "wagon tracks and popcorn sacks" would remain. The great age of the circus sideshow was long gone, truck shows by this time typically combining a few acts with their wild-animal menagerie. But here was Doc, a purist and a fine actor in his own right, proclaiming: *Don't let your friends tell you tomorrow what you missed today.*

Doc could stand with authority on the bally platform because he knew the circus business inside and out. Undertaking a one-night-stand circus tour, even one for three months, is a frightening investment of time and money. Staffing a circus with students in the turned-on, tuned-out 1960's and early Seventies was bold. Then, routing this outfit among the bigger, well-financed "pro" shows-this was near madness.

---

[1] Calvert, "A Three-Ring Summer Along the Sawdust Trail with a Student Circus."

A native of Harrisburg, Pennsylvania, Doc had received his doctorate in geography at the University of Michigan, but left teaching to become a professional clown and advance man. *Life* magazine in 1961 covered his family's defection to the big top. On the road with Carson & Barnes and Sells & Gray, Doc had learned well the hard truths of operating under canvas in modem times. The public might love the circus as an institution, but that fact did not guarantee long lines at the box office. He understood that selling tickets meant selling a unique idea, not just an event. He sought to promote the mystery and make the magic of the circus, inviting into his world some of the restless youth of the day with whom he was prepared to share some trade secrets. His long years as press agent and contractor of dates, combined with his faith in modern adventurous youth, produced Circus Kirk, a new kind of show, operated for and by students. A trial tour of its predecessor, Boas Bros., in 1968 confirmed for Doc that a crew of young people would honor his idea.

He joined forces with the Reverend L. David Harris, a pastor in Philadelphia, who saw the circus, according to an early Kirk program, as a "traveling ecumenical youth community stressing Christian ideals." The youth ministries division of the Central Pennsylvania Synod of the Lutheran Church in America provided some funding and a pastor, and helped recruit the crew. The name "Kirk," a Scottish word for "church," had the promotional advantage of being short, mono-syllabic, and different. The show would seek sponsors among churches across Pennsylvania.

Circus Kirk entered a showbusiness landscape growing inhospitable to the small traveling circus. Sweet and Habenstein[2] note that while the circus has "a clearly distinctive, highly traditionalized, social organization and culture," it is also affected by changes in society. They point out that the circus industry, by the 1970's, the era of Circus Kirk, had long since become vulnerable to what they call the inroads of "rationality, technology, and bureaucracy." The circus as an institution was no longer the emotionally triumphant, dominant, free-roaming enterprise it had once been. Now the onenight-stand circus was pitched on the outskirts of the American imagination, confined, if not to buildings, to parking lots and remote tracts awaiting conversion to suburban housing.

So it was all the more important for Circus Kirk to make a special statement about what the big top was and could be. As recounted by Carl T. Uehling,[3] the inaugural 1969 season was challenging logistically and artistically. Replacing the traditional circus caste system was a traveling community seeking to say something of importance in 72 days, and most of all, to be entertaining as a show, and convincing as a circus. The new show contended with mechanical

---

[2] Sweet and Habenstein, "Some Perspectives on the Circus in Transition," 583.

[3] Uehling, *Blood, Sweat and Love: The Circus K irk Story*, 7,8.

breakdowns, uneven attendance, and the crew's own inexperience. Uehling concludes that the inaugural tour was "a kind of a gift to the people of Pennsylvania" and points out the recognition among some pastors that the circus made a successful Christian witness in its role as part show, part celebration of life. These "children of the circus," in Uehling's words, had done something special indeed, but what exactly were they celebrating?

One is reminded of Frank E. Manning's discussion of the ingredients of celebration. He writes: "As a communicative agent, celebration embraces two modes: play and ritual. Play inverts the social order and leans toward license, whereas ritual confirms the social order and is regulated. The two modes are complementary as well as contrastive, and the tension between them gives celebration much of its piquancy and power."[4]

Tiny Circus Kirk, in the conventional sense of a circus, was not a spectacle, although its pageants and dramatic re-creations evoked something much older than the big productions of the American "golden age of the circus." Kirk's crew hoped to work joyfully within a rigid, ritualized tradition-the formula of an enclosed canvas arena offering intimacy, but enforcing creative distance. But in doing so, it could not achieve the quality of a community celebration. Kirk sought to step down from the pulpit and walk among the people. But it was not a participatory church-style meeting, for it was not a church. The stylized requirements of a circus performance-albeit with some messages in its early seasons-were the defining element. Kirk's audiences expected the entertainment values of the circus-any circus-to conform to their expectations of ritualized, escapist relief. As Kirk alumnus, magician and author Tom Ogden points out, Circus Kirk was not intended to offer opportunities to "witness in the center ring."[5] There was no mandate, Ogden says, from the church to be a church. Yet the creative tension that Manning refers to did exist. The performers had an opportunity each season to reinvent the show, to create their vision of a circus, drawing upon their own talents and perspectives as well as established circus performing arts available to them.

Circus Kirk offered a blend of ground and aerial acts, a few animals in the dog and pony tradition, and clown turns with a message. A presentation called "Bridge Building" offered "a new look at the divisions that prevent persons from working together," and asked, "Wouldn't it be great if people would cooperate these days? The clowns overcome their divisions-we hope society takes a lesson from them!"[6] The program cover from that season shows the

---

[4] Manning, *The Celebration of Society: Perspectives on the Circus in Transition,* 7.

[5] Ogden, "Circus Kirk," *Two Hundred years of the American Circus,* 81.

[6] Circus Kirk Program, 1971.

converging forces that had created the Kirk: circus images of a strong man and fire eater framed by the words "peace, love, joy."

Circus Kirk was still evolving, still finding its niche. The church affiliation ended, the 1972 program shows none of the social-consciousness themes of previous seasons. But Kirk remained a magnet for student energy and performing values-a training academy on wheels, but also an enterprise that sought legitimacy and brand loyalty in its own right. The show's creative orientation was changing, moving away from religious themes to a more conventional circus production. Its own sense of community, its unique culture, was becoming well established, too. This was not a summer camp, a recreational adventure, or a team-building exercise. Nor was Circus Kirk seeking to revolutionize the circus business. The troupe sought to offer a quality performance that drew upon the best circus traditions while keeping an open mind to the ideas of its youthful performers and managers. Above all, the troupe insisted on a total effort. Kirk had finally come to terms with what it was celebrating. There was room for play, room for ritual, in Manning's terminology. The troupe respected those who gave a hundred percent to finding the balance between them.

Meanwhile, this Circus Kirk family faced a crisis of biblical proportion. In June 1972, rains spawned by Hurricane Agnes lashed Pennsylvania. The show fled rising waters, finding refuge at Elizabethtown College, and struggled through weeks of mechanical breakdowns, poor business, even the destruction of its donniker (the bathroom trailer) in an accident. True to the Circus Kirk spirit, however, the crew built a new one and held a private pageant featuring a donniker king and queen to welcome the rolling outhouse. The creator, the show's father figure who, himself, had been caught up in the chaos of the '72 tour battling forces that stretched to the limit even his extensive experience and wisdom-Doc won the honor of christening the new facility.

In a way, the show lost its innocence that summer, washed away by the unforgiving realities of operating a small traveling circus in modern times. The troupe's simultaneous celebration of an emerging performing community and its introspective exploration of the show's identity seemed part of the past. Circus Kirk, once a summer youth project, had come into its own as a fullfledged, ready-for-battle, company of some 50 artists, promoters, and staff moving on six big semi-trailers well beyond its Pennsylvania home borders. Its performance was strong and spirited, even without exotic, four-legged professionals. Upgraded for our time were the methods and ballyhoo Doc, himself, had practiced. He ordered new paper that said "Bigger Than TV," "Big Tent, Big Show," and "All Hands Up for the Mighty Kirk"-a nod to the show's sawdust roots, but also its sense of humor about itself: playing David to the Goliaths of the road.

The giants of the circus world, however, weren't laughing. During the '73 tour, in Reno, PA, we found that the "world's largest circus" was due over in Oil City in 10 days. We knew that because their paper was everywhere-including our own lot. The "world's largest" advance crew had reminded the public who was king of the sawdust trail. Four posters filled the glass front of a nearby service station. Appearing above scenes of lions and tigers-the things our show lacked-was the word WAIT.

Doc was ecstatic. The big shows now knew who we were. That same summer, near Washington, D.C., Irvin and Kenneth Feld, of the Ringling organization, dropped by to check us out. We were honored to have their visit, fortunately during a straw-house matinee.

The Watergate crisis came and went. Nixon had folded, and that was that. What really seemed to matter to the crew, day to day, were grassy lots, friendly audiences, and proximity to "flushy" toilets.

Among sponsors, the Kirk had built a reputation for honesty and reliability. Doc made sure that his audiences saw a vibrant, exciting performance-never a half-hearted one. Our audiences received the best a circus could offer: a real live brass band, plenty of clowns who were truly funny, and all the popcorn anyone could want. (I sold lots of it.) Kirk's 3-Ring show was now "a model to the circus world, energetic with its talented youth," said the writer of the 1973 program. Circus veteran Boas put it another way. "We're the Cadillac of the mud shows," he told a reviewer. Promotional coverage by *Mademoiselle* magazine and *The New York Times,* a commercial tie-in with Planter's Peanuts, and national TV exposure, worked the angle of an established show run by students. The circus resumed its affiliation with the Lutheran Church in 1974 and '75, although the spiritual pageants were long gone. It boarded a boat for a historic tour of Martha's Vineyard, and celebrated the nation's Bicentennial with triumphant prose and pageantry. The performance was professional-grade. As a veteran of the business end of the show, I was tempted to think that Circus Kirk, the onetime youth project, was becoming almost too slick for itself. But like any business, it was locked into a battle for the dollar. And all the while, in the winters, Doc maintained his academic schedule, simultaneously routing the show, hiring the performers, and managing the marketing. He sought a big score, a national PR coup, maybe a TV deal that would help ensure the show's future.

The backside of the '76 tour, however, foretold what really lay ahead. Business fell, and for the 1977 season, the show cut back to one ring and extended its tour past its usual Labor Day closing. Fighting for its life, Circus Kirk pushed on to Florida where, shortly before Christmas of '77, it closed forever. The student crew stuck by it to the end.

The next spring, the equipment, parked where it had begun-in the backyard of a visionary, was sold to yet another man who dreamed of running a circus. The Big Top is a state of mind. Although Circus Kirk is all out, it is far from over. The show lives on as an extended family-as well as a catalyst for creativity. The Kirk experience has inspired circus films by Middy Streeter and Dave Fulton, a circus history by Tom Ogden, and a web site by Frank Gyondla. A number of Kirk alumni continue to tour as full-time show business professionals. If the troupe has passed from the world of the "Spinning Spanish Web" into the web of cyberspace, it had long since made a more profound journey into popular culture.

Thirty years ago, Doc Boas had encouraged students at the end of their formative years to cross the magical line between being entertained and doing the entertaining. He gave us a world of strange and shared ritual-the daily raising of our home, a language outsiders would not understand, a set of signs and symbols and anecdotal humor and, finally, a figure in whom we could trust-himself-when any authority, in those days, was suspect. He instilled in us pride in the circus profession, and our unique, collective contribution to show business history as the first, and at that time only, 3-ring traveling tented student circus. It all worked so well because it was *our* show. Our version of the circus had strong entertainment value and popular appeal, honoring many traditions and practices from the wagon mud shows to their over-the-road successors, trucks. In doing so, Kirk drew inspiration from circus ritual as old as the business itself, achieved the quality of professionalism, and awaited a leap to another creative plane. Circus Kirk was a laboratory for the development of leadership, demonstrating years before its time the possibilities of a diverse, working community operated largely by students who shared their skills and rejoiced together in meeting tremendous challenges.

But when all is said and done, Kirk's celebration was a form of homage to the living performance, a dream brought to life for an instant, up close and personal. The night show was magic, a wonderland of shifting shadows, glittering costumes, and a swelling of the spirit. Tumblers sprung free of the earth as the drummer's hands raced to keep up. People juggled flames in darkness. The wire walker danced at the top of the tent. Old Glory was unfurled. Our audience cheered.

Bibliography

Boas, Charles William. "The Circus," *Guideposts,* July 1973, 16-19.
Boas, Dr. Charles W.. Interviews with Mort Gamble, East Berlin, Pennsylvania, 1977-78.
—. Sideshow opening, Circus Kirk, 1973-74.

Calvert, Catherine. "A Three-Ring Summer Along the Sawdust Trail with a Student Circus," *Mademoiselle,* December 1973.

Circus Kirk, official programs, 1971, 1972, 1973, 1974 and 1976 seasons, and official route book, 1972 season.

Circus Kirk web site (www.circuskirk.org/history.htm). designed and managed by Frank Gyondla, 1999-2001. With excerpts from *Two Hundred Years of the American Circus: From Aba-Daba to the Zoppe-Zavatta Troupe,* by Tom Ogden, Facts on File, Inc., 1994.

Gamble, Mort. "A Hillbilly Under the Big Top," serialized memoir in *The West Virginia Hillbilly,* Richwood, West Virginia, 1982.

—. "Circus Kirk Troupers Look Back from Middle Age," *The White Tops,* official publication of the Circus Fans Association of America, July-August, 1999.

Manning, Frank E. *The Celebration of Society: Perspectives on Contemporary Cultural Performance.* Bowling Green, Ohio: Bowling Green University Popular Press, 1983.

Sweet, Robert C., and Robert W. Habenstein. "Some Perspectives on the Circus in Transition," *Journal of Popular Culture* VI (Spring 1973).

Uehling, Carl T. *Blood Sweat & Love: The Circus Kirk Story.* Philadelphia: Fortress Press, 1970.

Acknowledgements

I would like to extend special appreciation to Dr. Charles W. "Doc" Boas and his family and members of the Circus Kirk troupe for their assistance over the years in compiling the Circus Kirk story, part of which is presented above.

CHAPTER TEN

WEST MEETS EAST: THE WESTERN IMPACT ON TRADITIONAL CHINESE CIRCUS

TIM HOLST

From 1972 until 1983, I had the privilege of touring with Ringling Bros. and Barnum & Bailey Circus as clown, then Ringmaster, and then Performance Director. I am now the Vice President of Talent and Production for the three touring Ringling Brothers shows and seek out original acts on all six continents for them.

While touring with the shows, I had a firsthand view of America from the railroad car I called home, and I fell in love with the entire notion of circus entertainment. In the circus ring there is no beginning and no end; performers step into it, and out of it, as their lives evolve.

When I was touring, our performers came mainly from South America and Eastern Europe. Over the years, the owners of the Greatest Show on Earth, Irvin Feld, and then his son, Kenneth, gave me opportunities to grow in their family business. Shortly after President Nixon made his historic trip to China and began opening communication between China and the United States, our company made many attempts to bring the world renowned Chinese Acrobats to Ringling Bros. and Barnum & Bailey, but from the later seventies through the early eighties, all attempts failed.

Our organization has a unique way of operating. It then had two units, the Red and the Blue, and each toured for two years following essentially the same route. As each unit opens in alternate years, we are able to bring a new show to a venue every year. Our way of operating posed a problem for integrating the Chinese into our circuses. To understand the problem, we must look at the history of Chinese acrobatics which appear to have first developed among rural peasants in the Wuchaio District of the Hebei province in Northern China. To celebrate weddings, good harvests and other joyous occasions, farmers devised entertainments that used common household utensils or farm implements. By juggling and balancing them, the farmers invested these workaday tools with seemingly magical properties.

As the decades passed, the acrobatic skills were refined and numerous troupes sprang up to tour the countryside. When word of the astonishing acrobatics of the North reached the ears of the Emperors, the most illustrious acrobats were invited to perform at court and for visiting heads of state.

Near the end of the twelfth century, Marco Polo visited the opulent court of Kublai Khan in the land that was then called Cathay. He wrote about the tumblers and jugglers who exhibited their skills in the presence of the Great Khan. The very best of the acrobats were accorded royal patronage and were able to abandon their plows and farms and spend their full time refining their skills.

In 1984, when Kenneth Feld and I were invited to explore the possibility of employing Chinese acrobats in the Ringling shows, one of my first tasks was to study the Chinese performers from the viewpoint of American audiences. As I thought about what might be appropriate, I kept hearing about the Shanghai Acrobatic Troupe and proposed that we visit them.

Through the influence of attorney Edward Nixon, the President's brother, we were able to meet members of the Cultural Bureau of Shanghai with whom we had many discussions. One of the hardest jobs was to explain to them what the Ringling Bros. and Barnum & Bailey shows are. I presented them with promotional videos, press kits, programs, pictures, and souvenirs. As we did this, we followed every rule of protocol in selling not only our product, but convincing these very suspicious people that they could trust us.

The first problem that arose was that the Chinese authorities dismissed the idea of our two year tours, and would only allow their acrobats to have contracts that did not extend beyond twelve or sixteen weeks. After many trips to China, we arrived at an agreement that would allow us to feature their performers for six months at a time. We would then bring in a second group, rehearse them and continue the tour. And there was an additional complication. The Chinese had never allowed their acrobats to perform with other acts. So the first impact of Western circus on Chinese performers was getting them to perform with acts from different parts of the world.

Locating Chinese performers for our shows has been my responsibility. To do it, I have regularly visited every major acrobatic troupe in all regions of one of the world's most populated countries. I have traveled by train, boat, car, bus, and plane to find the best talent to bring to our shows. When the Chinese artists have joined the Ringling shows, bonds have been developed with the Western artists as they play, eat and travel together. Through the widespread use of video cameras, Western concepts, acts and costumes have made their way back to China.

In recent years, I have served as a member of every Festival hosted by China to support the acrobats. This has offered me perspective on the influence of the West on Chinese acrobats. At first traditional acts were accompanied by traditional woodwind instruments. That was to change along with costuming and the style of presentation.

As the socio-economic situation in China changed, some acrobatic troupes bought such businesses as hotels, restaurants, and shops. Different kinds of acts, for example The Globe of Death, based on Western traditions, appeared in China. As part of the change, we received permission to extend the stay for the acrobats from six months to 8 months, and since the 1996-1997 season, we have been allowed to keep the acrobats a full year.

During the continuing reform in the eighties and the first part of the nineties, cities began to manage their own business affairs and regulation from the Central government waned. The loss of control opened the flood gates and Chinese acrobats appeared around the world in theme parks, festivals, local events, and almost every conceivable venue or circus. Despite the changes, we continue to arrange our contracts, and do our business with the Ministry of Culture and the Ministry of Foreign Affairs. We have found it easy to keep our political differences apart as circus is apolitical. We visit the troupes, meet their performers and leaders, review all the details, but the final decisions are made in Beijing.

Another influence on circus performers worldwide has been the success of Canadian based Cirque du Soleil with its dreamlike style of performance. Its permanent and touring shows, which employ no animals, have caught the fancy of the public. This style of performance, music and costuming has influenced many circuses and performers including the Chinese. For the first years, performers in each Cirque production were given characters to portray although their faces were often covered by makeup. The Cirque production *Dralion* featured Chinese performers most of whom had previously toured with the Red Unit of Ringling Bros. where they learned their touring discipline. In *Dralion,* for the first time audiences could identify individual performers.

Traditionally, individuality is not characteristic of Chinese performance. Even the distinction between men and women was often difficult to discern. When Chinese acrobats were chosen to become part of a particular acrobatic troupe, their coaches determined the potential skill level of each performer based on body size, strength, and natural abilities. After the skills were learned, the performer was integrated into the act. As a result of this training, the acrobats, who see themselves as technicians rather than performers, show little emotion in presenting their acts. The word "artistic" is not often used by Chinese acrobats. However, as they travel, Chinese performers have seen the pleasure Western artists take in presenting their acts and the emotion that is part of their presentations. Even when Western performers' skills are not equal to the skills of the Chinese, audiences sometimes respond more positively to the less skilled performers. The enthusiasm exhibited in our pre-shows when the performers welcome our customers finds the Chinese on truly foreign soil.

However, the vocal and physical emotion of the Chinese performers is slowly changing. On the current Blue Unit, the Yunnan Troupe presents an excellent Russian Swing act, The final trick is performed as a catcher hangs upside down about thirty feet from the swing. Three other performers are swinging. On cue, they vault from the swing, execute a single somersault and land by their legs in the hands of the catcher. They perform this same trick three different times. It is very exciting to watch, and I have not seen it done by any other Chinese troupe.

The catcher is a bit older than the others. When he first arrived, he was a technician. He did the trick and caught these performers every time. I recently saw their performance ten months into the tour, and the catcher had come to life. After the trick was executed, he jumped down to the mat, and I was amazed at the emotion of his voice, and his clenched fist, as if he was saying, "Hey did ya see that? Good, huh?" The driving bass music and the movement of the dancers allowed the catcher to express himself freely. He was emotionally engaged in the moment. Here was an example of Western influence.

Yes, things are changing. The Kunming acrobatic troupe, one of the exceptional acrobatic troupes in China, has been influenced by Cirque du Soleil and chooses sportsmen, rather than acrobats, for its troupe. The Fujian Troupe that will join the Red show in 2007-2008 will not only do hand balancing, but an act that employs cowboy lassoes.

Sometimes the impact of Western ways has been surprising. In 2004, I brought the Hunan Troupe to replace the Beijing Acrobatic Troupe that had performed a handbalancing, contortion act. The members of the troupe from Hunan were mostly females, very young and cute. They were a strong replacement act and I was excited to have them with the show. Their costumes had mesh see-through material on their stomachs and, the costumes were tight fitting "jumbo spandex." The girls soon started rejecting the Chinese food prepared for them, and substituted fast food. They started to get heavy and it showed immediately. Their performance was exactly the same as their strength and years of hard practice allowed them to execute the same tricks precisely day after day, show after show.

I first heard of the situation from the pie-car manager. Normally, on a three-show day, we feed a hot meal to the performers who work the pre-show. Each performer is given a meal pass to present to the pie car. I was told that the Chinese girls chose chocolate bars and potato chips to equal the sum of the hot meal. They hoarded their goodies from their leader, to make them stretch over the next seven days.

I was called to task for letting this happen to these once thin girls who by now had been given the moniker, "fat potatoes." Perhaps I had picked the wrong troupe, but the reality is that there is a wide variety of choices in foods. Here is an example of the impact of Western style obesity on Chinese acrobats.

When Chinese acrobats began venturing into the West, social events, were always planned for the entire group. If they went to a museum, the entire group, including the cook, burst out with still and video cameras to see the sights. Today, group activities are not always attended by all as the idea of being alone as an individual has become more important. Some choose to sleep, as opposed to getting out to see the sights. Others choose to work out, read, or plan other activities with their new friends. There is less evidence of the old Socialist emphasis on the group over the individual.

Chinese performance has been influenced by the music industry. In China, pirated music, videos and DVD's are readily available on the black market. Familiar with these media, the Chinese were among the first to send prospective buyers videos and DVD's of their entire troupe and all the acts it could offer.

Despite the changes, Chinese acrobats remain among the most disciplined. Their strength is in acrobatics, juggling, and balancing acts. Their weakness is in clowning and aerial work. They are consistent winners of acrobatic festivals in Monte Carlo, Paris, and Budapest as they represent their country and their acrobatic circle. The influence of the West complements the Chinese system that continues to develop young performers and prepare them to share their talents with a world in which entertainment helps relieve the stress that has become so much a part of our lives.

Although the influence of the West has brought a new integration of music and performance art to them, I am not convinced that the influence of the West has improved the quality of Chinese acrobatic performance. I applaud the efforts of the troupes who pour so much energy, time and effort to create and continue the legacy of the Chinese acrobats. China is one of the few places that offers formalized training which is available to the Chinese and to students from different parts of the World.

It is clear that with the effort of the China Performing Arts Agency, the leadership of the different troupes, and the support of Ministry of Culture, Chinese acrobatics will continue to flourish. However, to do this they need to create acts that match the ever changing taste of the public. Originality needs more support. Some Chinese acrobats now emulate Russian acts that have themes or tell stories. To remain financially viable in the new economy, the Chinese must increase the market for their acts inside China so that it becomes a greater source of income. The Western influence, integrated into Chinese performance, provides a key to future success in maintaining the traditional acrobatic skills.

Part IV

The Dark Side

CHAPTER ELEVEN

CIRCUS NOIR: PEERING
INTO THE DARK CORNERS OF THE BIG TOP

MORT GAMBLE

A friend of mine, a fellow member of the Circus Model Builders, has a miniature big top. He comments: "When I'm setting up my tent, I just want to take it outside and rub dirt all over it." Striving for realism in his handcrafted, one-half-inch-scale, he speaks to the resplendent, but calloused world of the circus. The temptation to portray the circus as a battered enterprise may be as compelling as the inclination to celebrate its beauty and pageantry. Describing Edward Kelty's photographic record of circuses from the 1920's through the mid forties, Edward Hoagland notes how "these collective images telegraph the complexity of the circus hierarchy, with stars at the top, winos at the bottom." [1]

How the public has perceived the American circus has historically been shaped by the industry's successful promotion of itself as magical and family-friendly. This favorable view has been reinforced by children's literature, appreciative TV specials like George Plimpton's "Man on the Flying Trapeze," and the collective experience of the circus-going public. That the circus is not what it appears to be, or rather, that it may be more than it appears to be, is a favorite subject of writers.

Such non-fiction works as Fred Powledge's book about Hoxie Bros. and Bruce Feiler's account of his season with Clyde Beatty-Cole Bros. have introduced us to the gritty and lusty world of the traveling tent show. Who among us, as well, has not lifted the canvas flap to peer not into the tent, but outside it, into the earthy circus backyard where clowns smoke, pretty aerialists yawn, and lions grunt. The circus community has its personal and even dark side, and other entertainment media (novels, movies, TV) have at various times sought to explore, exploit, or fictionalize the big top's rougher, more private ways.

---

[1] Hoagland, "Circus Music: For Clowns, Lions, and Solo Trapeze," 35.

The purpose of this paper is to introduce you to my current research area: how have the family secrets of the circus fared in the hands of storytellers with the big top as setting and subject? The circus has inspired purveyors of the kind of popular entertainment that it helped to invent. The big top has been a regular character in numerous works. In some, the circus is a supporting player. In others, it is the star.

Circus society has been portrayed as heroic, exciting, and romantic, or seedy, sordid, and violent. Writers have directed our attention to the heights of aerialists' grace, or to the depths of workingmen's degeneracy. Circus traditions and culture have been used as props, or as central components of the story line. Plots have involved sabotage and backyard terrorism; center-ring tragedies; the return of vindictive former circus personnel to the show; the transformation of townspeople who join the circus; the ascendancy, decline and fall, or resurrection of star performers; families held together by the circus; couples torn apart, then reunited, by the circus; and all manner of accidents: burning tents, escaped wild animals, train wrecks, and daring feats performed in the nick of time. The demise of the show is sometimes linked to individual ego or self-centeredness. At other times, the survival of the circus hinges on one person's efforts.

Accurate portrayals of this world, in any case, have varied widely, revealing at best some of the true, complex nature of the circus; at worst, demonstrations of how, as Barnum might have said, the circus is the convenient peg upon which to hang a movie.

I would like to focus on two key works from different media which offer some treatment of the dark side of the circus. Although my research has revealed many books and some films worthy of discussion, the following are two of my personal favorites that invite examination.

Perhaps the best example of Hollywood's on-again, off-again affair with the circus is Cecil B. DeMille's *The Greatest Show on Earth,* winning 50 years ago the Academy Award for Best Picture. With its extensive coverage of star acts and documentary-style footage of the raising of the big top, the film captures some of the final days of the Ringling Bros. and Barnum & Bailey tented, railroad operation in all of its ponderous poignancy. Four years after the 1952 Oscars, the real show would succumb to internal disorganization and external reorientation of the public's interests in popular entertainment.

The film foreshadows some of the forces that compelled the 1956 closing of the Ringling big top in Pittsburgh. Confronted by declining attendance and rising costs, management acquiesces to general manager Charlton Heston's newest hire, the gifted but reckless aerialist, Sebastian (Cornel Wilde), who immediately displaces Heston's girlfriend, Holly (Betty Hutton), from the center ring. The two engage in a friendly trapeze duel for the audience's affection, and jointly challenge Heston's character, Brad, whose workload of running the big show leaves little time for romance. (Incidentally I once asked the late circus historian Joseph Bradbury if Brad's job description, with DeMille having him running all over the lot, doing everything, was true to life. Bradbury's answer was, "No.")

Lurking in the shadows is a criminal operation of crooked midway gamblers, backed by an unnamed syndicate, who fleece the public of their egg money. By 1955 the Ringling show would confront the real-life pressure of a very powerful organization, the Teamsters, whose president, Jimmy Hoffa, vowed to organize the show's laborers or put the show out of business.[2]

Adding to Brad's worries as the film reaches its climax, is the mysterious clown Buttons (James Stewart), a doctor in perpetual make-up who is wanted for murder. The character's anonymity correlates to the circus custom of honoring employee secrets and asking few background questions. Straight-arrow Brad, shown a photo of the doctor, does not lie to a detective, but merely says, "You won't see that face around here."

The Greatest Show on Earth is a celebration of the energy, beauty, and spectacle of a traveling tented society destined, in reality, for extinction. Under the bright lights of Hollywood, the show sparkles, its troubles confined for a time to the backyard soap opera of competition, romance, and mystery. The community thrives as long as its characters honor their obligations to the enterprise, pulling together to play a full season. When individuals and their needs supersede the organization, however, they and the show are punished.

Sebastian's fall from the trapeze as he tries to impress and win Holly ultimately reroutes the circus train toward its collision with criminality, leading to a tragic nighttime wreck and the disintegration of order. Guilt-ridden after Sebastian's accident leaves him with a ghoulishly crippled hand and finishes his career, Holly begins an affair with him, freeing Brad for the attentions of Angel, the elephant girl (Gloria Grahame). Her pathologically jealous suitor, Klaus (Lyle Bettger) first threatens to have her crushed by an elephant, then teams for revenge with the syndicate to rob the pay wagon, causing a spectacular pile-up of railroad cars careening through the darkness.

After the wreck, order is reconstructed as the circus clan rallies around the fallen symbol of original authority, the near-fatally injured Brad, to put on a show in the next day's sunshine, sans tent. (In real life, during the circus's disastrous 1956 tour when a windstorm ripped apart the main tent, the crew similarly vowed to do a DeMille and prevail "under God's big top," to use the words of Buttons the clown.) As for Buttons, his re-emergence as a doctor in clown make-up, performing a blood transfusion on Brad, offers almost

---

[2] Hamerstrom, *Big Top Boss: John Ringling North and the Circus.* 218

grotesque incongruity, but somehow it all works as the devilishly handsome Sebastian gallantly offers his rare blood type to save the "Boss Man."

The Greatest Show on Earth is classic DeMille spectacle, but it also functions as a sort of "circus confidential." It has mystery, violence, gangsters, wise-cracking and ironically constructed characters like Angel, who is naughty but needy, greed, passion, seduction, sin, darkness, and redemption. The show is a key player, rising from the wreck and reconstructing itself. The real Ringling show also metamorphosed into another, and eventually into two units now playing very successfully in arenas.

A radically different view of a large railroad show during this same period is offered by Edward Hoagland in his novel *Cat Man*. In place of sequined costumes and lavender rings, we see blood and vomit. Hoagland's view is from inside the belly of the circus beast in which the rhythm and order of daily set-up and work yoke together a kind of circus chain gang of winos, braggarts, and lost souls.

The novel takes place in and around animal cages, far back inside seat wagons, and in grimy train cars. Written from the workingmen's point of view, it describes a flophouse on rails, populated with employees as menacing as the wild animals they guard. The main character, Fiddler, views life through the hardened pupils of a circus survivor, finding little nobility in his fellow workers, but conforming nevertheless to the harsh social code inside the canvas wall.

The crew invades a local coffee shop one morning on the way to today's town:

> old mealy mushhead winos whose hair grew long enough to braid and kids trying to cultivate mustaches, people with glass eyes, cross eyes, wall eyes, clubfeet, gangling long-nosed men like herons, harelips, stringbeans, butterballs, ex-fishermen-sheepherders-orange-pickers, squat tough guys with smoked jailbird complexions, morons, Portuguese, Swedes, Texans, little pipsqueak drunks, mostly fly-by-night new faces, but some were old, that had been with the show a month or more.[3]

The workers grudgingly respect each other, and stare incomprehensively at those at the upper end of the circus caste system, the performers "at their glittering peak,"[4] whose rare appearance in the novel offers a break from a subculture whose members fight an ape at bedtime for his cage floor:

> Behind Hopalong an ape was cavorting, trying to entertain and postpone being caught. Daff and Robinson were after it and there wasn't much room. The chase was short. Once caught, the thing buttered up to them, hugging and whimpering

---

[3] Hoagland, *Cat Man*, 26.
[4] Ibid., 226.

and sentimental. But Robinson worked it over to a box in the comer and stuffed it in. Its arms were long, grabbing in all directions to escape from the box. Robinson rammed in the door and fixed the padlock. Daff and Hopalong were smoothing the straw in the cage to sleep on."[5]

What everyone seems to agree on is that townies are not to be trusted and contemptible, staring at the cookhouse, for example, "to find out whether circus people used knives and forks or ate with their fingers like cannibals."[6]

Fiddler finds solace where he can find it-in the messy machismo of the perennially nicknamed workingmen, in the "glorious home" of the rising big top, "wavy and resilient as the sea, day to day almost as magically changing... Who would have wanted to live in a house!"[7] and most of all, in the barely contained wildness and raw beauty of the big cats: the lions "throwing challenges in all directions,"[8] a tiger "with a gaze to shrivel an army,"[9] a leopard with a "clanging exultation in her eyes."[10]

In its suggestions of violence and loneliness, with humor as hard and frayed as the tops of pounded tent stakes, *Cat Man* paints a vivid, but unsentimental and unforgiving, portrait of the circus. Here, the show is an impassive machine, its workers kept in check by timeless, unspoken codes of behavior, hanging on to their limited prerogatives, and their precious freedom to leave after the next pay. The reader is immersed in an alien culture with a daily routine that has clarity of purpose, but little apparent significance to the world. The circus' mystery is compounded by familiarity.

Yet for any who have worked at a laborer's level in a traveling tented circus, who have found their lives distilled to buckets of water and rickety folding chairs, who have learned to look at everything through the lens of the circus, the novel offers grim pleasure and satisfaction. It is among the most authentic views of the big top from the ground up, a world that is right because it is there. Like all circus veterans, Fiddler finds security in transience and in the central icon-the cloak-of the big top:

> Not to have it going up by this time in the morning made Fiddler uneasy. Already the townies were making the rounds a second time, and they always began to get snotty the second time they saw a thing. By the third it got really rough. They disliked anyone in a circus because they thought he was doing so much that was strange and wrong. He was riffraff to all of them, respectable rich

---

[5] Ibid., 75.
[6] Ibid., 224.
[7] Ibid., 200.
[8] Ibid., 230.
[9] Ibid., 250.
[10] Ibid., 266.

or respectable poor. If they weren't given something constantly to watch they might do anything-throw stones, jail you. Without the full hugeness of the circus here, a town like this might run you out for a pack of gypsies or a shantytown of tramps.[11]

Often in books, film, and TV, the circus serves as a backdrop for human struggle. In the works cited above, its own culture is portrayed as at least as fallible and vulnerable as that of the world on the outside. The success of these two works also demonstrates the imperative of accepting the circus on its own terms, of suspending familiar everyday experience to enter its special world, a state of mind that should prove to be attractive to writers for years to come. We look forward to seeing how the circus is depicted in future works, and what new directions it may inspire the creative community to pursue.

Bibliography

Davis, Janet M. The *Circus Age: Culture & Society Under the American Big Top*. Chapel Hill: The University of North Carolina Press, 2002.

Feiler, Bruce. *Under the Big Top: A Season with the Circus*. New York: Scribner, 1995.

Greatest Show on Earth, The. Paramount Pictures, 1952.

Hammarstrom, David Lewis. *Big Top Boss: John Ringling North and the Circus*. Urbana: University of Illinois Press, 1992.

Hoagland, Edward. *Cat Man*. New York: Ballantine Books, 1955.

—. "Circus Music: For Clowns, LIons, and Solo Trapeze." *Harper's,* February 2002.

Powledge, Fred. *Mud Show: A Circus Season*. New York: Harcourt Brace Jovanovich, 1975.

---

[11] Ibid., 96.

Chapter Twelve

Circus-Related Crime and Deviance: Revisiting the Prevalence and Decline of a Circus Darkside

Joseph W. Rogers

WE PAY AS WE GO.—We stand between the grifting circus and the public and between the grafting public and the circus.

The Circus Fans Association of America (CFA) adopted this compelling motto in 1927 at its second annual meeting in a singular effort to refurbish the tarnished image of a beloved social institution. Otherwise dedicated to assisting these traveling shows, the CFA notified every circus owner and manager of its resolve to refuse aid to "any circus carrying 'grift.'" Simultaneously, this slogan gave warning to politicians, law enforcement officers, and merchants that unscrupulous victimization of circus people would not be tolerated either. The time had come for this growing organization to take an unequivocal stand.

Most authorities set 1793 as the advent year of the circus in America, and by 1927 it had just passed through a "Golden Age"--roughly a half-century of tented splendor carried to our nation's people wherever they lived.[1] Prior to radio, movies, and television, "You just had to let the townsfolk-and the people of neighboring farms, towns, and villages-know that the circus was coming."[2] The dark side of this panorama was a naive citizenry, vulnerable to fleecing by extraordinarily skillful predators.

In circus lingo, grift refers particularly to theft through crooked games (e.g., three card monte, shell game, spindle wheel) in which players had little or no

---

[1] May, *The Circus From Rome to Ringling*, 324
[2] Culhane, *The American Circus*, 163

chance of winning.[3] Grifters also included short-change artists, boosters (shoplifters), and pickpockets, among others engaged in relieving locals (aka "towners" or "suckers") of their money. Circuses regularly carrying such illicit activities, with payoffs to owners and managers, were known as "grift shows," with the controlled (i.e., sure-thing gambling) games being called "gaff joints".[4] Ogden relates some shows flagrantly advertised for grifters. "Often the more genteel word 'fakir' was used; but listings in some journals from the years 1890 to 1910 actually stated positions open for "Fakirs in all lines. Our people are ready to be took."[5]

Almost any examination of "Lot Lingo" or older circus glossaries will reveal that sizable portions of the entries are linked to deviance and crime, including the organization of grift. In addition to those mentioned elsewhere, consider just this small sample:[6]

BOOSTER - Shoplifters who specialized in stealing new merchandise from stores. They would take orders for any item, such as suits of clothing, with size and color specifics, promising delivery within a week. This term also designated a gambling confederate, a SHILL, CAPPER, or SURE-THING PERSON. A BOOSTER-HANDLER worked with shills to dispose of ill-gotten loot.

BROAD TOSSER - Three-Card Monte Dealer. "Broad" refers to the original guessing game in which the queen was hidden. The object of the game was to "find the lady."

BURN UP - Leaving a route or territory behind with such bad feeling, particularly from grift or clems (fights), but also poor shows, as to prevent returning for future dates. An especially bad combination of these was termed a "FIREBALL" which "BURNED UP THE TERRITORY." Some circuses changed their names to disguise themselves, and/or skipped certain towns to allow healing. Nevertheless, such events often hurt innocent troupes following too closely on the heels of a grift show.

CAKE CUTTER-Short-change artist who "cuts cake." The term SHORT-CAKE ARTIST might be given to a short-change expert making "short cake." This practice was also known as "DUKING." Ticket stands were built very high to conceal the exact location of change. Missed coins were quickly scooped into a built-in trough. Both the money and the short-changed customers were called

[3] McKennon, *Circus Lingo,* 41-2.
[4] Ibid., 38. Also see Inciardi and Peterson, *Gaff Joints,* 591-606.
[5] Ogden, *Two Hundred Years,* 182.
[6] McKennon, *Circus Lingo, 1980;* The White Tops, Vol. 12, Nos. 10-11, (Aug./Sept. 1939), *Circus Glossary,* 9-12.

"WALKAWAYS."

FIXER-Also known by the terms PATCH or MENDER, this is the "legal adjuster" who traveled with circuses to deal with complaining victims or customers and with local officials, including law enforcement. Often using payoffs even in advance, they were essential to minimizing conflicts and arrests.

NUT or **BURR-**The operating expenses of the show (daily, weekly, seasonal, etc.). Legend has it this term entered the circus lingo after a creditor came onto circus grounds and took the nuts (i.e., burrs) off the wagon wheels. These he kept until the circus paid what was owed, at which point the nuts went back on the wheels and the show could move on. "MAKING THE NUT" meant the circus made its expenses for the day (or tour).

OLIVER or **OLLIE-**An officer of the law.

Over time certain individuals, such as "Pogey" O'Brien[7] and Henry E. Allott, better known as "Bunk" Allen[8] established enduring reputations among circusdom's celebrated grifters. Bunk was so nefarious that former James gang outlaw, Cole Younger quit his job as general manager of their Wild West Show because of so many attached grifters.[9] Another infamous grifter, Eddie Martin, professed discriminating virtue through his claim that in "all his life he had never shortchanged a woman, or a cripple or a fool."[10] Successful grifting was enhanced by another role figure, the "fixer." For example, Martin collaborated with the resourceful master, Frank McCart of Fred Buchanan's 1909 Yankee Robinson Circus. McCart boasted he could fix any town, anywhere, with the possible exception of North Carolina where he had encountered uncommonly honest folks. "All it takes is guts and money," he asserted. "I will furnish the guts if someone else will furnish the money and enough, the thing is easy done."[11] In contrast, some shows, such as those operated by Charles Sparks, the Ringling Brothers, or the Gollmar family, became hailed for their straight dealings with employees and public. In some circles, the term "Sunday School Circus" was derisively applied to them, with the Ringling Bros. being maligned as the "Ringling Sisters" or the "Ding-a-ling Bros.!"[12]

---

[7] Sturtevant, *John V. O'Brien*, 4.
[8] Yadon, *Bunk Allen*, 32.
[9] Ibid., 38.
[10] Sharpe, *Circus Grift*, 32. Also see, Tully, *Circus Parade,* 1932.
[11] Ibid., 32.
[12] Interview with longtime circus man, Don Francis.

Occasionally grifting and related chicanery led to violence, even deaths.[13] Fights between circus troupers and towners were known as "clems" or "rubes," but some incidents involved only circus personnel with arguments over paychecks and gambling debts a frequent issue. One particularly heinous form of settlement was known as "redlighting," in which an opponent was thrown off the train onto the tracks, perhaps fatally.[14] Perhaps not all persons were disposed of from trains. In the 1930s, the supposedly accidental death of a performer was actually a murder for financial reasons when he was thrown off a truck. "At least that was the story on the lot."[15]

Criminologists Donald H. Sutherland and Donald R. Cressey define circus grifting as a behavior system in crime.[16] To be conducted safely and satisfactorily, they claim four elements are necessary: "grifters, victims, a dishonest circus management, and dishonest public officials." Grifters were trained and socialized, coming to form a cohesive in-group. While on the road, performers did not ordinarily associate with them. Performers often rode in a steel-lined "privilege car" on the circus train, thus protected from attacks by angry victims. They thrived on the general interest in gambling, enhanced by the contagious, party-like atmosphere of the circus itself and by "shills" (undercover assistants) who played and won, stimulating suckers to play and lose.

Dishonest public officials, especially those not opposed to gambling anyway, seem to have been readily available in most communities in exchange for a price, a ticket, or a favor. Dishonest circus proprietors could easily rationalize their compromise as gaining income essential to making the show's "nut," perhaps the difference between financial success and failure for the season. Moreover, some managers, such as Bunk Allen, started as grifters who gained power along the way.

Such prevalent dishonesty was abetted by four conditions of the time.[17] (1) The circus was a mobile organization, often moving daily. In the absence of permanent ties to the numerous communities visited, grifters possessed few or no responsibilities to locals and once departed, they provided elusive targets for law enforcement. (2) Many communities were hostile to circuses on economic and moral grounds. Some felt that these travelers took away money from the area, a loss to their hard-working citizens. The distinguished circus historian Stuart Thayer provides invaluable insight into efforts to regulate or ban circuses on

---

[13] King, *Only Show Coming*, 43-47.

[14] Editor, *The White Tops*, 1931, 6. Also see, Dean and Anderson, *Hot Rails*, 43.

[15] Interview with a former troupe member.

[16] Sutherland and Cressy, *Principles of Criminology*, 294.

[17] Ibid., 297.

religious and other grounds.[18] (3) Victimization could be a "two-way street" in that community officials, merchants, farmers, or residents were known to be dishonest in their dealings with circuses. Accounts of licensing hassles, contrived charges, excessive pricing, and bullying attacks are readily found in the literature. (4) The migratory nature of traveling shows, frequently encountering disapproval and conflict, was a hard life. Rather than a random selection of the country's populace, joiners were self-selected individuals hardy enough to survive amidst trying conditions.

In a cogent analysis, sociologists James A. Inciardi and David M. Petersen state that circus grift "persisted in its purest form for as long as the shows remained small, anonymous, and mobile."[19] Circuses often changed names to deceive communities and the media, thereby concealing ill-gained reputations as grifting shows. However, as the number of circuses began to increase in size toward the turn of the twentieth century, their titles became valuable assets; thus grifting became a liability. Such deviance did not disappear entirely, of course, with Inciardi and Petersen observing, "While the vintage grifter had operated from *within* the circus organization, his newer counterpart worked from *without*." And there were other itinerant organizations to join, such as medicine shows and carnivals, the latter offering especially expansive opportunities for grifters.[20]

***

More than a decade has passed since the 1993 celebration of the American Circus's bicentennial year, and today the story of the circus grifter can be looked upon like a long lost ancestor, a "skeleton in the closet" we can talk about in self-conscious humor, but not with pride. Considerable credit must be given to certain shows-Al G. Barnes, Gollmar Bros., Ringling Bros. and Barnum & Bailey, and the Sparks Circus-among others cited in the literature, that were as opposed to grift as to graft. Had it not been for such leaders, hindsight now tells us, the circus as a social institution would not have been alive to celebrate its 200th birthday in America.

---

[18] Thayer, *The Anti-Circus Laws,* 18-20; *Legislating the Shows,* 20-22. Also see, Shettel, *Early Circus Prejudice,* 7-8.

[19] Inciardi and Petersen, *Gaff Joints and Shell Games,* 597.

[20] Ibid., 598. Also see, Easto and Truzzi, *The Carnival as a Marginally Legal Work Activity,* 336-353.

Epilogue

Contemporary owners and managers have tried different practices from more careful screening of employees to hiring in-house detectives as deterrents. Strategies from professional, independent auditing to eliminating pockets in the clothing of ticket-takers have been utilized. Regardless of any claimed success, alertness remains a necessity.

If there must be a cautionary statement here, it should be to recognize that criminal and deviant behavior are about as sturdy in their survival as roaches and sharks that adapt to environmental change so effectively. In particular, although the shell game may be history, gambling is not; although the Volstead act vanished long ago, excessive drinking has not.[21] In 1998, this writer encountered a circus troupe, which allegedly fired their advance crew for chronic intoxication. A shortage of roustabouts may have stemmed from similar reasons, thus requiring impromptu recruitment from a local employment office or homeless shelters.

Crimes do occur. For example, in 1988 an ice-show promoter was charged with stealing $300,000 worth of free coupons from a forthcoming Circus Vargas appearance in El Paso, Texas. Using a false identity, the thief claimed the coupons had to be picked up because of misprinting. Some 100,000 circus tickets were discovered in his car, with Vargas estimating it would have cost it $40,000-$50,000 in lost revenues over the period of ten performances. The culprit was charged with felony-theft and jailed under a $20,000 bond. His motive? While Vargas was to play the El Paso County Coliseum on November 18-21, the ice show was to play the same building the following week.[22]

Another illustration: A Ringling circus manager was indicted in 1997 on charges of defrauding the company of $150,000 using wire fraud. Allegedly, he wired a collaborator $3,000-$5,000 increments under the pretense of funds needed for fuel and other transportation expenses. Prosecutors claim the pair then split their gain 50-50.[23]

Nor are incidents of violence unheard of. The celebrated clown Paul Jung was murdered during a Ringling Bros. and Barnum & Bailey 1965 stand in New York City. After the 5' 8," 140 pound Joey missed appearing for the familiar clown firehouse number, friends headed for his hotel. His body was found in his room; he had suffered a vicious beating about the head and his hands were tied behind his back. Blood was splattered on the wall, floor, and bed. Two months after the

---

[21] Clausen, *I Love You Honey, But the Season's Over,* 1961; North and Hatch, *The Circus Kings,* 1964.

[22] *The El Paso Times*, November 10, 1988, 1-2B.

[23] *Circus Report*, August 4, 1997, 15.

murder, it was learned that he was the intended victim of the old "badger game" by a 24-year old man and a partner prostitute with whom the married Paul apparently had sexual relations the night before. When Paul refused their demands, he was beaten to death with a fire hose. Both assailants were convicted. The man was given a life sentence; the woman two years.[24]

Two other clowns were much luckier during a later Ringling Bros. and Barnum & Bailey visit to New York. During a lunch break in the Penn Station area, four fellows pushed them against a building, taking their money and billfolds. One clown tried to fight back, but wound up with a bruised face, broken glasses, and some glass in an eye. The 18-year old victim was treated at St. Vincent's Hospital where he received some pointed counsel from a police sergeant. He was advised to buy the largest pair of electrical pliers he could find and to carry them in a leather holder on his belt. "Go back to work," the officer said, "and if any street people ever lay a hand" on you, hit them with those pliers and knock them down. He added that electrical pliers are a tool, not a weapon; thus, it is legal to carry them. After this story was told to Boss Clown "Frosty" Little, he and a friend followed the policeman's advice which saved them a few weeks later in a similar incident![25]

In 1994 while the Bentley Bros. Circus was playing in Merced, California, Alfredo Gaona, a circus flyer, was the victim of a drive-by shooting when a bullet struck him in the neck. At the time of this incident, one of four youths was captured after a high-speed chase. Their car was reported stolen. Fortunately, Gaona's wound was sufficiently minor to allow his hospital release after four hours.[26]

And obviously we cannot depend on all circus people to be honest as this "Hotline" discloses. "June 27-Walla Walla, Wash.-Samuel M. Richardson, 20, was arrested on felony forgery and burglary charges. Richardson was performing as a clown with a local circus and authorities waited until the performance was over before arresting him."[27].

Potential confrontations with animal activists present a serious, possibly the greatest, threat of future conflict, even violence. Among several reported incidents involving circus personnel, this account reveals one scenario:

The incident took place at Goleta, Calif. on June 2, 1997 on the Carson & Barnes Circus lot. (Mike) Echols was helping the circus and the protester was picketing the circus because of its use of animals. Prosecutors alleged that

---

[24] Audibert, *The Paul Jung Murder,* 18-19.

[25] Little, *Frosty,* 9-10.

[26] *Circus Report*, June 13, 1995, 12.

[27] *Circus Report*, July 3, 1995, 12.

Echols broke the law when he grabbed the protester's arm and pulled it down. Echols told the court that the protester raised her sign and 'it looked like it was coming to hit me.' Then he said, 'I put my arm up to block it. I did not attempt to strike her or grab her.

Jurors were unable to agree on a verdict, with 10-2 voting for acquittal, so the misdemeanor battery charges were dropped. Afterwards, Echols said he was considering taking his own legal action against the activists' group leader, whom he accused of orchestrating the event, and damaging his reputation.[28]

Two additional incidents illustrate the ongoing threats of crime and violence.

Nineteen persons dressed in striped prisoner pajamas and wearing elephant masks were arrested when they tried to disrupt a Ringling Bros. and Barnum & Bailey Circus publicity performance in the parking lot on the east front of the U. S. Capitol....The estimated 150 protesters chanted "Free the elephants" in response to instructions from a woman with a bullhorn....They stalled traffic as they dashed toward King Tusk's trailer, where television cameras were congregated. Capitol police...locked arms and gently but firmly started moving the group back. Clearly outmanned, the youthful protesters began throwing themselves on the ground....the police methodically began fitting them with plastic handcuffs, which cinch up like garbage bags ties, and toting them to the paddy wagons. In some cases, an extra officer was needed to carry the arrestee's elephant mask. The 19 were charged with unlawful entry and obstructing passage on Capitol grounds, both misdemeanors. [29]

Two months after sabotaging a Bergen county fur shop, a militant animal-rights group claimed responsibility for a midnight firebombing that destroyed two circus vehicles in a Somerset county park. In a statement sent to *The Record* on Wednesday, members of the Animal Liberation Front said that on March 27 they used gallon containers with gasoline and topped with candles to set fire to equipment owned by the traveling Big Apple Circus.[30]

Despite the overblown claims by PETA (People for the Ethical Treat of Animals) of cruelty to circus animals, relatively few such charges have been substantiated. However, on occasion an incident occurs wherein the show personnel were not faultless. Consider, for instance, a 1997 case in Albuquerque, New Mexico when police discovered three circus elephants and eight llamas crammed in into a trailer that had only two small openings for ventilation. An

---

[28] *Circus Report*, March 2, 1998, 2.

[29] *Circus Report*, May/June, 1995, 23.

[30] *The Record Online*, April 1, 1999, 1.

eight-year old African elephant named Heather, died in the trailer of complications from salmonella bacteria infection. The driver, son of the circus owner, was convicted of 10 counts of improper care and maintenance of animals and one count of interference with police, all misdemeanors.

The driver was assigned to 300 hours working at animal shelters, and a payment of $3,000 to the Rio Grande Zoo, which cared for the surviving animals after their confiscation by the city. Additionally, the Department of Agriculture fined the circus $200,000 and stripped it of its license to show animals.[31] These and other legal issues are apt to continue to plague circus owners as animal activists lobby with government officials at every level to ban animals and add licensing restrictions.

And there is still much to learn about what Ernest Albrecht calls "The New American Circus." As traditional circuses vie with the likes of *Cirque du Soliel* or *Big Apple,* one can easily wonder what competitive impulses might emerge in battles for contemporary audiences. For now at least, three viable predictions are possible.[32]

One, that there will never be a return to the criminal and deviant practices characteristic of earlier decades. Second, although the general health of most traditional circuses remains good, many smaller shows shall continue to face year-to-year struggles for survival. Seemingly, as one circus folds, another blossoms to "follow the arrows." Third, rather than entirely replace the "traditional" circus, the "New" is far more likely to impact it through such avenues as technology, logistics, music, artistry, displays, themes, characterization, and a revival of some of its theatrical roots. Optimistically, we may come to enjoy the best of both circus worlds!

Bibliography

Albrecht, Ernest. *The New American Circus*. Gainsville, Florida: University Press of Florida, 1995.

Audibert, Chris. "The Paul Jung Murder" *The White Tops* 60. May/June 1987.

Bradbury, Joe. "Letter to the Editor." *The White Tops* 67. Jan/Feb. 1994.

Chindahl, Georg L. "Fred Buchanan." *The White Tops* 30. Nov/Dec. 1957.

Chipman, Bert J. *Hey Rube*. Hollywood, California: Hollywood Print Shop, 1933.

Clausen, Connie. *I Love You Honey, But the Season's Over*. New York: Holt,

---

[31] *The Albuquerque Journal,* July 10, 1998, B3. Also see, *The White Tops,* March/April 1998, 21.

[32] Albrecht, *The New American Circus, 1995.*

Rinehart and Winston, 1961.

Coates, June. "How the Mabie Brothers Put Delevan on the Map." *The White Tops* 66. July/Aug. 1993.

Culhane, John. *The American Circus: An Illustrated History*. New York: Henry Holt, 1990.

Day,Charles H. "Fakirs, Freaks and Frauds." *Billboard* . May 11, 1907.

Dean, Loomis and Ernie Anderson. "Hot Rails!" *The White Tops* 65. Nov/Dec.1992.

Easto, Patrick and Marcello Truzzi. "The Carnival as a Marginally Legal Work Activity: A Typological Approach to Work Systems." In *Deviant Behavior: Occupational and Organizational Bases,* ed. Clifton D. Bryant. Chicago: Rand McNally, 1974.

Harris, "Kid". "The Grafting Circus: An Expose." *Bandwagon* 39. July/Aug.1995.

Inciardi, James A. and David M. Petersen. "Gaff Joints and Shell Games: A Century of Circus Grift." *Journal of Popular Culture* 6. Winter, 1972.

Jensen, Dean. *The Biggest, the Smallest, the Longest, the Shortest*. Madison, Wisconsin: House Book Publishers, 1975.

Kunzog, John C. *One-Horse Show*. Jamestown, New York: John C. Kunzog, 1962.

King, Orin Copple. "Only Show Coming: A Grand Autochthonic Collection" *Bandwagon* 33. July/Aug. 1989.

—. "Only Big Show Coming: Kill the Son of a Bitch." *Bandwagon* 40. May/June 1996.

Lano, David. *A Wandering Showman, I*. East Lansing, Michigan: The Michigan State University Press, 1957.

Lentz, John. "Circus Lawyer." *Bandwagon* 20. Nov/Dec. 1976.

Little, Glen "Frosty." as told to Barry DeChant. *Circus Stories by Master Clown Glen 'Frosty' Little*. Rupert, Idaho: Published by Frosty and Pat Little, 1996.

May, Earl Chapin. *The Circus from Rome to Ringling*. New York: Duffield and Green, 1932.

McKennon, Joe. *Circus Lingo*. Sarasota, Fl: Carnival, 1980.

Mills, Bertram. "Rogue Circuses." *The White Tops* 19. Sept/Oct. 1946.

North, Henry Ringling and Alden Hatch. *The Circus Kings*. New York: Dell Publishing Co., Inc., 1964.

Ogden, Tom. *Two Hundred Years of the American Circus*. New York: Facts on File, Inc., 1993.

Otis, James (pseudonym of James Otis Kaler). *Toby Tyler or Ten Weeks with a Circus*. New York: Harper & Brothers, 1881.

Pifer, Gale. "Circus Lore from the Dakotas." *The White Tops* 66. Nov/Dec. 1993.

Sharpe, Adrian D. "Circus Grift on the 1906 Yankee Robinson Circus." *Bandwagon* 14. Nov/Dec. 1976.

Shettel, James W. "Early Circus Prejudice." *The White Tops* 12. April/May 1939.

Sonnenberg, C. A. "Red". "The Old-Time Circus Fixer (Legal Adjuster)." *The White Tops* 45. March/April 1972.

Staley, John M. "The Great Circus Liquor Raid." *Bandwagon* 16. Nov/Dec.1972.

Sturtevant, Charles G. "John V. O'Brien." *The White Tops* 2. February, 1929.

Sutherland, Edwin H. and Donald R. Cressey. *Principles of Criminology*, 7th ed., New York: J.B. Lippincott, 1966.

Thayer, Stuart. "The Anti-Circus Laws in Connecticut 1773-1840." *Bandwagon* 20. Jan/Feb.1976.

—. "Legislating the Shows: Vermont, 1824-1933." *Bandwagon* 25. July/Aug. 1981.

Toll, Joseph F. "From the Circus to Juvenile Court." *Survey Graphic* 79. December, 1943.

Tully, Jim. *Circus Parade*. New York: Continental Books, Inc., 1932.

White Tops Editors. "'Redlighting' Victim Dies." *The White Tops* 5. November, 1931.

Yadon, W. Gordon. "Bunk Allen-Memorable Circus Grifter." *Bandwagon* 29. Jan/Feb., 1985.

—. "Holland-McMahon's World Circus, Framed a Century Ago, Had Turbulent Existence." *Bandwagon* 29. May/June 1985.

Part V

Circus in the Arts and the Media

CHAPTER THIRTEEN

THE CIRCUS HIPPOLYTA

MARY M. GRIEP

Over the past thirty years I have been interested in comparative mythology, and the myriad ways the narratives of myths have been given visual form. Appropriating mythological content has been a way for artists to join a long-standing dialogue concerning the largest questions of life. Myths form the deep underpinnings of cultures and, as we enter the 21st century, the clash of cultural myths has taken on many disturbing aspects. What follows is my tracing of an interest in several myths and visual forms those mythological figures might take today.

The *Circus Hippolyta,* a series of paintings and small sculptures, was begun in 1994. This circus consists of paintings and collages of circus wagons, sideshow banners, and boxes/suitcases to carry the characters' belongings. This paper is an attempt to put these pieces into an intellectual and personal context, since for most artists the finished objects are but one part of the creative process. The artist's mapping of the idea is generally private and inaccessible to the viewer.

The first mythological Greek character to appear in my artwork was Ariadne, daughter of Minos of Crete. She was a weaver and rescuer of Theseus from the Minotaur in the Maze. *Wedding Dress for Ariadne* (1983) was a large-scale ceremonial robe made from paper that had been printed, painted and then stitched together with metallic thread. The rich ultramarine blues and cadmium reds of the dress glowed when set off by the gold thread. The sewing of the piece referred to: Ariadne the weaver, the work of art as symbolic clothing, and a reference to previous work inspired by my great grandmother, a quiltmaker. To complete Ariadne's story I felt compelled to make *Mourning Blanket for Ariadne* (1983), given that after she had led her lover, Theseus, from the Maze to safety with one of her threads, he deserted her. The *Mourning Blanket* was predominately black and silver, fashioned in the same way as the wedding dress. The two pieces were so large and complex they took six months of steady work to complete. After such a long, labor-intensive project, I moved on to explore more expressive and immediate figurative work, beginning with an exhibition on the theme of a circus.

Three years later I returned to a large-scale mythological subject. This time the characters were the three Fates; Clotho, Lachesis and Atropos. They were powerful figures to me, a haunting evocation of my own struggles with the actions of fate or chance in everyday life. It was natural for me to personify the Fates in a large painting given the figurative nature of my work at the time and the fact that Greek mythology gave Fate the female form. It was comforting to give Fate, or Necessity, larger-than-life female bodies. Yet this was not a completely satisfying solution to me. Over the intervening years, I have come to think that the very fact that I personified Fate was what limited the piece. The figures, although powerful, were too specific and did not address the underlying issues of chance and luck.

When I returned again to Greek mythological figures, I combined them with circus images. In 1994 I began a series titled *Circus Hippolyta*, after the Amazon Queen of that name. I based the paintings on antique circus wagons at the winter quarters of the Ringling Brothers Circus in Baraboo, Wisconsin. I made paintings of wagons rather than using the human form, hoping to avoid my creative dissatisfaction with the earlier painting of the embodied Fates. The image of wagons seemed appropriate because elaborately decorated wagons have a long association with women (seeresses and/or shamanesses) who traveled from town to town in an imitation of the moon's wanderings.[1] These rites were the forerunners of Lenten carnivals, which welcomed spring and celebrated the expulsion of winter, death and demons destructive to crops. "The word carnival is believed to come from carrus navalis, or 'cart of the sea,' a boat-shaped vehicle on wheels like those used in the ship-cart pageants of Egypt, the Near East, and the processions of Dionysus."[2] Aside from historical allusions and their potential for beauty and color, wagons were appropriate because they implied movement both through a landscape and through a life.

The wagon pieces are constructed with mixed medias. including paint, chalk, photos, maps, beads, and small objects such as keys, charms, and religious amulets. Each collage has an elaborately decorated frame. The inner wooden frame is covered with small

Fig. 13-1. Circus Hippolyta Wagon.

---

[1] Johnson, *Lady of the Beasts*. 279-281.
[2] Ibid., 282.

bits of paper cut from various sources and glued to the frame in a quilt like pattern. Some frames have pieces from color photographs whose colors and images relate to the central image. Others have excerpts from literature or reference works related to the image. Once the "quilting" of the pieces is done, the original sources are jumbled and less obvious so the visual effect becomes primary, and it is necessary to hunt for clues to the sources.

The decorated wooden frame acts as an elaborate spacer to keep the painting away from the glass. This has the effect of making the images within the frames seem more surreal. The wagons become objects situated in a strange space, not part of the real world. They are not illusionistic objects pretending to share your space. They exist in their own space where a different set of rules applies, much as the circus or carnival is set outside of everyday life. Circuses have their own rules and values where a person or a culture can explore the "other" or the "dark side." My circus also has a sideshow with images from various parts of the world. We live in a culture that says we are not to look at certain types of difference, but the sideshow exists to titillate our voyeuristic impulses. The sideshow is a place where boundaries are blurred, between genders, races and even species. I confess to an interest in the idea of how we handle difference even as we feel uncomfortable. No circus is an entirely happy place; there are always dark corners.

Fig. 13-2, 13-3. Character Boxes

The painted wagons are useful for hauling all the baggage accumulated over the years (and these characters have thousands of years of baggage to haul.) So as the *Circus Hippolyta* grew, I constructed boxes for each character to use to haul their belongings. The boxes were more narrative and poetic in their accumulation of details. Creating the boxes was like writing to me, but more personally satisfying because they are filled with concrete objects, reminiscent of game boxes of the Fluxus artists where the player spelled his or her name with objects placed into small boxes. Each character's box or suitcase was painted or gold-leafed. The characters "belongings" are recycled; found at garage sales, rummage sales and salvage yards. The use of recycled objects is one answer to the dilemma of the artist; how to express ideas without   adding to the clutter of consumer society. I returned to the Greek characters because I had come to see them as a beginning point in an ongoing dialogue about issues that resurface in my work. The idea of an Amazon Queen opens the topic of female power; the Muses join an ongoing dialogue about creativity; and the Fates examine free will, luck, and one's lot in life.

The choosing of characters was an intuitive process. They are mostly female, and can be described as minor characters from Western mythology. None are goddesses with fully described attributes. This relative ambiguity gives me room for more invention and personal associations. (Also attempting to reinterpret a Goddess seems faintly presumptuous.) Some of the chosen characters, such as Atalanta and Hippolyta, are personifications of the heroic. The heroic characters are only given painted wagons since their narrative potential is limited. Given the specificity of the heroic stories accumulated over the centuries, I don't have room to supply much more than an illustration of their feats, or a representation of their genealogy. In contrast, characters that are personifications of attributes, such as Mnemosyne (Memory) offer more fertile territory. Personified attributes allow room to create narrative through the interactions of the paintings and the boxes. These figures allow me to play with ideas of the "marvelous, and ...as a place to explore the imagination's necessary connection to the irrational...." [3]

What interests me about the Greek theology/cosmology is articulated in a book of essays by Curtis Bennett, *God as Form*. Bennett's thesis gives Greek gods their reality in the human soul, not in some transcendent realm, in contrast to the Christian notion of a godhead that is transcendent by its very nature. Bennett posits that Judaism, Christianity and Islamic monotheism are "the most insistent anthropomorphism the world has ever known as it hypostatizes human into divine will that tolerates no other." [4] Bennett's discussion of the Greek gods as Nature, with the express purpose of making us understand ourselves as powerless before nature, speaks to my childhood experience of the power and terror of nature. Growing up in Montana, I had a vision of people as small and often insignificant parts of an immense world. The view of a storm rising hundreds of miles away, the isolation and sheer scale of the surrounding landscape convinced me of both my insignificance and my incredible good fortune to have been so privileged to see the world in all its splendid indifference. The experiences of my extended family are proof of the vagaries of agricultural life. The progressive loss of almost all family lands west of the Missouri River, while the midwestern branch prospered, gave me a view of the Western land, so desperately loved and diligently worked, as uncaring. On the

---

[3] Heartney, "Report From Greece: Contemporary Oracles," 63.
[4] Bennett, *God As Form*, 3.

High Plains ordinary mistakes were magnified into life threatening events in a way unfamiliar to these hardworking Midwesterners. Given this world-view, it was no surprise that Bennett's theory of the form chosen by the Greeks for their gods, which did not place the human at the center, struck a chord of recognition. In the Greek theology, man was not the measure of all things. And in the journey of my work from the earliest student landscapes, I have been interested in the power and mystery of the physical world.

It has taken me thirty years to gain some understanding of what I see as my process of making images, and how that process differs from writing. My understanding of the writing process is one that accumulates details in hopes of illuminating an idea. In contrast my process of making a good painting is one of paring away, cutting the unwieldy and word-ruled idea down to one seamless and ultimately mysterious image that can carry weight and metaphor. Yet, as a visual artist I understand western civilization as one ruled by the word: "In the beginning was the word. And the word was God." Words have ruled us while images are suspect. Many artists of the 20th century have struggled to combine word and image. According to W.J.T. Mitchell, the changing relationship of art and language that is central to postmodernism has its roots in Dadaism, in works by artists such as Raoul Hausmann and Carlo Carra, and in surrealism, with works like Rene Magritte's *This is Not a Pipe*.[5] By mid-century, Pop artists, including Robert Indiana and Jasper Johns, were using the form of words and letters as subject matter. It seems from the point of view of the early 21st century, it is hard to disagree with Craig Owens' description of postmodernism as "an eruption of language into the aesthetic field."[6] This eruption can be seen in artists as diverse as Jenny Holzer with her *Inflammatory Essays*, and in the work of Barbara Krueger and John Baldessari.

In my work, the combination of word and image has to do with giving the viewer an entry into a dialogue. The use of Greek myths is a way of starting a multilevel dialogue, first between me and the many versions of the myths, and the many works of art these myths have inspired; then with the issues raised by these stories, and with the viewer's ideas about the stories and themes explored; and finally and most importantly, between the viewer and the works of art themselves.

Myth is a tool to forge a distance from the contemporary American art world, which in the words of critic Eleanor Heartney, has a "current distrust of tradition, transcendence and the very notion of the sacred."[7] The idea of art as an exploration of the sacred is one articulated by Georges Bataille in his book, *The Absence of Myth*. Bataille sees that the ancient role of myth was to mediate

---

[5] Mitchell, *Picture Theory*, 245.
[6] Owens, "Earth Words, 125-26.
[7] Heartney, 61.

between humankind and the natural world, while contemporary society believes it has no dependence on myth and exists in a world where humans assert dominion over nature.   In the introduction to Bataille's book Michael Richardson writes,

> Both Bennett and Bataille stress the role of myth as one of acknowledging human's place in a world of mystery ruled by forces other than that of the human. Hence my attraction to the Greek myths is as one way for art to try to communicate and speak of the sacred. And in a world where images are immediately commodified and usurped by a capitalistic culture, it seems the hopeful path to see art as a way to explore the sacred. The fear is that as art holds a marginalized place in contemporary society it becomes a 'prayer in the void' that only other artists can hear. I agree with Bataille that art needs to be an "affirmation of a basic humanity," and it embodies the complicity of our intimate relations with other beings. It stands against the reality principle, which requires the very destruction of those same human qualities and turns us into things.[8]

The use of myth is also a way to explore the surreal in the sense defined by Bataille. It is a place, as Heartney says, to focus on myth as the outlet for the marvelous and irrational. But, of course, the danger is in a nostalgic use of myth in a society that denies it has myths. My hope is to use myth as a starting point for communication and dialogue. Do old myths say anything to us? When were the "Halcyon Days?" Is it hubris to think that a contemporary artist has anything to add to the dialogue? Is it foolish to think that the dialogue is a living one? To answer these questions, we must assert that we are all concerned with fate, creativity, and power.   And the attempt to make images is an invigorating and intimidating type of participation. But any artist who wishes to participate must take heed of Heartney's warning, given in a review of mythologically based paintings,

> Without an acknowledgment of the continuing costs of the battle between matter and spirit, chaos and order, and reason and madness, Greek mythology can seem little more than a set of comfortable bedtime tales. By pushing just a little further, and bringing their observations into the present, the artists…might…clinch the argument for the continuity of a sacred realm, which embraces the contradictions of human existence.[9]

To return to Ariadne the weaver is appropriate here as I wrestle with the three Fates: Clotho, the spinner of the thread of life; Lachesis, the measurer: and Atropos, who cuts the thread when life is done. I see the role of the artist as a weaver of disparate threads encompassing the contradictions of life. As an artist

---

[8] Bataille, *The Absence of Myth*, 23.
[9] Heartney, 63.

at mid-career, I have a vision of a life's work in art as a web of images. Like any web, it is delicate, easily torn, tirelessly added to, sticky, collecting dust, and existing in out of the way spots. It is full of the husks of ideas sucked dry as well as juicy ideas still struggling to get loose. The woven web includes pieces from outside as well as inside an individual life and, if successful, must ultimately transcend personal interests and observations. A web is not quite an autobiography even though it is a map of a process.

Fig. 13-4. Circus Hippolyta, *The Fates.*

Bibliography

Bataille, Georges. *The Absence of Myth.* Ed and Translator Michael Richardson. London:Verso, 1994.

Bennett, Curtis. *God As Form.* Albany: State University of New York, 1976.

Heartney, Eleanor. "Report From Greece: Contemporary Oracles." *Art In America.* May 1995.

Johnson, Buffie. *Lady of the Beasts: Ancient Images of the Goddess and Her Sacred Animals.* San Francisco: Harper and Row, 1981.

Mitchell, W.J.T.. *Picture Theory.* Chicago: University of Chicago Press. 1994.

Owens, Craig. "Earth Words." *October 10.* Fall 1979.

CHAPTER FOURTEEN

MARÍA IZQUIERDO:
IMAGES OF WOMEN IN THE CIRCUS

MARÍA DE JESUS GONZÁLEZ
WITH LUCELLEY GALLEGOS

María Izquierdo's (1902-55) painting career began in Mexico City in the early 1920s at a time when the role of art in post-revolutionary culture was being challenged and debated. It was the height of the Mexican mural renaissance when much of the art was created in service to propaganda. The muralists were extremely powerful and received government-sponsored commissions to support their work. Artists not aligned with the movement (known as the *counter-current*) had to be creative, independent thinkers. For a woman to place herself and her art in this position was especially risky. In the midst of this political, social, and artistic ferment, María Izquierdo, through her own tenacity and talent, overcame the obstacles of her humble provincial origins, as well as her gender, to assume a place of some significance in the Mexican art world.

Izquierdo entered the Academy of San Carlos in 1928, but soon left tired of the rigidity of the teaching methods. She ended her formal studies, broke away from the academic style, and developed her own unique vision. Her new style favored color and motion over realistic proportion and perspective. The colors in her paintings are not accidental, but carefully selected and integrated. For the next twenty-six years, she produced a body of work that included still lifes, allegories, and portraits; however, the theme she always returned to was the circus.

The characters she presents all seem close-knit and entirely of themselves, inhabiting a peculiar world of frozen motion and dark spaces. Women are central figures in Izquierdo's circus paintings, both as paid performers and as individuals who hold status and power within the family. It is the circus

paintings, and the representations of the female circus performer, that will be the
focus of this paper.   Izquierdo's representation of female circus performers
reveals, and parallels, the notion of the 'modernized' woman in the circus as
well as in society in general. Essential to this analysis will be a discussion of the
role of female performers, and the history of the Mexican circus.

Fig 14-1. *María* Izquierdo, *Caballista del Circo [Circus Bareback Rider]. 1932.*
Watercolor and gouache on paper. Rick Hall photo. Blanton Museum of Art,
The University of Texas at Austin, Gift of Thomas Cranfill, 1980.

Although Izquierdo painted the circus throughout her career, it was the
years 1939 and 1945 when the theme appears most frequently in her work.
Undoubtedly, her inspiration came from her childhood memories when she went

to the circus in her native town San Juan de los Lagos, Jalisco (a state in the western part of Mexico). These recollections of the circus were probably some of the happiest moments that she had during her strict Catholic childhood.[1] Izquierdo's fondness for the circus never diminished. Even as an adult, Izquierdo continued to be impressed by the circus, and would often spend entire days there accompanied by her friends. Among them, the now famous Mexican photographer, Lola Alvarez Bravo (1907-1993). Izquierdo was not only a patron of the circus, but also an insider. She befriended many of the circus performers. Of all the performers, she was especially fascinated by the women of the circus. Her admiration of the female circus performer is evident in her paintings.

By the 1930s, Izquierdo's artistic style was maturing. She was an artist who was in tune with the artistic tendencies in Mexico, but also in Europe. It could be stated that Izquierdo was aligned with the *counter-current* movement in Mexico. Artists associated with this movement paid close attention to European modernism. While Izquierdo never went to Europe, she was familiar with these trends through reproductions in monographs and journals that were published in Mexico. She purchased journals and monographs regularly and kept abreast of the newest artistic trends. Izquierdo was also a subscriber to *Art News* (published in the U.S.). The theme of the circus was not a theme confined to Mexican art nor one period in the history of art. Many artists painted circus themes, among them Pablo Picasso (Spanish, 1881-1973), and Georges Seurat (French, 1859-1891). Journals such as *Art News*, as well as others, many times reproduced works with circus themes. For example, the October 11, 1930 issue of *Art News* reproduced Auguste Renoir's (French, 1841-1919) *Claude As A Clown in White* (1877). Izquierdo would have seen this picture and perhaps it inspired her own painting *Payaso* (Clown) of 1945.

Izquierdo's most direct contact with European modernism occurred in 1930 when she traveled to New York City. The trip marked an important milestone in her life when she became the first Mexican women to have a one-person exhibition in the United States. The exhibition at the Art Center displayed Izquierdo's still lifes, landscapes, and portraits.

While in New York, she must have visited the city's major museums and galleries, and seen works by European modernists. Marc Chagall (Russian 1887-1985), for example, was exhibiting his paintings with Russian backgrounds. Certainly Chagall's vivid reds and blues made an impact on Izquierdo's color palette. At the Sidney Ross Gallery, an exhibition featured circus themes and vaudeville acts. America was certainly interested in the circus and popular culture in general. Interest in documenting the "American Scene" was evident on the pages of major newspapers. *The New York Times* and

---

[1] Birbragher, "María Izquierdo," 91.

the magazine *Life* devoted full page spreads to the circus. In the March 31, 1940 issue of *The New York Times Magazine*, an article titled, "The Circus and Art", announced the coming of the circus to Madison Square Garden, and heralded the circus as the show for all Americans.

From the 1920s to the 1940s, the circus was a popular form of entertainment in the United States and in Mexico. According to art historian Kathleen Spies, the circus female figure became especially important. The female circus performer was the "figure loaded with meaning, regarding sexuality, gender, ethnicity, and class."[2] She was, on the one hand, a mysterious female body of desire, while at the same time, she could also be a working mother. Many times, the female circus performer was a housewife and/or a mother working outside the domestic realm.[3]

The female stage performer, as a subject in art, was approached by artists in different ways. According to Spies, in the 1930s artists in the United States pictured the women as 'low' female performers including strippers, singers, showgirls, and circus performers. Female performers labeled as 'low' also served as subjects for, novels, articles, short stories, and Hollywood films. The objective for all was "to echo and reinforce a wider cultural interest in this figure and her places of performances." In effect, the representation of the 'low' female figure gave a sense of the authentic American scene. However, there were artists who took a different approach and interpreted these women as glamorous.[4]

Rather than marginal figures, Izquierdo paints female circus performers as graceful and fashionable women. From her paintings of the circus, it is evident that she paid careful attention to the female figure. To understand Izquierdo's image of the female circus performer in a larger context, one needs to consider the status of women in Mexico in the early 20th century. The proscribed role of women at this time dictated that she be submissive, abnegated, completely dedicated to her family, and dependent on her husband. A female circus performer did not fit the mold of the traditional woman. Female circus performers were working women who made their living by their talents— especially if they were the principal performers. These women were not dependent on any man. Because of their hard work and talent, female circus performers were respected individuals. Izquierdo found a kindred spirit with these women and could relate her own life to that of a female circus performer. Izquierdo was an independent woman who raised her three children on her own. At the age of 14, Izquierdo was forced by her mother to marry an older man.

---

[2] Spies, *Burlesque Queens and Circus Divas: Images of the Female Grotesque in the Art of Reginald Marsh and Walt Kuhn*, 3.
[3] Ibid., 4.
[4] Ibid.

Izquierdo eventually divorced, and began the difficult balance of being a single mother and   maintaining a professional artistic career.   Among the many economic and emotional challenges, Izquierdo struggled to negotiate a place for herself in Mexico's male dominated society and art world.

Izquierdo expressed her feelings in 1939, when she stated, "women should have a broad spirit of self criticism, a sense of struggle, and should never lose their femininity."[5]   In this light, many of her circus paintings can be read as Izquierdo's deep felt sentiments about her life.   Many of Izquierdo's circus paintings show women walking tightropes or balancing themselves on horses. Could this be a metaphor for having to balance her life as a mother and as a professional artist? She was struggling financially to support herself and her children just as many female circus performers.   In an interview, Olinka Wallenda of the *Flying Wallendas*, recalls having to work to support her four children.[6]   Motherhood was important to the performers, just as it was for Izquierdo. In her painting titled, *El Circo* (*The Circus* 1939), Izquierdo paints various performers practicing their acts.   A woman in the painting holds a child's hand. Maternity in women's art production is a legitimate subject. Here Izquierdo demonstrates her debt to Mary Cassatt and Berthe Morisot, prominent painters of the 19th century.   Izquierdo probably saw paintings by Cassatt and Morisot during her trip to New York in 1930.   In October, of that year, the, Durand-Ruel gallery held an exhibition of Cassatt and Morisot. Among the paintings was Cassatt's *Young Mother with Two Children* (1892). Like Cassatt and Morisot, Izquierdo believed that women should be profoundly feminine and happy to be mothers, because motherhood itself is a creative force.[7]

Izquierdo favored the advancement of women. She recognized the unjust past shared by the whole female sex.[8] She criticized women who called themselves 'feminists' and was deeply feminine. She identified herself first, as a painter, and then, as a woman.[9]   Paintings such as *Les Écuyeres* (*The Horsewomen*, 1939) are a testimony to the femininity Izquierdo embraced.[10]   In

---

[5] Lozano and del Conde, *Maria Izquierdo 1902-1955*, 46.

[6] Personal interview, 15 March 2005.

[7] Lozano and del Conde, 46.

[8] Ibid., 12.

[9] Iquierdo's memoirs contain a transcription of a radio conference dated July 1939 in which she expresses her thoughts on the role of women in post-revolutionary art in Mexico. Titled "Women and Mexican Art," she states, "I think feminists have not conquered anything for humanity nor for themselves, and instead of helping women grow (who for so many years have been slaves of everything), they get in the way of emancipation." Izquierdo criticizes women she identifies as "feminist" and labels them, "pseudo." See Lozano and de Conde, 46.

[10] Lozano and del Conde, 12.

the painting, two women performers hold hands as they gracefully balance their swaying bodies on their horses. They are dressed in colorful costumes and wear ribbons in their hair.

One must also bear in mind that women in the circus also played a vital part in the day to day business activities. In his book, *The Fabulous History of the Circus in Mexico*, Cárdenas reveals the importance of women in many circuses. An example is *Circo Union* founded by the Gasca family. Founded in 1938, the women of this circus troupe were not only the principal performers, but also administrators. For example, Rosa, the youngest daughter, was famous for her feats—riding a bicycle on the tightrope.[11]   The talents of Licha, the eldest daughter, were announced in their 1948 program. Maria Luisa Gasca, the matriarch of the family, ran the family business. Women in circus families, like Maria Luisa Gasca, were not only performers, but had learned the daily administration of the business from their fathers.[12]   It was a family run business that many times had very modest beginnings. A circus like *Circo Union*, toured throughout Mexico entertaining audiences in small and large towns.[13]

It would have been circuses like *Circo Union* that Izquierdo would have attended. Inspired by them, Izquierdo pictured her circus performers with femininity, but also very glamorous. Let us consider how Izquierdo points to the 1920's ideal of fashion and glamour in her circus paintings and emphasizes the modern woman's youth and sexuality. First, one needs to note that during the 1920s in New York, the slogan "New Woman is the Modern Woman" was headlined in mass market publications. Modern fashions took up much of Izquierdo's time.   A long subscriber of *Vogue,* she was in tune with up-to-the moment fashions and hairstyles. She wore the most sophisticated and chic apparel, groomed herself with make up artfully applied--penciled thin eyebrows --and finished the look with a sleek upswept hairdo. Transformation in fashion was introduced in Mexico after the Revolution in the 1920s.   Women, like Izquierdo, looked to America for new trends in fashions just as circus women looked at the American culture to add a 'twist' to the costume.   Female circus performers   incorporated elements from vaudeville to form a style called 'fantasia.'[14]   The word 'fantasía' referred to the clothing style that was modified

---

[11] Cárdenas, *La Fabulosa Historia del Circo en Mexico,* 433.

[12] Ibid., 432.

[13] Circo Union's beginnings were humble. Initially, they traveled and performed out of two carts. There were few roads in Mexico so the troupe traveled by train and set up their tent by the train station. In 1939, Circo Union began a tour throughout Mexico which lasted almost 20 years entertaining audiences in small towns. See Cárdenas, 433. There were many similar circuses that traveled to many towns in Mexico.

[14] Haney, "Fantasia and Disobedient Daughters Undressing Genres and Reinventing Traditions in the Mexican American Carpa," 1.

from the traditional costume to a modern, more sexy, version. Female performers did not mean to "Americanize" the costumes, but to "modernize" them. They wanted to make their costumes more sexually appealing by altering the outfits--making the skirts shorter and the sleeves short or even off the shoulders.

Another type of character arose at this time called the 'vedette.' She was the Mexican singer-dancer stage idol. Women who fit this role were both respectable and sexually alluring. According to Haney, this character most probably emerged because of the crisis of traditional gender roles that occurred in Mexico in the 1920s. "She [the vedette] was neither a fallen whore, nor blessed virgin, nor suffering mother, but the inaccessible woman for those who lacked money and power, whom they entrust with playing the accessible and dazzling woman."[15] In addition, women began to style their hair in more 'modernized' hairstyles. Izquierdo, a circus aficionado, was familiar with the latest costume styles and hair fads in the circus. These changes are visible in her paintings. For example, in *El Camerino* (*The Dressing Room*, 1939) the women's costumes are plain and not revealing. Five women are preparing for a performance by slipping on their solid color tights that cover all their skin. However, by 1945, a change can be seen in the fashions women were exhibiting in the circus. In the painting *Escena de Circo* (*Circus Scene*), women have exposed their legs by not wearing tights and wearing short 'ballerina' style costumes. The costumes are very much in harmony with the Haney's notion of 'fantasía.' The 'modernization' of hairstyles also becomes evident in Izquierdo's paintings.

Early images of women have either long black hair or they have a short 'bob' haircut. Women with a short haircuts are pictured in *El Circo* (*The Circus* 1939), and in *Ballerina Ecuéstre* (*Horseback Ballerina,*1932.) In the 1920s, young women in Mexico City were cutting their hair in a 'bob'—going against parental approval. Traditionally, It was not considered feminine for a woman to cut her hair short. Long hair was considered part of a woman's femininity. The craze for the 'bob' may have started in Paris in 1922 and became fashionable in the United States in 1925.[16] Izquierdo painted female circus performers with 'bob' hairstyles. The 'bob' was a symbol of the independence and liberation women had achieved. Izquierdo's female performers, like Izquierdo herself, were liberated women.

In other paintings such as *Los Caballistas Lolita y Juanita* (*The Equestrians Lolita and Juanita*, 1945), the women's hair is not aggressively short, but

---

[15] Haney, 7.

[16] According to writer Robin Bryer, a New York barber, Signor Raspenti, claimed to have created the "bob" when a well known artist asked him to cut her hair short. See Robin Bryer, *Fashion and Fantasy Down the Ages,* 116.

definitely feminine. The hairstyle is accentuated with a flower. Flowers accenting the hair is the way the women from *Circo Suárez* styled their hair. In *Equilibrísta (The Tightrope Walker)* of 1945, the woman's hair is loose and her head tilts back in a provocative manner. The performer's face shares elements with many of Izquierdo's self-portraits: wide face, large lips, dark red lipstick-a clear sign that Izquierdo identifies with the free and sensuous woman. In 1938, the Mexican writer Octavio Paz encountered Izquierdo at Café Paris, a place in Mexico City where intellectuals and artists gathered. He later stated, "Maria seemed like a pre-Hispanic goddess, her face was like sun-baked clay, and her make-up was heavy, but rather than it being contemporary, it was of ancient ritual."[17]

Izquierdo's women were modern. They paid attention to fashion, hair and makeup, but they were also strong in character. Their bodies are fragile, but robust and strong. In *Caballista del Circo*, (*Circus Equestrian*, 1932), the woman's body is masculine looking. The image may reflect Izquierdo's knowledge that women in the circus had undertaken the feats of muscle normally done by the male performer.[18] The balance of femininity and masculinity was difficult to maintain with circus performers because females faced criticism of appearing too masculine.[19] Women had to depend on men for maneuvers because physically men were the stronger of the two sexes. Gender roles in the circus dictated that men did most of the work in the performance while the women would assist.[20] Yet in Izquierdo's painting of 1932, *Equilibrísta (Acrobat)*, the woman is the one performing the dangerous maneuver. Izquierdo presents us with a woman of strength and courage.[21]

The women Izquierdo captures in her paintings are like snapshots of history. The women are physically powerful and proud, but always feminine. Izquierdo was a woman who was well aware of her surroundings, and she portrays this in her paintings. Izquierdo was a working women in a male-dominated society and art world. She took it upon herself to present scenes of independent women like herself creating an art that was an alternative to the masculine, political art of her day.

Bibliography

Beal, George L. *Through the Back Door of the Circus*. Mass.: McLoughlin Bros., 1938.

---

[17] Paz, Octavio. *Essays on Mexican Art,* 257.
[18] Kiblar, *Rank Ladies: Gender and Cultural Hierarchy in American Vaudeville,* 146.
[19] Ibid.
[20] Ibid., 147.
[21] González, *María Izquierdo: Formative Years 1928-1934,* 132.

Bransten, Ellen H. "The Significance of the Clown in Paintings." *The Pacific Art Review.* 3 (1944).

Bryer, Robin. *Fashion and Fantasy Down the Ages.* New York: Philip Wilson Publishers, 2000.

Chindahl, George L. *A History of the Circus in America.* Idaho: Caxton Printers, 1959.

"The Circus." *New York Times.* 27 April 1930.

"The Circus in Art." *New York Times.* 13 March 1940, Sec 7.

Cotter, Holland. "Painter on a Pendulum, Swinging from Innocent to Elegiac and Back." *New York Times.* [Late Edition (East Coast)] 30 May 1997.

"Demotte Opens Gallery of Modern Art." *Art News.* Volume 29, Oct. 18, 1930.

Exhibition, Durand-Ruel Galleries. *Art News* 29 (Oct. 25, 1930).

González, María de Jesus. *María Izquierdo: Formative Years 1928 to 1934.* Diss. University of Texas at Austin, 1998.

Haney, Peter D. "Fantasía and Disobedient Daughters Undressing Genres and Reinventing Traditions in the Mexican American Carpa." *Journal of American Folklore* 112 (1999).

Kanellos, Nicolas. "A Brief Overview of the Mexican Carpa." *Journal of American Folklore.* 112 (1999).

Kibler, Alison M. *Rank Ladies: Gender and Cultural Hierarchy in American Vaudeville.* Chapel Hill: The University of North Carolina Press, 1999.

Leal, Fernando. "El Circo al Gran Payaso Pirrín."

Martín Lozano, Luís and Teresa del Conde. *María Izquierdo 1902-1955.* Exhibition Catalog. Chicago: Mexican Museum of Fine Arts, 1996.

Paz, Octavio. *Essays on Mexican Art.* New York: Harcourt Brace, 1987.

Reid, Leslie. "'The Last Closet' Maternal Life and Canadian Women Artists," *The Magazine of Women's Art,* Number 75, Apr.-May 1997.

Revilla, Federico, *Diccionario de Iconografía y Simbología.* Madrid: Catedia, 1999.

Revolledo Cárdenas. Julio. *La Fabulosa Historia del Circo en Mexico.* Mexico: Escenología, A.C., Consejo National para la Cultura y las Artes.

Spies, Kathleen. *Burlesque Queens and Circus Divas: Images of the Female Grotesque in the Art of Reginald Marsh and Walt Kuhn.* Diss. Indiana University, 1999.

Taber, Bob. "The Circus in Mexico." *The Bandwagon.* April (1966): 4-6.

—. "The Escalante Circus from Mexico." *The Bandwagon.* Jan.-Feb. (1961).

Tibol, Raquel. *María Izquierdo y su obra.* Instituto Nacional de Bellas Artes. 1971.

"The Treasury of the Circus." *Art News Annual* 19 (1949).

Villaurrútia, Javier. "María Izquierdo." *Mexican Folkways.* July-Sept. (1932).

Wallendas, Olinka. Personal Interview. Sarasota, Florida. 15 Mar. 2005.

CHAPTER FIFTEEN

CIRCUS IN A BOX: THE BIG TOP ON TV

MORT GAMBLE

Continuing my research into how the circus has been portrayed by other media, "Circus in a Box" examines the big top as television star in several dramatic programs of the 1950's and 1960's, while providing an overview of the sometime marriage of convenience between an entertainment medium designed to impress on a grand scale, and one aimed at audiences on a much smaller one.

As it was for the movie industry, television became destructive competition for the circus during the post-war period. Although the so-called "Golden Age" of the big top was in clear decline by the Depression years of the 1930's, circus day remained a popular event through the 1940's. Then came TV. Invading American households, menacing the film industry, altering even people's bathroom habits, television was transformational to American society. Except for occasional collaboration on the airing of actual circus performances, TV was a formidable distraction for circus audiences. Perhaps adding insult to injury, some TV shows sought to squeeze the spectacular art form of the big top into short-lived dramas for the tube.

Hungry for material, early TV used what many people already knew well—vaudeville, radio star power, the circus. Many of us recall the circus kiddie shows of the period, "Super Circus" and "Sealtest Big Top"; the rise of the popular TV clown Bozo, a grinning and zany homage to his more artful colleagues still sweating out their craft under circus tents on the road; and "International Showtime," hosted by the fine actor Don Ameche.

Ameche's program was especially engaging, combining the best of what TV could do with some of the best that the circus could do. The show featured Ameche in European circus buildings, introducing show royalty from Denmark, Germany, and other nations. He turned in his seat toward the camera to provide the context for the acts—often drawing curious but respectful stares from audience faces—and, turning back toward the single ring, enjoyed along with us the formal feast of the circus, continental style.

Ameche's was an appreciative exploration of circus art and traditions, as opposed to cursory use of variety and some animal acts on "The Ed Sullivan Show" and "The Hollywood Palace" in the Fifties and Sixties. Ed's show was live, of course, and there were occasional circus moments that could not be edited out. Wild animal trainer Clyde Beatty once appeared on Sullivan's stage when a cat acted up; the camera pulled away as Ed gamely proceeded to the next entertainer's introduction—to the audible accompaniment off camera of snarling and cracking of whip as Beatty restored order.

Circus specials of Ringling Bros. and Barnum & Bailey highlights were scripted and more tame. Ringling and TV had found each other of use as early as the 1950's—The Greatest Show on Earth still touring under canvas, with TV sometimes providing promotion of the season's debut from the old Garden. Celebrities such as Dale Robertson and Mike Douglas appeared years later, hosting ringside the taped highlights and often joining the clown brigade or other performers for special bits. These "coming to a city near you" specials relied in later editions on TV tricks of the trade like dubbed sound effects, slow motion, and instant replay—as if the thrilling acts themselves were not enough, in the confines of the TV box, to impress increasingly detached viewers.

It fell to journalist George Plimpton, whose quixotic inclinations had led him to try professional boxing, football, and stand-up comedy, to use television to its best advantage as a rare window on the circus world. Plimpton rehearsed for ten days on the Clyde Beatty-Cole Bros. Circus as a guest trapeze performer with the Flying Apollos for a special released during the 1970-71 TV season. With his writer's eye for detail, his appreciation for human foibles, and his curiosity about the inner sanctums of professional sports and now the big top, Plimpton wove a delightful documentary tale about a world in which he was an aspiring trespasser. His "Man on the Flying Trapeze" offers fascinating glimpses of a tent show and of a dream to be a part of it. Here his camera, like him, is in awe of the true human drama of the circus, showing contrasting views of its people in ways both heroic and commonplace, exotic and familiar.

A footnote: In recent years, premium channels like HBO have featured the artistry of performers in the Big Apple Circus and Cirque du Soleil, taking us inside the ring and bringing us even closer to the magic of these innovative productions.

TV circus fiction has largely failed to capture on a weekly basis what Plimpton did in under an hour. Convenient plots were easily exhausted, and most circus serials lasted but a season. Adherence to circus realism was uneven, often sacrificed to fit the confines of the tube's tried-but-true plots and script timelines.

The longest-running of them, "Circus Boy," starred Mickey Braddock, a.k.a. Micky Dolenz of later Monkees fame. Set in the wild west, the half-hour drama was formulaic, as were most TV westerns of the 1950's. Mickey played Corky, an orphaned twelve-year-old whose sidekick pet was "Bimbo," a young elephant.

In the premiere episode, airing on September 23, 1956, the Burke & Walsh Circus confronts a local mob bent on collecting debts from the previous owner of the show. The new show's owner, Big Tim Champion, played by Robert Lowery—a sort of TV version of Clark Gable—arrives on the scene in time to see his new place of business being wrecked by the cowboys. The cry of "Hey, Rube!" goes up; Champion prevails, drives the mob off, and sets about making changes in his new enterprise. Boss canvasman Pete says Tim is "tough as they come, but honest and fair." The new boss fires the crooked shell-game operator (who sets him up for a later ambush by the same mob that attacked the circus), and insists that Corky leave the show for a Kansas City boys' home.

Corky's "Uncle Joey," played by Noah Beery, tries to change Big Tim's mind to no avail, and the clown quits the circus in protest. Corky says goodbye to Bimbo, vowing to come back when he grows up and buy the show. Later, Corky rallies the circus canvas crew and the sideshow's strongman to fight off the marauding cowboys. "Look out, circus is coming!" yells the head of the mob. A grateful Big Tim welcomes Corky back as "the heart of the circus," orders everyone "to get this show on the road," and thereby sets up the program for two seasons of entertaining, if not original, and yes, sometimes corny, stories.

Another western with a circus theme was "Frontier Circus." Appearing during the 1961-62 season, it starred character actor Chill Wills as Col. Casey Thompson, John Derek as his partner Ben Travis, and Richard Jaeckel as their hard-riding advance man, Tony Gentry—as in Gentry Bros. Circus.

The show followed similar plot conventions as "Circus Boy"—the "T & T Circus," too, is threatened with destruction by a band of outlaws, suffers through painful jumps over rough roads, endures poor business—Derek plays in a high-stakes poker game to raise money for the show, at one point—and wraps its plots around guest stars like Mickey Rooney who played a deranged clown, as I recall.

This big top "Wagon Train" was rescued occasionally by the tension between the Barnum-like Chill Wills character and the hard-nosed realism of Derek's role. Derek's character spends one episode trying to retrieve their show after the Colonel, without consulting with him, sells out to a competitor. Like "Circus Boy" and many other shows of the time, "Frontier Circus" was built around a gimmick, and lacked the depth of character found in other period TV westerns like "Gunsmoke," "Rawhide," or "Bonanza," and honoring only superficially the circus connection. Here, the circus served as backdrop and prop for variations on familiar, predictable scripted themes.

Television made one more interesting attempt to tell a circus story, not just a story at a circus, with the 1963 premiere of "The Greatest Show on Earth," starring Jack Palance as the boss of Ringling Bros. and Barnum & Bailey. By then some seven years out from under the big top and appearing in arenas and stadiums around the country, post-tent Ringling was a different kind of show. It had shrunk, its downsized spectacle a better fit for the Box. No DeMille homage to the panoramic circus drama here. In this TV version, second-unit footage of the circus unloading its modern tunnel cars and scooting inside a building had to suffice for any circus fan interested in glimpsing the real show.

Palance, who had played heavies much of his career, has more of a sense of humor about his role than had Charlton Heston in the movie of the same title. Similarly preoccupied with the daily challenges of running the show, Palance's Johnny Slate also frequently steps off the train and immerses himself in the lives of co-stars. Frequently he finds himself balancing the needs of circus people with those of the organization. He tracks down skid-row Houdini Jose Ferrer, and entices him to escape back to the circus. He probes horse trainer Lucille Ball's demons, wire walker Gilbert Roland's past (a great line in this episode as Roland holds up a pair of costume slippers to a young protégé and advises that "your grandfather died in these shoes"), and the circus memories of Betty Hutton in an episode titled "The Glorious Days of the Used to Be" (airing March 31, 1964). Hutton and Cornel Wilde, stars of the DeMille film, and other Hollywood guests helped to carry the show's one season. The plots were tightly constructed around each week's celebrities, the series not aspiring to replicate any of the broad, colorful canvas of the film version in which the circus, as much as anyone, was the star.

One of the best episodes, "You're All Right, Ivy," (airing April 28, 1964) mixes Joe E. Brown, Joan Blondell, and Buster Keaton with Ted Bessell—later of "That Girl" fame—and Lynn Loring in a piece about the changing times that afflict the circus and the possibilities that it always seems to symbolize. Brown, Blondell, and Keaton play over-the-hill circus workers inspired by a sexy, over-the-top young dreamer named Ivy Hatch who catches the magic of the circus from Keaton's lyrical pantomime as Pippo, an old clown—Keaton's great sad face in whiteface. Ivy gives the three false hope of resurrecting their circus careers, before Palance puts the oldtimers back in their places. "It's not a matter of talent," he tells the three senior citizens of the big top, "it's a matter of the times." And of Pippo, he concludes: "People don't always want to laugh at the same things."

Bessell plays the son of a legendary showman whose will directs him to spend six weeks learning the circus business. Palance, who directed the episode, balances unconvincing scenes of circus backyard life and low-budget arena sets with smart-alecky lessons to his apprentice, Bessell: "This is an elephant. It is very big. This is a hose. It squirts water."

Ivy, the idealist, connects with Bessell the cynic, who eventually succumbs to showmanship himself, and builds up the no-talent Ivy's possibilities for circus stardom—as Brown, Blondell, and Keaton shower her with their accumulated circus skills and wisdom.

Somehow, this and other episodes of "The Greatest Show on Earth" satisfy—even 40 years later. Perhaps it's because the ever-fascinating Palance as a wooden-faced circus boss is often on the edge of losing his temper or even turning violent, exhibiting a hint of the stoic menace that marked one of his great roles, Wilson the gunfighter in *Shane*. Perhaps it's because, like its film ancestor, the TV series just works as a circus soap opera.

As "The Greatest Show on Earth" left town, television was already turning to other material. The decade that began with "Frontier Circus" gave way to one featuring "MASH" and "All in the Family." The circus had done its TV time and would find its own resurgence in the 1980's and 1990's, drawing from television some valuable lessons: Keep it moving, keep it short, and make it marketable. The audience will as soon *click* as look at you.

Acknowledgements

I am especially grateful to Jessica Schneider and the reference staff of the Edward John Noble Scholar's Room of the Museum of Television and Radio, New York, NY, for their assistance in making available for viewing at the Museum three archival episodes of "Circus Boy" (1956) and one of "The Greatest Show on Earth" (1963).

Other sources for the paper include "TV.com," a website devoted to listings of episodes, cast members, and other data pertaining to past television programs, and "The Official Micky Dolenz Website." A lifetime of personal TV viewing and a good memory for episodic detail also provided inspiration for this paper.

Chapter Sixteen

Sanitizing *Toby Tyler* — Disney's Making a Children's Circus Classic "Socially Correct"

Joseph W. Rogers and Suzanne Rogers Brannan

Among children's books, few would challenge *Toby Tyler or Ten Weeks with a Circus* by James Otis in its standing as a genuine classic. Written in 1881 (265 pages, Harper & Brothers), Otis tells the moving story of a young boy who runs away with a small circus passing through town. Its classic status in the realm of children's literature has been frequently reaffirmed, and remarkably, Toby still remains in print in at least two different editions, long after most of its contemporaries have vanished from the American scene.

The first film version was made was made in 1923. The film is known to exist, but in an unidentified archive. The story was credited to James Otis.[1] Like other favorites from children's literature (e.g., *The Incredible Journey, Pollyanna,* and *Treasure Island*), *Toby Tyler* found its way to Walt Disney's movie studio.[2] Disney's 1960 film release, as well as three books published that same year under the title of *Walt Disney's Toby Tyler*, allow us to compare and contrast the Otis version with the revisionist approach and product of the Disney studio.

As we pinpoint Disney's adaptations of *Toby Tyler* for twentieth-century audiences, our mission is not to enter a "Disney-debate" as does Frances Clarke Sayers who takes Disney to task "for his debasement of the traditional literature of childhood" and "showing scant respect for the integrity of the original

---

[1] *Circus Days,* a silent film, featured the famous child star Jackie Coogan as Toby Tyler.
[2] Griswold, *Shooting the Monkey*, 121-124.

authors."[3] Rather, we seek to recognize the *cultural* quality of story telling. That is, as society and its culture(s) change, we can view *Toby Tyler* as a specimen of *social evolution,* or evidence of *social correctness,* through the vehicle of story telling.

Therefore, once Otis' original work is examined as a classic of children's literature, this comparison and contrast study will focus on Disney's adaptation of *Toby Tyler* for twentieth-century audiences through such basic story elements as setting, characterization, and fundamental events.

The Classic Status of Toby Tyler

> Now there is no yardstick for measuring ordinary people. They must grow in fiction, as they grow in real life, from their environment, and when it is a question of bringing them out of the past, that environment must be built, stone by stone, from the ground upwards.[4]

Cynthia Harnett's statement captures both the strength and weakness of this exceptional children's story. Toby's character of the discontented runaway boy fits comfortably with late nineteenth-century imagery. The notion of an unwanted orphan seeking escape into the world of a small traveling circus provides essential ingredients for an enchanting novel that has continued to be read for more than a century. The story is plausible, interesting, dramatic, and sad.

Jerry Griswold asserts that, structurally, *Toby Tyler* is typical of the American children's classics produced during the "Golden Age of 1865-1914."[5] Like Tom Sawyer, Toby is an orphan; like Huckleberry Finn, he willfully embarks on a journey away from home; like so many fictional children, he is adopted by surrogate parents; like Dorothy Gale in the *Wizard of Oz*, he discovers "there's no place like home."

The mud show to which Toby escaped hardly afforded him the haven that he expected; indeed, his daily encounters with indifference, dishonesty, loneliness, and cruelty convey the tale of the lad's constant conniving to return "home."

Toby Tyler's lofty position as a classic can be partially substantiated by reviewing its publication record. The story was initially published in 1881 in serial form through the magazine *Harper's Young People*, and soon thereafter in its first of several hard bound editions by Harper & Brothers; two have recently been listed as "still in print." Although this is significant in itself, another fact must be

---

[3] Sayers, *Walt Disney Accused,* 602-611.
[4] Harnett, *From the Ground Up,* 98.
[5] Griswold, *Shooting the Monkey,* 121-124.

attached: A minimum of fifteen other companies also published *Toby Tyler* in its original narrative form, and employed the skills of over a dozen different illustrators. As recently as 1997, it appeared as a softbound copy by Dover Press with thirty-three illustrations. Even a four and a half-hour audiocassette tape is now available.

A longitudinal study conducted by W. W. Charters also supports the book's classic status.[6] In 1907, he conducted a survey of children's libraries in twenty-four of the largest cities of the United States, asking each library to identify the twelve most popular books for boys. Of the twenty-seven books listed by three or more libraries, *Toby Tyler* was the top listed book with eleven citations, exceeding *Treasure Island* (10), *Tom Sawyer* (7), and *Huckleberry Finn* (4)! Charters repeated this survey during the next three decades in 1917, 1927, and 1937. Although eclipsed during the next three polls by the Stevenson and Twain masterpieces, Toby remained on Charters' "Hall of Fame" roll call through the first quarter of this century. How do we account for such early acclaim and uncommon longevity? The following observations yield considerable insight, starting with those of the *original* publisher, Kirk Munroe.

It happened one morning in the early 'eighties,' while I was the editor of *Harper's Young People*, that a shabbily clad stranger, unwashed and unkempt, appeared, unannounced, at my office door...[the stranger demanded to see the editor and explained,] "I am desperately in need of a little ready money. Two weeks ago I was the editor of a bankrupt American paper in London. At the final smash I had barely enough to pay for a steerage passage home. I have here a story that I wrote on the way over, working at it night and day; and it is a bang-up yarn, if I do say so. Now if you will just let me read it to you—"...

The editor explained it was the custom to leave manuscripts to be read at a later date, and continued,] "Now if you will excuse me, I am about to go to lunch."

"Lunch!" repeated the stranger. "That generally comes after breakfast, doesn't it?"

"Generally," I laughed. Then noting the hunger lines on the man's face, I added, "If you have no other engagement, won't you join me?"...

A few minutes later we were installed in one of the small dining rooms of the old Astor House. Here a waiter had no sooner taken our order and departed than my surprising companion again produced his MS. and, without apology, began to read aloud the story of *Toby Tyler, or Ten Weeks with a Circus*. He utterly ignored the waiter's return and the placing of food on the table, together with my

---

[6] Charters, *Sixty-four Popular Boys' Books*, 399-400.

suggestion that he defer his reading until we had eaten.[7]

Munroe, absolutely enchanted by the story, arranged at the author's insistence to pay Otis immediately. Two days later, a clean-shaven, neatly dressed Otis returned--subsequently becoming a regular contributor to the magazine.[8]

At the time James Otis Kaler (1848-1912) was in his early thirties, and as noted above, an experienced journalist. Equally significant, he had also been a publicity man for a circus (unidentified), with which he had toured in this country. As another editor put it, "So he knew real people who were much like Toby, the fat woman, her paper-thin husband, Old Ben, and Mr. Stubbs, the monkey, too."[9] This observation echoes that of Anne Thaxter Eaton in *A Critical History of Children's Books* where she asserted *Toby Tyler* was "still a favorite because of its genuine portrait of a boy and its true picture of circus life and what the young hero thought of it." [10]

Also adding anecdotal support to Toby's position as a classic, the General Editor for Rainbow Classics wrote an introduction to the 1947 World Books' edition of *Toby Tyler.* She vividly recalls her enthusiasm as a seven-year old at receiving *Harper's Young People,* and her anxious anticipation while awaiting each subsequent installment of the Otis serial,

> To find out what happened next to Toby...The boys and girls in our neighborhood followed Toby's experiences—and those of his friend and consoler Mr. Stubbs the monkey, from one week to the next, while circus life, glittering and chattering, went on around us.[11]

Becker connects her anecdotal testimony of *Toby Tyler* as a significant work in children's literature with this definition of a classic:

> *Toby Tyler* has kept itself alive for more than fifty years...(and) you can call it a children's classic, if you accept my definition of one. For when someone asked me the difference between a child's book and a children's classic,...I said any child's book was read once, but a children's classic was a book that was re-read many times by the same child or by successive generations of children.[12]

Everett Shinn, illustrator of the 1937 Winston edition, remembered over

---

[7] Griswold, 124-125.

[8] We have been able to identify 26 additional books written by Kaler between 1882 and 1923.

[9] Hogarth, *Editor's Note*, Preface.

[10] Ibid.

[11] Becker, *Introduction, How this Book Came to be Written,* 7-11.

[12] Ibid., 8-10.

forty-five years earlier his older brother taunting him, "Idiot! Simpleton! Who do you think you are? Toby Tyler?" At the time, Shinn was clad in crudely made pink tights as he was trying to walk atop a wooden fence. As his brother's intimidation ("Toby Tyler! Huh, Smarty, why he wouldn't even look at you,") took effect, little Everett fell into an asparagus bed. The now adult illustrator fantasizes:

> Had I caught, for one fleeting second, at the top of that fence, a vision of myself, at the far distant length of forty-five years, feverishly illustrating the book of *Toby Tyler*, I am confident that my elation would have winged my spirit to such a dizzy height that I would have, in all confidence, attempted to walk a fragile cobweb from the top of the hotel flagpole to the towering water standpipe at the edge of my home town.[13]

In sum, these testimonials reveal that *Toby Tyler* from its inception caught the imagination of its young readers. Its impact was enduring long after original exposure; it was a story, well told for its time period; and its classic status was assured from the very beginning through the support of enterprising editors.

A 1961-reminiscence by novelist Hamlin Garland embraces well the setting and the sentiment:

> There were always three great public holidays,--the Fourth of July, the circus, and the fair... Of all these, the circus was easily the first of importance... No one but a country boy can rightly measure the majesty and allurement of a circus. To go from the lonely prairie or a dusty corn-field and come face to face with the "amazing aggregation of world-wide wonders" was like enduring the visions of the Apocalypse.[14]

Let us now turn to five major categories of change brought about by Walt Disney.

Circus Structure and Size

> We just try to make a good picture. And then the professors come along and tell us what we do.
> —Walt Disney, Time, 1937.[15]

Even for the 1880s, the Otis outfit was a pretty bedraggled circus. As Toby awakens his first morning on the road, this is what he sees:

---

[13] Shinn, *A Boy's Dream in Action*, iii-viii.

[14] Flint, *The Evolution of the Circus*, 187.

[15] Watts, *The Magic Kingdom*, v.

The horses were tired and muddy, and wore old and dirty harness; the gilded chariots were covered with mud-bespattered canvas which caused them to look like the most ordinary of market wagons; the elephants and camels looked dingy, dirty, almost repulsive; and the drivers were only a sleepy-looking set of men, who, in their shirt sleeves, were getting ready for the change which would dazzle the eyes of the inhabitants of the town.[16]

Although any traveling show had to endure its battles with the elements, the overall description of this company makes it hardly comparable to such better-known troupes of the period as Barnum & Bailey, Adam Forepaugh, or Sells Brothers.[17] It is this combination of strong points and *flaws*, which provided Walt Disney a platform in 1960 to revise the story for a different generation of readers and viewers whose images of their environment and the circus had so drastically changed in eighty years.

While considering major changes from the Otis show of 1881 to Disney's much larger 1898 circus depicted in the 1960 film, it should be remembered Otis was writing just ten years prior to the 1891 death of P. T. Barnum, world renowned for his amazing "humbug," museums, plus such special features as the famous midget "General Tom Thumb," and Jenny Lind, the "Swedish Nightingale." When Walt Disney recast the story, he moved it about two decades later; thus, facilitating his presenting a much better developed show than that of Otis.

Disney and his writers had the dual advantages of circus history and global hindsight. For instance, 1872 marked the year the ingenious circus manager William C. Coup placed the Barnum show on rails, initiating a great evolutionary period throughout the United States. Then in 1881, the same year *Toby Tyler* was published, James A. Bailey and P. T. Barnum merged their circuses and introduced their celebrated three-ring production. With the approach of the twentieth century, the railroad shows boasting three rings became a standard with which other troupes were compared.[18]

While the little untitled one-ring show of Otis featured only a few animals and performers, Disney's show provided a much larger set of parade wagons,

---

[16] Otis, *TobyTyler*, 1881, 43.

[17] Chindahl, *A History of the Circus*, appendix; Flint, *The Evolution of the Circus*, 192. By the 1870s, circuses placed great emphasis on the number of elephants they featured.. By 1882, Adam Forepaugh had 21 elephants, while the Otis show had only four, and these had no major part in his story.

[18] Flint, *The Evolution of the Circus*, 192. It is noteworthy that in contrast to our American shows, those of Europe remained steadfastly dedicated to the one-ring circus. Ironically, today there is a trend back to the single-ring format.

animals for the three rings, and concessionaire treats for *"Colonel Sam Castle's Great American Circus."*[19]

The Addition and Deletion of Key Characters

During the nineteenth century when Toby was written, an age of discovery was in full bloom. Circuses of that day cheerfully catered to human curiosity by providing traveling zoos in the form of menageries; entertaining with the antics of clowns; thrilling audiences with feats of daring; and displaying oddities of nature through the sideshow.[20] For his story, Otis created several such individuals through the two key characters of Lilly Treat, the "Fat Woman," and her devoted husband, Sam Treat, the "Human Skeleton," plus four lesser figures: a "Sword Swallower," two "Albino Children," and a "Snake Charmer." Interestingly, they played crucial roles for the author as friendly, supportive persons for the lonely, abused lad desperate for acceptance. In one respect, "social outcasts" were helping another outcast, the runaway boy, Toby.

By 1960, the term "freak" had so disappeared from acceptable public vocabulary that Disney chose to delete all of Otis' human oddities, a logical move in light of changing social mores. The plot is sustained, by his shifting emphasis to other more socially acceptable individuals such as "Ben," the wagon driver, whom Disney promoted to additional roles as the circus strong man and equestrian trainer.

It was essential, however, for Disney to find a suitable substitute for the Treats which he chose to do through a talented, benevolent clown with the coincidental name of "Sam Treat," (same as the Otis, The Human Skeleton). His casting of Gene Sheldon, (the mute compadre of *Disney's Zorro*) was a perfect choice.

Disney's revision also cried out for a major female figure for which he incorporated Toby's silver haired "Aunt Olive," who made only a very brief appearance in 1881. This important addition served as a major "softening"

---

[19] The Disney Studios at that time owned an array of at least seven attractive wagons, including the beautiful *Swan Bandwagon*. They enabled Disney to open his movie on a much grander scale with an exciting old time street parade combining color, beauty, animals, twelve-piece band, and even a steam calliope! Disney used the parade sequence wisely as the initial plot magnet to lure Toby as a runaway. By comparison, the Otis outfit appears pretty drab. In 1962 Disney donated all of the wagons to the Circus World Museum in Baraboo, Wisconsin.

[20] Truzzi, *Circus and Sideshow*, 176. This sociologist notes that almost from its beginnings the circus added special entertainment forms. These were generally presented to the public as supplemental exhibits for which an extra fee was usually charged.

mechanism to balance the stern demeanor of "Uncle Daniel," from whom Toby had fled.

The Otis story also portrayed Toby as the subject of excessive brutality, perhaps too much so for audience tastes in the 1960s. The three main circus persons responsible for Toby's 1881 misery were Job Lord, the concessionaire; Mr. Jacobs, his partner; and Mr. Castle, the equestrian trainer. Disney elected to drop the latter pair from the adaptation, and alter the substitute for Job Lord in the fashion described in the next section.

With the omission of the above pair of cruel antagonists, Disney found one even more fitting through the utterly unlikable, arrogant, snob of a circus-riding star, "Monsieur Ajax." He fulfills the role very well, and his demise contributes appropriately to the revised story with Toby's rise to stardom in Ajax's place.

Re-drawing Characters' Appearances

The principal villain in *both* versions is a concessionaire, called "Mr. Job Lord" by Otis; "Mr. Harry Tupper" by Disney. While Otis draws Lord in dark, near-Dickens-like garb, Disney paints Tupper as a sharp witted, carnival dandy wearing a straw hat and colorful arm bands. In the 1960 movie, actor Bob Sweeney, while still a conniving shyster taking advantage of the naive Toby, actually gives this character something of a humorous, almost endearing veneer.

In contrast, ponder this description by Otis:

> Mr. Lord was thoroughly enraged when Toby left the wagon, and saw the boy just as he stepped to the ground. The angry man…caught him by the coat-collar and commenced to whip him severely with the small rubber cane that he usually carried.

> Mr. Job Lord lifted the poor boy entirely clear of the ground, and each blow that he struck could be heard almost the entire length of the circus train….

> "Oh, please stop! Please stop!" shrieked the poor boy in his agony. "I'll do everything you tell me to, if you won't strike me again!"

> This piteous appeal seemed to have no effect upon the cruel man, and he continued to whip the boy, despite his cries and entreaties, until his arm fairly ached from the exertion, and Toby's body was crossed and recrossed with the livid marks of the cane.[21]

Lilly Treat is certainly the most "lovable" character drawn by Otis. She

---

[21] Otis, *Toby Tyler*, 1881, 138-139.

constantly showers Toby with affection, food, plus other favors, and stands out as a strong adversary to Job Lord. Nevertheless, today's audiences would be taken aback by many references to her weight.

> "You ought to have seen my wife Lilly shake with laughing when I told her who Mr. Stubbs was!"

> "Yes," said Toby, at a loss to know just what to say, I should think she *would* shake when she laughs."

> "She does," replied the skeleton. "If you could see her when something funny strikes her you'd think she was one of those big plates of jelly that they have in the bakeshop windows." And Mr. Treat looked proudly at the gaudy picture which represented his wife in all her monstrosity of flesh. "She's a great woman, Toby, an' she's got a great head."[22]

Although we believe that Otis wrote without *intended* malice, he repeatedly utilized a number of offensive descriptive expressions such as: "enormous Lilly;" "Mrs. Treat waddled;" "his fleshy wife;" "the fat lady ceased the exertion of clapping her hands;" and "the mammoth lady." Otis through the voice of her husband, identifies Mrs. Treat's weight at "pretty nigh" 400 pounds, despite the show's claim of her being over six hundred.[23] Ironically, Lilly would be on the slim side compared to such real-life circus women as "Dolly Dimples," 555 pounds and "Baby Ruth," about 800 pounds, and less than half the *Guinness* record of 850.[24]

Otis describes Toby as "a very small boy, with a round head covered with short red hair, a face as speckled as any turkey's egg, but thoroughly good-natured looking..."[25] However, as Ruth MacDonald read the book, she considered Toby to be "fat, gluttonous, and often as conniving as that of his taskmasters." In contrast, she describes Disney actor Kevin Corcoran's Toby as

---

[22] Ibid., 103.

[23] Ibid., passim.

[24] Fiedler, *Freaks, Myths & Images*, 130. Also see, Bogdan, *Freak Show*, 210-212 who mentions the 1870 marriage uniting 40-pound human skeleton John Battersby with 688-pound Hannah Perkins. They exhibited for years. The proximity of their marriage date to Otis' 1881 book makes us wonder if he knew of this couple.

[25] Otis, *Toby Tyler,* 1881, 15. William Slout (1972:83) calls attention to the important development of the beloved stock character "Toby" in tent-theatre repertoire with plays about the turn of the twentieth century. Compare Slout's description with that of the 1881 Otis youth. "Toby, when he emerged as a stock figure, was a redheaded, freckle-faced, country boy, dressed in rural attire–a Huck Finn or Peck's Bad Boy, at various times brash, shy, shrewd, natively bright, stupid, industrious, lazy."

"a more appealing type, with large blue eyes, younger than Kaler's original, and....more wholesomely innocent, i.e., without Kaler's originality of language and slang."[26]

Mr. Stubbs also underwent significant alteration from being "old, mangy, and melancholic." As MacDonald puts it, "Such a pathetic, morose character would not do for a cleaned-up Disney version, so the studios substituted a chimpanzee who was more human and therefore more visually attractive than a sickly monkey." [27]

With the strokes of an illustrator's pen, some we suspect of never having read the book, the appearances of the original Otis characters change, sometimes drastically. Disney's illustrations are based on the movie actors who were cast to play the various roles. The studio chose relatively familiar, likable character actors with broad expressive faces possessing few wrinkles, blemishes, or other disfiguring facial marks.

Addition or Omission of Events

The plot-outline of Otis (1881) provides a definitive contrast with the Disney movie screenplay and/or Dorothea J. Snow's (1960) adaptation for Disney. Aside from the boy's initial meetings with the various characters, at least five events stand out in each story.

The Original Story

(1) For Otis, the "dinner party" hosted by the Treats looms large in introducing us not only to the nature of that circus, but also to a desperately needed "support group" for Toby. Here we discover the genuine affection of an odd couple for one another, plus their willingness to protect Toby from Job Lord.

(2) The breakdown of Ben's wagon and the monkeys' escape, enabling Toby to become an instant hero is pivotal. Previously the low-level, insignificant "Job's new boy," Toby gains a bit of status and respect.

(3) Mr. Stubbs' losing the boy's carefully saved coins lengthens the tale by forcing Toby to remain with the show until he saves more money.

(4) The cruel Mr. Castle's persuading Job Lord to let him train Toby as an

---

[26] MacDonald, *Mouseketeer in the Center Ring*, 40. We could not locate a specific age for Toby in either version, but Snow (1960:252) has Harry Tupper pegging it "about eleven years old."

[27] Ibid.

equestrian; thus, setting the youth up for ring stardom.

(5) The final scenario of Toby's escape from the circus, the death of Mr. Stubbs, and Toby's return home to Uncle Daniel.

The Disney Revision

(1) Toby's immense excitement watching Colonel Castle's grand parade. His thrill sets in motion not only the lad's desire to travel with the circus, but triggers Uncle Daniel's rage which pushes the boy toward running away.

(2) Clown Sam Treat's rescue of Toby from the demeaning taunts of youthful rider Monsieur Ajax. Here we simultaneously encounter not only Ajax's arrogance and Mademoiselle Jeanette's charm, but also the initiation of a friendship bond replacing that of the Treats in the original.

(3) The Fourth-of-July parade when the firecrackers panic Ben's horses, wreck his wagon, and allow the monkeys to escape. Obviously a substitute for the monkey's flight in Otis, Disney plays this escapade with great humor featuring Mr. Stubbs as a pistol-waving chimp.

(4) Ajax's brash attempt to show off in front of Jeanette and Toby. His accidental fall after removing his safety harness, is a case of "just deserts" which opens the plot for Toby's training and subsequent stardom as a talented equestrian.

(5) The abbreviated escape scenario, during which Mr. Stubbs is wounded (rather than killed); Tupper forcibly returns Toby to the show; hunter Jim Weaver brings Mr. Stubbs back; concluding with both Aunt Olive and Uncle Daniel proudly watching the skillful and humorous equestrian act of Toby, Jeanette, and Monsieur Stubbs.

Alteration of Particular Attitudes and Behavior

The two most significant changes, we believe, concern (1) Toby's concluding relationship with his Uncle Daniel, and (2) Toby's overall view of the circus. The Otis ending is a real "downer" with Uncle Daniel pleading:

> "Stay here, Toby, my son, and help to support this poor old body as it goes down into the dark valley of the shadow of death; and then, in the bright light of that glorious future, Uncle Daniel will wait to go with you into the presence of Him who is ever a father to the "fatherless."[28]

And in Uncle Daniel's kindly care we may safely leave Toby Tyler. Moreover,

---

[28] Otis, *Toby Tyler,* 1881, 262,265.

in Otis, Toby's view of his circus experience was one of almost total unhappiness and disillusionment. As nearly as we can tell, the boy has no desire to see or join another circus.[29] Ironically though, MacDonald claims that despite such observations, "children and adults who remember the book, notice and remember only the scenes of bright circus life." If she is correct, we have another instance of the recurring mystique of "happily running away with the circus."[30]

We have previously mentioned the importance of Disney's expanded role for Aunt Olive who mitigates the entire relationship with Uncle Daniel. Whereas in Otis, *Toby begs his uncle's forgiveness*; in Disney it is reversed with *Uncle Daniel seeking Toby's forgiveness!* Moreover, we gain the impression they will approve the lad pursuing his career as a star circus performer. Indeed, one gains a sort of *deja vu* image as described by Snow .

> Toby saw the tousle-headed boy who had taken his place at the lemonade stand. The boy was standing in the aisle, eyes wide and mouth agape, watching Toby. Toby grinned and bowed in the boy's direction. He knew exactly how that boy felt. He had felt the same way not so long ago when he carried the tray and stood looking at Jeanette and Ajax.[31]

A third notable factor has been delineated by Griswold, who points to Toby's almost constant eating in the Otis tale. He thoroughly documents this behavior to such an extent, one readily concedes the boy's habitual eating was wisely deleted by Disney.[32]

Linda Granfield describes the original *Toby Tyler* as "ten weeks of cruelty and pain with brief glimmers of love." She points out that the characters' acceptance of such barbaric treatment is shocking to modern readers, but does demonstrate how few rights children possessed a century ago. [33]

The noted film critic, Leonard Maltin, in an extended review of the Walt

---

[29] This observation does NOT take into account a lesser known continuation of Toby's life in *Mr. Stubb's Brother*, published in 1882. This sequel sets a very different tone, with a kindly, supportive Uncle Daniel and a warm Aunt Olive. Moreover, Toby is a "hero" to the local youngsters who make him their leader for planning their own backyard circus. One plot highlight returns Old Ben, the Treats, and little Ella to town. Toby again gains celebrity status among his friends as he provides them with personal introductions. Before the show departs, Ben gives to Toby his new friend, "Mr. Stubb's Brother."

[30] MacDonald, *Mouseketeer in the Center Ring,* 39.

[31] Snow, *Walt Disney's Toby Tyler,* 277.

[32] Griswold, *Audacious Kids,* 168-9.

[33] Granfeld, *Circus: An Album,* 84.

Disney movie admits he failed to appreciate the "supposedly hilarious antics" of Mr. Stubbs who "caused nothing but trouble and hardship for Toby and everyone else in the circus." This and some other flaws aside, Maltin relates that the film won Disney some of the producer's best reviews in years. He quotes Howard Thompson of the *New York Times*: "The very smallness of the setting pulls the gallery of circus people into *cozy* focus ... this little picture ... shines from within, mildly, but sweetly."--then the *Herald Tribune's* Paul V. Beckley, who called it "a minor classic among children's movies."[34]

When these observations are added to the other modifications from Otis to Disney, what we see is more than just a variation on a theme. We witness transition from a small struggling mud show to a thriving three-ring circus. We move from a morality tale told with Dickens-like cruelty to a children's story conveyed with color, humor, and likable characters despite their flaws. And we trade a rather dismal story ending for one with an upbeat vision of Toby's future. As such, Toby has a story to share with children of all ages, especially for those children from dysfunctional families. It is they who need to seek acceptance, a sense of belonging, and to discover elsewhere their value as persons.

In the process of "sanitizing" the original, Walt Disney tampered with a circus classic. But in doing so, he was sensitive to the audience of eight decades later. In our view, "Uncle Walt" did not so much "re-invent the wheel," as give it a new "paint job."

Bibliography

Becker, Mary Lamberton. "Introduction: How this Book Came to be Written," in *Toby Tyler*, the 1947 World Publishing Company edition.

Bogdan, Robert. *Freak Show: Presenting Human Oddities for Amusement and Profit.* Chicago, Illinois: The University Press, 1988.

Charters, W.W. "Sixty-four Popular Boys' Books." *The Library Journal* 63 (May 1938).

Chindahl, George L. *A History of the Circus in America.* Caldwell, Idaho: The Caxton Printers, Ltd., 1959.

Dickinson, Peter. "Afterword," in *Toby Tyler*, the 1990 Signet Classics edition.

Disney, Walt. *Walt Disney's Toby Tyler.* Story adapted by Carl Memling. Illustrated by Sam McKim. New York, NY: Golden Press, 1960. -- "A Little Golden Book." (All illustrations in color.)--24 pages.

—. Story adapted by Carl Memling. Illustrated by Mel Crawford. New York,

---

[34] Maltin, *The Disney Films*, 167.

NY: Golden Press.--"A Golden Reading Adventure." (All illustrations in color; end papers.) – 60 pages.

—. Story adapted by Dorothea J. Snow. Illustrated by Ben Franklin. Racine, Wisconsin: Whitman Publishing Company, 1960. (All illustrations in red, black, and white; end papers.) -- 282 pages.

—. This abbreviated version, only thirty-five pages, is part of an anthology entitled *Disney's World of Adventure Presents The Circus Book.* Neither the adapter nor the illustrator is identified. New York, NY: Random House, 1978. All illustrations are in color. -- 35 pages.

—. MOVIE: *Toby Tyler, or Ten Weeks with a Circus* (1960). Technicolor. 96 minutes Directed by Charles Barton. Screenplay by Bill Walsh and Lillie Hayward. Starring Kevin Corcoran, Henry Calvin, Gene Sheldon, Bob Sweeney, Richard Easthan, & James Drury. Copyright Walt Disney Productions. Distributed by the Buena Vista Distribution Co., Inc.

Fiedler, Leslie. *Freaks: Myths & Images of the Secret Self.* New York: Simon & Schuster, 1978.

Flint, Richard W. "The Evolution of the Circus in Nineteenth-Century America. *American Popular Entertainment: Papers and Proceedings of the Conference on the History of American Entertainment.* Ed. Myron Matlaw. Westport, Connecticut.

Fox, C. P. "Chappie". *America's Great Circus Parade: Its Roots...its Revival...its Revelry.* Greendale, WI: Reiman Publications, 1993.

Granfield, Linda. *Circus: An Album.* New York: DK Ink, 1998.

Griswold, Jerry. *Audacious Kids: Coming of Age in America's Classic Children's Books.* New York: Oxford University Press, 1992.

—. "Shooting the Monkey: Taming Oral Greed in *Toby Tyler. The Lion and The Unicorn* 12 (1988).

Harnett, Cynthia. "From the Ground Up." *Horn Book Reflections On Children's Books and Reading: Selected from Eighteen Years of The Horn Book Magazine* -- 1949-1966. Ed. Elinor Whitney Field, Boston: The Horn Book, 1969.

Herne, Betsy. "Disney Revisited, Or Jiminy Cricket, It's Musty Down Here!" *The Horn Book* (March/April 1997).

Hogarth, Grace. "Editor's Note." In *Toby Tyler,* the 1971 American Education Publications edition, (pages unnumbered).

MacDonald, Ruth K. "Mouseketeer in the Center Ring." *Children's Novels and the Movies.* Ed. Douglas Street, New York: Frederick Ungar Publishing Company, 1983.

Maltin, Leonard. *The Disney Films.* New York: Hyperion, 1995.

Mitchell, Joseph B. *The Badge of Gallantry: Recollections of Civil War*

Congressional Medal of Honor Winners. New York: The Macmillan Company, 1968.

Ogden, Tom. *Two Hundred Years of the American Circus.* New York: Facts On File, 1993.

Otis, James (pseudonym for James Otis Kaler). *Toby Tyler or Ten Weeks with a Circus.* Illustrated by W. A. Rogers. New York: Harper & Brothers, Franklin Square, 1881.

—. Illustrated by Everett Shinn. Introduction by Everett Shinn. Philadelphia: The John C. Winston Company, 1937. (Frontispiece in color; 3 colored plates; numerous illustrations; illustrated title page; end papers.)

—. Illustrated by Louis Glanzman. Introduction by May Lamberton Becker. Cleveland, Ohio: The *World* Publishing Company/The World's Popular Classics, 1947. (Colorful front and back covers; frontispiece in color; numerous b & w illustrations, supplementing 6 in color; check interesting end papers.) This "Rainbow Classic" edition vies with the 1971 "Lifetime Library" edition for most attractive Toby Tyler.

—. Illustrated by Charles Mozley. Introduction by General Editor, Grace Hogarth. Published simultaneously in the United States and the United Kingdom. Middletown, Connecticut: American Education Publications; Rickmansworth, Hertfordshire, Great Britain: Everyweek Educational Press Limited, 1971. (Front and back covers in color; numerous illustrations, with 8, including 2 double pages in color). This "Lifetime Library" edition is, in our judgment, the most beautiful of all the Toby Tyler books--exceptional! But compare to the 1947 "Rainbow Classic."

—. Afterword by Peter Dickinson.   New York: Penguin Books USA, Inc./Signet Classic, 1990.

—. *Mr. Stubbs's Brother: A Sequel to "Toby Tyler."* Illustrated by W.A. Rogers. New York: Harper & Brothers Publishers, 1882.

Sayers, Frances Clarke. "Walt Disney Accused." *The Horn Book Magazine* 41 (December 1965).

Schickel, Richard. *The Disney Version: The Life, Times, Art and Commerce of Walt Disney.* New York: Simon and Schuster, 1968

Seelye, John. "Preface." In *Toby Tyler*, the Garland edition, 1977.

Shinn, Everett. "A Boy's Dream in Action." – A preface in *Toby Tyler*, the John C. Winston Company edition, 1937.

Slout, William Lawrence. *Theatre in a Tent: The Development of a Provincial Entertainment.* Bowling Green, Ohio: Bowling Green University Popular Press, 1972.

Snow, Dorothea J. *Walt Disney's Toby Tyler*, Racine, Wisconsin: Whitman Publishing Company, 1960.

Truzzi, Marcello. "Circus and Sideshow." *American Popular Entertainment: Papers and Proceedings of the Conference on the History of American Entertainment.* Myron Matlaw, ed. Westport, Connecticut, 1979.

Watts, Steven. *The Magic Kingdom: Walt Disney and the American Way of Life.* New York: Houghton Mifflin Company, 1997.

CHAPTER SEVENTEEN

JOYCE'S "CIRCE" AND THE CIRCUS: SYMBOLISM AND MYTH

CAROLINE A. NOBILE

For over 2500 years the circus has served, in one way or another, as a cultural and, simultaneously, a metacultural phenomenon. Considering its longevity, the way in which the circus "reads" and reflects its culture is apparently universal. Its code of communication includes such "language" as props, lighting, music, costumes, animals, and, of course, the social behavior of the performers. At the circus, all is surface, and yet all is equally subliminal, metaphorical. No modern writer understood the literary possibilities of this symbolic goldmine, the circus, better than James Joyce. For the phantasmogoric climax of his most celebrated novel *Ulysses* (1922), Joyce borrowed copiously from the naturalistic and symbolic medium of the circus.

True, though Joyce himself identified the "art" of his "Circe" chapter (the novel's climax) as "magic," and his "technique" as "hallucination," it is my contention that Joyce appropriated the nonlinguistic code of communication, the archetypal meanings, and the metaphoric structure of the circus, because, in short, his artistic purpose in "Circe" was to move beyond the inherent constraints of language per se (most of "Circe" is deeply subliminal) in order to express the mythic as well as the psycho-sexual dimensions of this key chapter. Like the ringmaster who orchestrates, yet remains apart from, the acts occurring simultaneously in the ring, Joyce, the artist-ringmaster, shapes, integrates, and vitalizes the seemingly-unintelligible fantasies and unconscious thoughts of his novel's hero, Leopold Blood, as he journeys through nighttown (literally, the red light district of Dublin).

Since this paper's thesis builds upon a previous study of mine published in the *James Joyce Quarterly* that linked the circus allusions in *Ulysses* to external sources, it will be helpful first to describe the somewhat complicated source history behind Joyce's circus allusions.

In a graduate class taught by the late Joyce scholar Michael Begnal, I became intent on locating the origins of one of *Ulysses*' more elusive sources,

Ruby: The Pride of the Ring, a title mentioned only twice in the novel. In searching through Raymond Toole-Stott's definitive bibliography *Circus and Allied Arts*, I found several titles of circus dime novels, a genre popular in the early twentieth century, that looked promising, but no actual *Ruby: the Pride of the Ring*. Though all were long out of print, I acquired one of the novels, Henry T. Johnson's *The Pride of the Ring* on microfilm from the British Museum. Its plot convinced me that Joyce had borrowed a number of details from this circus novel to serve his climactic chapter in *Ulysses,* the "Circe" episode.

However, in the *Quarterly* article, I went on to argue that Joyce's *Ruby: The Pride of the Ring* is a fictionalized composite, rather than a distinct source, which Joyce created by attaching the name *Ruby* to the common circus epithet *Pride of the Ring*, thus meshing two literary genres: adolescent adventure and adult pulp fiction, the latter befitting the brothel setting of "Circe." In conclusion, I suggested that further exploration of Joyce's circus analogies might provide a better understanding of his enigmatic, at times linguistically unintelligible, key chapter.

Following that suggestion, this paper examines the non-verbal and mythic parallels between the circus and "Circe" with attention paid to the way Joyce exploited the sensational and subversive qualities of the circus in order to provide a symbolic context for the psycho-sexual fantasies of the novel's hero, Leopold Bloom.

To begin, Paul Bouissac, in his *Circus and Culture* (1976; rpt. 1985), studies the circus as highly communicative cultural artifact. Nevertheless, the circus is not a "normal" mode of communication in a way that, for instance, a theatrical production or musical concert are normal cultural events. Circus acts demonstrate a freedom from the constraints of a given culture, notes Bouissac, and so are inversions of the norm. Furthermore, the circus, like myth and folklore, exhibits instinctual and primordial qualities of human nature, aspects that rely less upon linguistic elements than upon nonverbal signs of communication. In fact, circus performances often discourage explicit discourse. As a whole, the circus program derives its mythic, or archetypal, dimensions from its very deliberate and purposeful sequencing of the acts.

Let's examine more closely the individual constituents of a typical circus performance:

1. linguistic messages (minimal, performers talk to audience, to animals, to each other)
2. social behavior of performers (may be aggressive, heroic, humble, idiotic, fearless)
3. Music (sets the mood, conveys meaning by sound)
4. Lighting (spotlights, backlighting, soft lights, strobe lights, etc.)

5. Costume (may be practical, outrageous, sensual, exotic, primitive, noble)
6. Accessories (props, hoops, ropes, chains, nets, cages, set scenes, clown cars)
7. Technical ability of performer (balance, grace, agility, toughness, clumsy)
8. Colors (usually bright primary colors that help evoke mood).[1]

Each of these elements represents a code, which, when combined, form the supercode that is the circus, and there are any number of variations possible. In deciphering the code, it is important to consider the *ordering* or the structural sequencing of the acts that comprise the whole program. Their meaning is conveyed in two ways: their complementary associations. and their internal cross-referencing.

These two techniques of meaning are, in fact, quite compatible with Joyce's artistic intentions in "Circe," as we shall see. Moreover, the mythic connotations of the circus are well-suited to Joyce's myth-making purposes, as *Ulysses* is modeled upon Homer's *The Odyssey* and each of Joyce's chapters has its Homeric counterpart. Joyce also provided what became commonly known as his "schema" (or gloss) on his novel, in which he identifies the technique (hallucination) and art (magic) he selected for "Circe" (Gilbert). Befitting fantasy, the linguistic constituents of this chapter are random, disconnected, and free-associative. Such are the techniques of stream of consciousness. Although point of view has been widely discussed in the literature on "Circe," there are hints in this chapter that Joyce meant to move beyond stream of consciousness towards a mode of communication that pre-dates language. Those clues, I believe, are embedded in the novel's circus allusions and circus imagery.

The first clue comes in Joyce's fourth chapter, "Calypso," in the scene in which Molly Bloom is reading *Ruby: The Pride of the Ring.* She comes across the word "metempsychosis" and asks Bloom to define it:

—Metempsychosis, he said, frowning. It's Greek: from the Greek. That means the transmigration of souls.
—O, rocks! She said. Tell us in plain words.
He smiled, glancing askance at her mocking eye. The same young eyes. The first night after the charades. Dolphin's Barn. He turned over the smudged pages. *Ruby: The Pride of the Ring.* Hello. Illustration. Fierce Italian with carriagewhip. Must be Ruby pride of the on the floor naked. Sheet kindly lent. *The monster Maffei desisted and flung his victim from him with an oath.* Cruelty behind it all. Doped animals. Trapeze at Hengler's. Had to look the other way. Mob gaping. Break your neck and we'll break our sides. Families of them. Bone

---

[1] Bouissac, *Circus and Culture,* 15.

them young so they metempsychosis. That we live after Death. Our souls. That
a man's soul after he dies. Dignam's soul . . . .[2]

This is good example of Joyce's use of stream of consciousness. It begins
with outward dialogue as Bloom responds to Molly's question, but quickly
shifts inward as Bloom associates his and Molly's lovemaking at Dolphin's
barn, an incident from the past--before they were married--to the picture in
Ruby: The Pride of the Ring. Bloom then associates this sexualized image of
the innocent Ruby victimized by the sadistic ringmaster with another memory of
a trapeze accident he witnessed at a popular circus event. This thought leads to
Bloom's feeling that the circus is inherently cruel both to animals and human
performers. The thought process is momentarily recursive as "metempsychosis"
is reiterated, and then moves on to thoughts of Paddy Dignam's death and
subsequent funeral Bloom will attend later that morning.

This passage also exemplifies Joyce's use of internal cross-referencing and
complementary associations, which signify Bloom's own pattern of mind. The
initial allusion to the circus, via *Ruby: The Pride of the Ring,* makes that
connection possible. Moreover, the meaning of the word *metempsychosis,* and
its link to the circus story Molly is reading, is key to understanding how Joyce
adapts the mythic and structural codes of the circus in the later "Circe" episode.
Although Joyce never uses the exact title *Ruby: The Pride of the Ring* again in
the novel, the title (and the circus in general) undergo a bizarre metempsychosis
as *Ruby* the novel is alluded to via props and fantasy figures such as,
respectively, a "ruby ring"; "ruby buttons" on Bloom's deceased son's lapel; a
woman named Ruby; and a Scarlet Woman, the archetypal whore.

The figure of Ruby and the sinister ringmaster Signor Maffei appear again
in the "Circe" episode. As Joyce's schema indicates, the setting is nighttown,
the red light district of Dublin, at a brothel at midnight. Leopold Bloom has
followed Stephen Dedalus into the brothel. Bloom has been thinking all day of
Molly's imminent sexual encounter with her stage agent, Blazes Boylan. The
surface plot in this episode is pretty thin: Bloom and Stephen merely meet, talk
with some whores, and leave the brothel together. Stephen is drunk and nearly
gets into a street fight. Bloom comes to his aid, and they walk together to
Bloom's home, where in "Ithaca" they part after urinating together.

Most of the "action" in "Circe" takes place beneath the narrative surface, on
the unconscious level; at times the fleeting display of sounds, props, dialogue,
characters, and images seem to exist outside of Bloom's unconscious mind
altogether. It is at this level that Bloom's manhood is severely challenged,
stripped, and ultimately regained so that by the end of this climactic experience
he has achieved a stature worthy of his Homeric counterpart. This is also the

---

[2] Joyce, *Ulysses,* 64.

level at which the circus and "Circe" are linked. Like the circus clown who sheds one dirty shirt only to find another underneath, Bloom removes his metaphoric dirty laundry as his psychosexual fantasies are played out. Stephen, when he enters nighttown, rather drunk and pontificating, seems to understand the limitations of language, when he says that "gesture, not music, not odours would be a universal language, the gift of tongues rendering visible not the lay sense but the first entelechy, the structural rhythm."[3] And Bloom says it more simply: "Instincts rule the world. In life. In death." "Words? Music? No. It's what's behind."[4]

The individual components of the circus act are evident in "Circe" and communicate meaning in the same way: Colors, mainly red, purple, blue, are directly related to sensation and define mood ("Colors affect women's characters. . . . This black makes me sad;"[5] lighting affects memory ("Confused light confuses memory";)[6] props have the power to speak and everything is vital, alive (The calls, the answers.[7] the bells, the gong,[8] the soap;[9] the yews and waterfalls,[10] and even Stephen's cap.[11] Costumes, mainly hats, have metaphoric significance. They signal changes in the context of a particular fantasy or hallucination and help convey the role Bloom acts out in them. When Bloom courts Mrs. Breen, for instance, he wears a Napoleonic hat,[12] and his whole costume changes with each suggestive role. When Mrs. Breen tells him he was always a favorite with the ladies, Bloom turns Casanova, sporting a dinner jacket with silk facings, a black bow-tie and mother of pearl studs, and a glass of champagne tilted in his hand.[13] When he is later accused of indecent behavior towards his domestic, Bloom acquires a housejacket, flannel trousers, heelless slippers, and a disheveled appearance.[14] When he soars to grandiose heights, Bloom is decked out in formal governor-of-state attire.[15]

Bloom's fantasy transformations, signified by costume shifts, each denotes a "psychic" metempsychosis, so to speak, that will eventually prepare him to acquire the kind of hero status worthy of his Homeric counterpart. Interestingly,

---

[3] Ibid., 432.
[4] Ibid., 274.
[5] Ibid., 526.
[6] Ibid.
[7] Ibid., 429.
[8] Ibid., 435.
[9] Ibid., 440.
[10] Ibid., 553.
[11] Ibid., 504.
[12] Ibid., 445.
[13] Ibid.
[14] Ibid., 460.
[15] Ibid., 481.

Bouissac refers to "a formal dinner jacket occasionally enhanced by glitter" as one of the standard costumes in circus acts that denote a performer's hero status.[16] Another circus association implied by Bloom's frequent change of costume is what was known as the "quick change act" popular both in the circus and in vaudeville in Joyce's time. In fact, a quick change act is described in Henry T. Johnson's *The Pride of the Ring,* and there is strong evidence that Joyce borrowed from that description in various places in "Circe."

Musical accompaniment, street noise, and the like, add to the atmosphere which circumscribes the particular fantasy. Gestures are especially significant: Bloom gives the secret Masonic sign, for instance. And often the reader must rely on gesture alone to sense what is taking place between verbal exchanges.

Because the spatially open circus ring allows acts simultaneously to take place in the air as well as on the ground, it allows for an artistic stratification of performances that convey more than one level of meaning at a time. In "Circe," the non-linearity and simultaneity of action that characterize its structure make the circus ring an apt metaphor for its context. As "Circe" begins, Joyce implies this spatial dimension by including a "pigmy woman [who] swings on a rope slung between the railings."[17] Moreover, *Circus* and *Circe* also both mean "circle" or "ring." *The Pride of the Ring* thus becomes a clever double entendre as well.

Curiously, upon first encountering Bloom in nighttown, the reader sees him simultaneously from three dimensions:

> Bloom appears flushed, panting, cramming bread and chocolate into a side pocket. . . . A concave mirror at the side presents to him love-lorn longlost lugubru Booloohoom. Grave Gladstone sees him level, bloom for Bloom. He passes struck by the stare of truculent Wellington but in the convex mirror grin unstruck the Bonham eyes and fatchuck cheekchops of Jollypoldy the rixdix doldy.[18]

This first image is the self-pitying Bloom from "Sirens" episode, a negative self which Bloom must shed before regaining his manhood and leaving nighttown ("When in doubt persecute Bloom" he says;)[19] the second image is the practical, level-headed Bloom whom we associate with the surface narrative; and the third self is Bloom the circus clown, the comic butt of Jew-baiting jokes his acquaintances crack, and the cuckold of Molly. As the experiences in nighttown become more subterranean in fantasy, Bloom's multidimensionality is augmented by all the transpersonal roles he enacts—as Odysseus, as Christ, as

---

[16] Bouissac, 94.

[17] Joyce, 429.

[18] Ibid, 433-4.

[19] Ibid, 464.

Moses, as the New Parnell (Irish hero), and ultimately as the female Miss Ruby Cohen.

Within the mythic context of the circus ring, Bloom is put through a series of feats that he must successfully complete in order to gain hero status. Like the circus performer's, Bloom's progress through "Circe" parallels these stages of the hero's journey:

1. the identification of the hero
2. the qualifying test
3. a warmup for the real feat
4. the main test
5. the glorifying test, which gives the doer hero status
6. and the public acknowledgement of the fulfillment of the task.[20]

The sequencing of Bloom's fantasies in "Circe"—and their aggregate effect upon him—symbolize the myth sequence. Bloom is announced, or identified, in the above quoted passage of "Circe." His qualifying test is represented by all the women from his past about whom he's had erotic thoughts (Gerty McDowell, Mrs. Breen, Martha). Some put him on trial for obscenity (Mary Driscoll, Mrs. Yelverton Barry, Mrs. Bellingham, and Mrs. Mervyn Talboys). They also mock his cukoldry.[21] With the audial signal of cuckoo sounds, this hallucination fades out and Bloom, who survives the warmup test, passes through various compensatory fantasies before encountering his main test at the brothel. In this fantasy the whore Bella becomes a man, Bello, and threatens Bloom with castration. Bloom's glorifying test is his greatest challenge: the witnessing of Molly's sexual encounter with Blazes Boylan.[22] By confronting, at least unconsciously, the one thought he has been avoiding the whole day, Bloom purges himself of guilt and fear, and regains his manhood along with his capacity for forgiveness. Public acknowledgement of the fulfillment of this task[23] is presented in the catalogue of Dublin citizens, the "hue and cry" which crowd around Bloom as he intercedes on Stephen's behalf in the street brawl (a literal occurrence).

The metaphor of the circus ring provides a perfect context for the performance of Bloom's hallucinations, with one added dimension of meaning: Joyce transmutes the circus ring to the Pride of the Ring, and by so doing, imbues the context with all sorts of kinky, sexual innuendoes.

---

[20] Boussiac, 25.
[21] Joyce, 469.
[22] Ibid., 567.
[23] Ibid., 585-608.

As the hour of Molly and Bolyan's rendezvous draws near, Molly becomes transfigured in Bloom's fantasy from cruel wife to dark seductress; dressed in alluring Turkish costume, she sadistically taunts Bloom,[24] who has become a camel "stooping his back for leapfrog."[25] His transformation into beast of burden complements and reiterates his own comment about "the prevention of cruelty to animals." He announces: "All tales of circus life are highly demoralizing"—which summarizes the main theme of the circus fantasies performed within the Pride of the Ring.   That announcement evokes the appearance, once again, of the Italian liontamer I mentioned from the Calypso chapter:

> (Signor Maffei, passion pale, in liontamer's costume with diamond studs in his shirtfront, steps forward, holding a circus paper hoop, a curling carriagewhip and a revolver with which he covers the goring boarhound).
>
> SIGNOR MAFFEI (With a sinister smile): Ladies and gentlemen, my educated greyhound. It was I broke in the bucking broncho Ajax with my patent spike saddle for carnivores. . . . (He glares.) I possess the Indian sign. The glint of my eye does it with these breastsparklers. (With a bewitching smile.) I now introduce Mademoiselle Ruby, the pride of the ring.[26]

On the level of the Homeric myth, Signor Maffei is Circe—he has the same bewitching power to transform human into beast and the same possessive, sinister will. As a figure in *Ruby: the Pride of the Ring*, Maffei is a fantasy-projection of Bloom's desire to dominate Molly rather than being subservient to her. Maffei possesses the mysterious "Indian sign"—which gives him power over Ruby—Bloom's gimmick is, ironically, the ineffectual Masonic sign. Bloom's desire to dominate—and hence, be a real man—is thwarted by the inability to sustain, on the fantasy level, the illusion of himself as aggressor. In fact, Bloom's encounter with Bella-the-whore results in his becoming a woman and a victim, the female "Miss Ruby Cohen," while Bella assumes a masculine role (as Bello).

Bella/Bello also epitomizes the archetypal whore; she is Circe, on the Homeric level, and she is Maffei, on the circus-myth level. When she transforms Bloom into the role of the submissive Ruby Cohen, she tells him:

---

[24] Ibid, 439-40.
[25] Ibid., 440.
[26] Ibid., 454.

What you longed for has come to pass. Henceforth you are unmanned and mine
in earnest, a thing under the yoke. . . . You will shed your male garments, you
understand, Ruby Cohen?[27]

Under her spell, Bloom is forced to expose all acts of perversion he
committed in the past and to play out to extremes the inverted domestic role he
wittingly assumed in the marriage relationship. Bello taunts him—

By day you will souse and bat our smelling underclothes, also when we ladies
are unwell, and swab out our latrines with dress pinned up and dishclout tied to
your tail. Won't that be nice? (He places a ruby ring on her finger.) And there
now! With this ring I thee own. Say thank you, mistress.[28]

Rings as props in "Circe" take on meanings that subvert their conventional
or cultural connotations. Normally associated with romantic love, signifying the
bond between lovers, here the ring is a lewd symbol of bondage and
subjugation. In accepting the ring from Bello, Bloom has indentured himself as
her slave and accepts her emasculating demands. In transferring the ring/prop to
the ring/context, the circus ring represents the contextual boundaries within
which the hero's journey is enacted. We recall Bloom's comment about the
circus in "Calypso" that there is "cruelty behind it all."[29] In "Circe" he has been
exposed as a sexual pervert as well as himself being sexually exploited. In a
mock marriage, Bloom is further taunted by Bello, disguised now as a castrating
Nymph, who scorns Bloom's "pride": "UP! UP! Minx cat! What have we
here? Where's our curly teapot gone . . . Can you do a man's job?"[30]
As the words *pride* and *ring* are puns for male and female genitalia,
respectively, they mock Bloom's inability "to keep it up / to keep it up."[31] Thus
Ruby: The Pride of the Ring perverts the culturally known context of the circus
ring to the sexually mysterious context of Bloom's unconscious. Ironically, the
fusing of male and female genitalia implied in *this* circus ring allow Bloom the
courage to escape this ego-deflating trap set by Bello. In a cathartic response to
Molly's infidelity ("I forgot! Forgive! I have suff . . .,"[32] Bloom sees Bello for
the whore she is: "Fool someone else, not me (He sniffs)." The narrative
appropriately shifts to the surface, and Bloom, armed now with an affirmative
memory and the willingness to forgive, goes into the street (an actual

---

[27] Ibid., 535.
[28] Ibid., 539.
[29] Ibid., 64.
[30] Ibid, 541.
[31] Ibid., 553.
[32] Ibid., 544.

occurrence) to receive, symbolically, a public acknowledgement of his heroic achievement.

Bibliography

Bouissac, Paul. *Circus and Culture.* Bloomington: Indiana University Press, 1976; rpt. 1985.

Gilbert, Stuart. *James Joyce's Ulysses.* NY: Vintage, 1955 (Rev. ed).

Joyce, James. *Ulysses.* Paris: Shakespeare and Company, 1922. NY: Random House, Corrected Ed. 1961.

Nobile, Caroline A. "Who is Signor Maffei? And Has *Ruby: The Pride of the Ring* Really Been Located?" *James Joyce Quarterly.* 21.4 (1984): 321-28.

Toole-Stott, Raymond. *Circus and Allied Arts: A World Bibliography 1500-1962 III.* Derby, England: Harpur & Sons, Ltd., 1962, pp. 90, 94, 104. Henry T. Johnson's *The Pride of the Ring* [#5199] is also cited in Thornton, W. *Allusions in Ulysses.* Chapel Hill: University of North Carolina Press, 1968, pp. 73-74.

Part VI

Perspectives

CHAPTER EIGHTEEN

MASKING VERSUS MAKEUP: PRESENTING
PARADOX THROUGH THE FACE OF THE CLOWN

RODNEY A. HUEY

Introduction

The typified face of the contemporary American circus clown, with its exaggerated eyes, oversized mouth and red bulbous nose, is not only an instant icon of the American circus, but is perhaps its most recognizable signifier. The clown's facial makeup appears to be as necessary in defining the circus clown as its motley costume and zany antics. But if you ask any performing clown whether or not makeup is absolutely essential in defining the clown, nine out of ten would most likely tell you that true clowning comes from the inside the heart of the clown, rather than from outside physical appearances; and that the costume and makeup only accentuate the clown's persona. However, ask that same group of clowns if they ever perform without makeup, or even if they can assume their individual clown personas without the use of makeup, and one will soon learn that in the execution of their performances, makeup is quite likely the single-most significant identifier of the clown in its performance narrative.

But is the clown's makeup a culturally defined, standardized and easily recognizable mask; or is it an extension of each individual clown's facial features? Moreover, what does the grotesquely exaggerated face of the clown represent? This paper explores the relationship among the clown, its facial makeup, and the presentation of paradox through the lens of "masking."

Historical Antecedents of Masking

The idea of masking appears to be endemic to the human condition, and conveys powerful cultural meanings. Mary Douglas suggested that changes to, or manipulation of, the body symbolically reflect an individual's encounter with the larger society in that the "physical body is a microcosm of society"[1] which symbolizes "the relation of an individual to his society at that general systemic level."[2] John Nunley and Cara McCarty argued that masking is one of the "most ancient means of changing identity and assuming a new persona," and the desire, or "perhaps even universal need," to intentionally change physical appearances has "coexisted with the development of human society."[3] The mask, according to the authors, bestows the "power of anonymity [which] gives us the protection to behave in ways we otherwise might not, to act aggressively or to break rules."[4]   Michel Thevoz suggested that masking recalled the savagery inherent in early humanity, originating with man's "problematic relation with his own image," and leads a person to "retouch his body in various ways."[5] He stated: "The fact is that man is confronted with his own body as the initial object of 'cultural retouching,'" and the concept of body painting and adornment is an attempt to stave off the repressive, sterilized confinements of society.[6]   Likewise, Johan Huizinga proposed that the mask "carries us beyond 'ordinary life' into a world where something other than daylight reigns," transporting us "back to the world of the savage, the child and the poet, which is the world of play."[7]

Efrat Tseelon examined the role of masking from a more individualistic perspective, distinguishing the differences among the concepts of the mask, disguise and masquerade.   He argued that the *mask* represents, *disguise* conceals, and *masquerade* is a "statement of the wearer." Masquerading, or taking on an entirely new persona through masking and costumery, evokes "the notion of identity" to create a space in which "the notions of 'self' and 'other' are constructed."   It is this representation of identity that "alerts us to the inevitability of difference" and "provides the basis for understanding what holds us together, but also what sets us apart;" and at the same time injects the symbolic and necessary Other into our midst:

> To place oneself as Other or as masked is already to position oneself in a resistive position, whereby difference is threatening to (the logical explanations,

---

[1] Douglas, *Natural Symbols,* 77.
[2] Ibid., 87.
[3] Nunley and McCarty, *Masks: Faces of Culture,* 15
[4] Ibid., 17.
[5] Thevoz, *The Illusions of Reality: Painted Body,* 7.
[6] Ibid., 11.
[7] Huizinga, *Homo Ludens: A Study of the Play Element in Culture,* 26.

habitual practices and unquestioned assumptions of) the established order and its defined categories.[8]

Tseelon also pointed out that it is "only by breaking rules that one discovers which rules exist." [9]

Perhaps the most cogent study into body adornment, manipulation and masking, particularly through transgressive and symbolically inversive public performance, was penned by Russian literary critic Mikhail Bakhtin in *Rabelais and His World*. Bahktin argued that masking and motley dress during carnival season not only reflected a unique symbiotic, yet adversarial relationship between the individual and the forces of authority in the medieval social, religious, economic and political hierarchies; but they also created necessary public expressions that invoked the liberating *carnivalesque* spirit by revealing "the essence of the grotesque." It was through "grotesque realism," or the intentional exaggeration of bodily orifices, such as the mouth, eyes, nose and ears (parts of the body that connect the individual directly with the social world), that the concept of masking was inextricably connected to "transition, metamorphoses, [and] the violation of natural boundaries."[10] The *carnivalesque* image may be carried over into non-carnival periods, because according to Bakhtin's thesis, the fully costumed clown outside carnival becomes the carrier of the *carnivalesque* spirit into everyday life that creates a "gay and ambivalent laughter" to free us from the constrictive and hegemonic social and cultural bonds.

I am willing to argue that the typified clown of today's circus, with exaggerated facial features, motley dress and socially disruptive behavior, represents a modern-day version of Bakhtin's *grotesque realism*, creating a "gay and ambivalent laughter" in an attempt to liberate us from society's hegemonic constraints and confinements. More importantly, it is through the notion of masking, or facial makeup of the clown, that this becomes true; thus confronting us with the persistent presence of the alien Other, or symbolic outsider who "poses both a constant threat and a necessary corollary to the classification system itself." The clown becomes society's sanctioned mischief-maker who establishes social boundaries by transgressing them, rendering "a permissible rupture of hegemony."[11]

---

[8] Tseelon, "Introduction" and "Reflections on Mask and Carnival," *Masquerade and Identities: Essays on Gender, Sexuality and Marginality*. Edited by Efrat Tseelon, 6.
[9] Ibid., 27.
[10] Bakhtin, 39.
[11] Tseelon, 28.

Development of the American Circus Clown

The typified American circus clown did not originate in the American circus. Its traceable roots reach back to antiquity. But more pertinently, the origins of the modern circus clown may be found on the 18th-century English stages of London's Sadler's Wells, Drury Lane and Covent Garden in the CLOWN figure of Joseph Grimaldi (1778-1837). Grimaldi is generally credited by most circus historians as the father of circus clowning, and the originator of the grotesque, or exaggerated clown face that eventually morphed into the auguste clown. [12] During that same period, a French actor named Jean-Gaspard Deburau (1776-1846) introduced a more romanticized, whitefaced clown in the stage character of Pierrot. [13] These two clown types, with contrasting makeup styles, dominated the European stage before they found their way into the circus ring– a new entertainment format created by equestrian Philip Astley in a riding exhibition outside London in 1768. A riding clown named Fortunelly was introduced into Astley's riding exhibition as a comical relief. A spin-off of Astley's circus found roots in American soil when Scotsman John Bill Ricketts presented the first circus in America in Philadelphia in 1793. Ricketts' circus also featured a comedic riding act by a clown named Mr. McDonald.

Within a half century, the riding clown evolved into a central performer as best personified by Dan Rice (1823-1900), circus owner and performer whose clowning performance and popular political satire from the circus ring reflected the essence of the independent and populist 19th century American character. Biographer David Carlyon noted that although Rice wore minimal makeup, he still served the subversive role of political commentator, proposing that today Rice would be considered to be "Will Rogers, Robin Williams and [Senator] John McCain rolled into one."[14] However, the one-ring clown of Dan Rice soon gave way to a diminishing clown with the advent of the three-ring circus, relegating the mid-19th century talking clown to a silent role on the hippodrome track. But during the first half of the 20th century, clowning refused to take a back seat to the other popular acts, and comedic artists, such as Lou Jacobs (1903-1992), Felix Adler (1898-1960), Otto Griebling (1896-1972), and Emmett Kelly (1899-1979) began to emerge as America's dominant circus clowns.

The early 20th century American style of circus clowning relied on the historical whiteface and auguste clown types, but a third type developed in the 1930s–the character clown, which was most often in the trope of a tramp or hobo. The tramp clown got its inspiration from the many homeless wanderers during this country's Great Depression, and quickly gained popularity primarily

---

[12] Dishler, *Clowns and Pantomime,* 85.
[13] Ibid., 135.
[14] Carlyon, *Dan Rice: The Most Famous Man You've never Heard Of,* xiii.

due to Emmett Kelly's "Weary Willie" and Otto Griebling's unnamed tramp character. For more than a half-century, these three clown types dominated the American circus through the faces of Lou Jacobs (who set the standards for the auguste clown); Felix Adler (who defined an important model of the whiteface); and Emmett Kelly and Otto Griebling (who advanced the idea of the character clown).

But hard times fell on the American circus after the end of World War II, and the tradition of circus clowning itself was threatened with the temporary closing of practically all American circuses during 1955 and 1956. It was the regeneration of the circus by a business group of concert promoters–brothers Irvin and Israel Feld and Houston Judge Roy Hofheinz–that added new life to the three-ring spectacle, and brought about a brighter future for the American circus clown through the establishment of Ringling Bros. and Barnum & Bailey Clown College in 1968.

Clowning becomes a Formalized Regimen

From 1968 through 1997, Clown College held annual sessions whereby young clowning hopefuls were taught the art and skills of clowning. Under the tutelage of six directorships and literally hundreds of professional faculty members, 1297 fledgling clowns earned their diplomas from "the only school in the world solely dedicated to the ancient and honorable art of Circus clowning."[15]

To anyone who ever attended or even visited Clown College, it was obvious that from the first day of class, devising one's facial makeup was an extremely important priority. Early photographs indicated that the first Clown College class in 1968, under the inaugural directorship of former Ringling Circus Museum curator Mel Miller, yielded mostly whiteface clowns whose makeup tended to resemble one another. In 1969, author and illustrator Bill Ballantine took over as director, and it was apparent that makeup was important to him in the creation of the new American circus clown. In his book *Clown Alley*, he stated: "The most important element of a circus clown's appearance is his comical face. By wearing a bizarre makeup, the clown easily achieves rapport with his audience."[16] By the end of Ballantine's tenure, the three clown face types had been firmly established as a certain pedagogical formula that set rigid standards for clown faces–the whiteface, the auguste and the character clown.

When Ringling graduate Ron Severini (class of 1971) and his clowning wife Sandy took over the directorship of Clown College in 1974, makeup

---

[15] Clown College Press Release, 1987.
[16] Ballantine, *Clown Alley,* 82.

remained front and center. Severini approached the development of the clown character as a smorgasbord whereby students were allowed to select from a vast assortment of cloths and colors for their costume. He did the same for their clown faces. Severini set up a room with dozens of rubber noses tacked to a wall with a mirror and large sign that read: Pick your nose! From the Severinis' directorship (that ended in 1984) through Steve Smith's directorship (1985-1994), Clown College continued to support the idea of three basic clown faces to the point of codifying standard characteristics and palates for those facial types. Clown College brochures, distributed in educational school packages aimed at elementary children, proclaimed: "All Circus Clown Faces Come From Only Three Types" and "Every Clown Face in the World is a Variation of One of These Three." The Clown College Bulletin addressed the importance of students experimenting with "a rainbow of colors" to create their "own *variation* [italics mine] of these basic makeup categories."[17] In other words, students were expected to experiment with an infinite number of facial designs and combinations to create their own unique clown face, but *only* within the framework of the three proscribed typologies. Even in both Dick Monday's and Rob Mermin's joint directorship (1995) and eventually Monday's sole directorship (1995-1997), in which he indicated that changing the makeup from the idealized auguste to a more subtle stage and character makeup was a priority set by circus owner and producer Kenneth Feld, the face of the circus clown remained the single most important element of concentration and development for Clown College students.

Clown College graduate Ruth Chaddock (class of 1974) spent several years performing with the Ringling Bros. and Barnum & Bailey show before turning her attention in 1980 to teaching makeup at Clown College, a position she held for 13 years. Recognized as one of the foremost authorities on clown makeup, Chaddock also created numerous "lifecasts" of Ringling clowns (a plaster replica of individual clown faces) which she painted in authentic detail. More than 200 of her lifecasts are housed at Ringling or on display around the country in various shows and museum exhibits.

Commenting on the suggestion that a clown's face is a mask, Chaddock retorted: "We're not masking. I am trying to teach them [Clown College students] and help them develop clown makeup that is going to accentuate their own face, and [what] is going to work for them." She continued: "I don't design someone's face for them, not ever." Chaddock's philosophy of clown face development is that makeup must follow the natural lines of the individual human face, only in an exaggerated form. Makeup accentuates, enhances and brings out the inherent facial tendencies, and according to Chaddock, a makeup

---

[17] Ringling Bros. and Barnum & Bailey Clown College Bulletin, 1989.

line that is slightly off can prevent a smile from becoming an intended frown. She explained: "Move this [makeup line] over an eighth of an inch, and instead of it being a smile when you bring your face into a frown, it'll bring the whole face into a frown and you'll be able to see that."

As open and individualistic as Chaddock's approach is to clown makeup, there tends to be rigidity in the clown face typologies that she offers the students. "There's three basic kinds of makeup," she said, referring to the whiteface, auguste and character, "and as a teacher, I would teach you [the student] how to apply the different kinds of makeup." Chaddock also found a definitive theatrical reasoning for developing a strong clown face: "The reason you have makeup in the circus is to project to the top of Madison Square Garden."[18]   Finally, within the contrasting strictures and freedom with which Chaddock teaches her aesthetics of clown makeup and development, she adheres to one over-riding principle–the facial makeup has to fit the overall character, because as important as makeup is to the clown, it is only one part of the clown's persona and performance.

Another Clown College graduate Mark Renfro (class of 1983) joined Clown College's teaching faculty in 1994, and continued as a makeup instructor through the close of Clown College in 1997. Renfro agreed with Chaddock that creating a circus clown face through applying makeup is vastly different from masking.   And, also like Chaddock, he believed that makeup is "simply a theatrical conceit to exaggerate and build upon the human face" with the intention of accentuating and enhancing the individual clown's natural face. When Renfro worked with a student, he tended to guide that student toward creating a makeup style to a much greater degree than did Chaddock.   To Renfro, a mask is a static representation which is frozen in time as opposed to the clown's makeup which "must be a living thing."   But he indicated that both masking and makeup share a common element–the power to transform.   He said: "The mask has the power to transform, and makeup has the power to transform, but just because they have the same power, they're not the same thing."[19]

The Presentation of Paradox

To return to the original question of whether a clown's face is a cultural mask or an individual's makeup, an answer may be found within one inherent characteristic of the clown figure–the presentation of paradox.   The clown is an agent for paradox, or as David Napier described, "something that appears self-

---

[18] Chaddock interview, July 2002.
[19] Renfro interview, August 2002.

contradictory, a thing that at some time, or from a particular point of view, appears to be what it is not. . .contradictions that we accept as genuinely irreconcilable." Napier argued that to accept the concept of paradox demands the recognition of *illusion*, or the "acceptance that things may look like what they are not."[20] He defined the mask, or disguise, as "the primary way of expressing this ambiguity," rendering masks as "hypothetical and make-believe." [21]

If we apply Napier's thesis to the idea of the circus clown with its painted face, we can easily understand that the made-up clown becomes the very embodiment of paradox; and often presents irreconcilable differences through a comical, yet subversive narrative. Through masking (via makeup), motley dress and subversive behavior, paradoxically the clown is able to occupy many spaces and tropes simultaneously. The clown is both universal and individual, historical and contemporary, funny and sad, conformist and non-conformist–a cultural figure that stands at the center and margins of society at the same time. Through subversive narratives, the clown uses these irreconcilable differences to present society with ambiguity through its grotesqueness; transgressing recognized boundaries to establish rules by breaking rules. The clown represents everything about us, and nothing about us. It is a part of us, yet apart from us; a *cultural imperative* that defines our civility through incivility.

Following the illogic of paradox, makeup instructor Renfro pointed out that the clown's face is the *most important* and *least important* element of a clown, arguing that when a clown applies greasepaint, it becomes "printing on the outside to represent something that's on the inside. You're covering up, but you are revealing . . . its a lie, but in that lie, you can tell the truth." He continued:

> It's the balance between those two things [where] you can find the magic in it that will transform you as a performer and allow you to do things with an audience that they would not allow someone [else]. When you get into areas where those opposites are so closely tied together, you can find moments of real magic.[22]

It is within that magic that the transformation from individual performer to cultural figure takes place to construct a new persona. Perhaps this is what circus historian Lowell Swortzell meant when he stated that clowns are like "sacred personages" in that they "expound the law, explain the order of the cosmos, and may even assume the personalities of the gods themselves,"

---

[20] Napier, *Masks, Transformation and Paradox,* 1.
[21] Ibid., 3,4.
[22] Renfro.

because clowning "is the expression of an individual, a culture, and of a universal need."[23]

Conclusions

In conclusion, I once again must raise the question: "Is the face of the circus clown a cultural mask that carries significant meanings; or is it simply makeup that enhances and accentuates an individual's unique facial features?"

Considering that the clown is the constant purveyor of paradox, then the only acceptable answer has to be YES to both. The clown's face is indeed a culturally defined, standardized mask; yet it is also an individualized representation of the human face upon which it is painted.

Bibliography

Publications

Bakhtin, Mikhail. *Rabelais and His World.* Translated by Helene Iswolsky. Bloomington: Indiana University Press, 1984.

Ballantine, Bill. *Clown Alley.* Boston: Little, Brown and Company, 1982.

Carlyon, David. *Dan Rice: The Most Famous Man You've Never Heard Of.* New York: Public Affairs, 2001.

Dishler, M. Wilson. *Clowns and Pantomime.* Salem, NH: Ayer Company, Publishers, Inc., 1985 printing.

Douglas, Mary. *Natural Symbols.* London & New York: Routledge, 1996.

"How to Make Your Own Clown Face." Ringling Bros. and Barnum & Bailey Combined Shows, Inc. 1982.

Huizinga, Johan. *Homo Ludens: A Study of the Play-Element in Culture.* Boston: The Beacon Press, 1950.

Napier, A. David. *Masks, Transformation and Paradox.* Berkeley: University of California Press, 1986.

Nunley, John W. and McCarty, Cara. *Masks: Faces of Culture.* New York: Harry N. Abrams, Inc., 1999.

Ringling Bros. and Barnum & Bailey Clown College Bulletin, Ringling Bros. and Barnum & Bailey Combined Shows, Inc., 1989.

"School's in Session . . . Students Off to Sterling Year!" Ringling Bros. and Barnum & Bailey Clown College Press Release for 25th Anniversary Year Celebration. 1987.

---

[23] Swortzell, *Here Come the Clowns: A Cavalcade of Comedy from Antiquity to the Present,* 2.

Swortzell, Lowell. *Here Comes the Clowns: A Cavalcade of Comedy from Antiquity to the Present.* New York: The Viking Press, 1978.

Thevoz, Michel. *The Illusions of Reality: Painted Body.* New York: Rizzoli International Publications, 1984.

Tseelon, Efrat. "Introduction" and "Reflections on Mask and Carnival." *Masquerade and Identities: Essays on gender, sexuality and marginality.* Edited by Efrat Tseelon. New York: Routledge, 2001.

Interviews

Clown College Makeup Instructor Ruth Chaddock, July, 2002

Ringling Bros. and Barnum & Bailey Vice President Tim Holst, March, 2002

Clown College Director Dick Monday, August, 2002

Clown College Makeup Instructor Mark Renfro, August, 2002

Clown College Director Ron Severini, April, 2002

Clown College Director Steve Smith, April, 2002

CHAPTER NINETEEN

RUSSIAN CIRCUS, AMERICAN CIRCUS: POLITICS, ECONOMICS AND PERFORMANCE

ROBERT SUGARMAN

An assumption shared by many at this conference is that there is a dynamic relationship between popular culture and the society in which it exists. As we explore areas of special interest, we often find ourselves confronting the larger society. This paper considers the relationship between Russian and American circuses and the contexts in which they operate.

In pre-Revolutionary Russia, the Russian social structure was arranged around the nobility and the peasants and there was a rising middle class that Anton Chekhov wrote about at the beginning of the twentieth century. Russian circuses were influenced by French and Italian models and, like them, Russian circuses were often managed by performing families. Russian circuses featured the traditional elements–trained animals, acrobats, jugglers, and clowns who used the extreme make up we are familiar with in this country. The audiences for Russian circus, like the audiences for ballet, theatre and opera, were drawn from all segments of the population. The poor were in the cheap seats in the Gods, but they did attend.

After 1917, Lenin, the leader of the Revolution, saw two forms of popular art that could spread word of the Revolution, especially to the illiterate masses–motion picture and circus. Circus because the acrobats with their well trained bodies and their physical skills would represent the glory of the new Soviet citizen. Clowns would no longer be grotesque. They would abandon extreme make up and be witty, earthy citizens commenting on the social system. Anatol Lunacharsky, who was in charge of the arts, undertook to fulfill Lenin's mandate. By the 1920's schools were set up to create performers for the new circuses. After World War II, when the Soviet Union sent circuses to this country–the Moscow Circus and the Moscow Circus on Ice–to earn dollars, people here were awed by the artistry of the performances. This was because under the Soviet system, not only were performers trained, but acts were created. An act, with performers from the circus schools, would be assigned a director, a choreographer, composers and designers. After being nurtured in subsidized studios, the act would travel throughout the Soviet Union performing in more than 70 permanent circus buildings. After the acts had performed a while, they would be brought back to the studios to be refurbished by new directors, designers and musicians. All this circus activity took place at state expense because the state saw the social value in circus that Lenin had annunciated. Soviet circus performers had guaranteed employment and, when their careers were over, subsidized retirement. They did not get rich, but they had guaranteed housing, health care, and support for their acts. What was called the Moscow Circus here, was a selection of the acts that toured continuously throughout the Soviet Union.

After Lenin's death and Stalin's rise to power, things changed for clowns. They were denied the freedom to criticize, and their words, like all the words in the media, were censored. However, within these constraints, performers like Oleg Popov were still remarkable. While American clowns had lost their voices and were mostly relegated to covering equipment changes in the vast three ring circuses that had emerged late in the nineteenth century, Russian clowns, performing in one ring, were always important. A Russian circus performer only became a clown after mastering other acts. Popov is a wonderful juggler and slack wire performer. Under each Five Year Plan the goals for circus were redefined and methods to achieve them revised. [1]

Under Free Enterprise, circus in this country was very different. In the early part of the 19th century there were one ring shows that featured talking and singing clowns. The great mid-nineteenth century clown Dan Rice told topical jokes adapted to the locality where he was playing, sang songs, and did Shakespearean parodies. The American shows traveled in horse drawn wagons, performed in some permanent buildings, but mostly in tents they carried with them. In the latter part of the 19th century, railroads united the nation and made possible giant industries. Circuses emulated these industries. Small family circuses, like the horse and pony show started by the five Ringling brothers in Baraboo, Wisconsin, grew into giant entities. Two rings had been added so that everyone in the vast tents would have something to watch and later, four stages were added to the three rings. Competition was keen and sometimes brutal. As Horatio Alger had it, with Pluck, and Luck you could succeed. Circuses with Pluck and Luck became as awesome as steel mills.

Ringling, Sells-Floto, Christy, Barnum and Bailey and others became engineering triumphs. A great circus would arrive at the local train station in the morning in as many as 100 railroad cars. Personnel, equipment, and animals

---

[1] For a fuller description of the Soviet circus system, see Sugarman, *Circus for Everyone: Circus Learning Around the World.* 75-78.

would disembark, trek to the circus lot where they would create a self-sufficient tent city. They then turned around and paraded through the town to drum up business before returning to the lot where they presented two Big Top shows and sideshows. After the second Big Top show, the circus packed up, returned to its train, and headed to its next destination. These capitalist ventures, like the new industries and the mansions in which the industrialists who owned them lived, were only possible because of cheap labor that the nation's immigration policies made available.

Although the American circus still bore traces of its rural Midwestern roots –circus music was based on that of the small town band-it had transformed. Due to the size of the tents, the focus switched from individual clown acts or acrobatic acts or animal acts to spectacle. In addition to the multitude of acts, giant extravaganzas-*specs*-presented visions of history that reinforced popular ideas about The Age of Chivalry and America's wars. There were featured center ring stars like the stars that had arisen in motion pictures-Lillian Leitzel doing her one-arm *planges*, the Flying Codonas, the Riding Hannefords, the Great Wallendas on the highwire–but all the performing space had to be filled.

This was the Golden Age of American circus. It lasted from the last quarter of the nineteenth century to the Great Depression when fortunes were lost, people had little spending money, and the restrictive immigration policies instituted in the twenties, cut off the supply of cheap labor, although there was still cheap African-American labor. As circuses performed in the South and some moved their winter quarters to the South, segregation was observed as it was in less overt ways throughout the nation. There were no black performers, except as in baseball, those who could pass as members of dark skinned ethnic groups. There were segregated black work gangs, but they could not fill the gap. As segregation ended and more employment opportunities became available to African Americans, even this source of cheap labor vanished. It is interesting that today circuses, especially those like Carson and Barnes and Kelly-Miller that are based in the southwest, are dependent on seasonal laborers from Mexico. However, fears of terrorism have threatened to compromise that labor force.

When *perestroika* came to Russia, the impact on Russian circuses was as profound and unsettling as it was on the rest of society. Oligarchs took over vast segments of industry and the utilities. A frontier mentality emerged not unlike this country's unbridled capitalism in the 19th century. At this time, Alla Youdina, who has been a source for this paper, worked in the Russian circus system as a performer, and then as an administrator. With the new freedom to travel and uncertainty at home, she came to this country to join Ringling Brothers and Barnum & Bailey as a trainer and then as "Creative Director– New Circus Acts." Youdina sees her journey as nothing unique. She says,

"Circus has always followed money."[2]   She contends that Russian circus reached its peak in terms of the technical skill of its performers and the quality of its acts in the nineteen sixties and seventies. There had been schools for fifty years, the skill level had kept improving, and so had the circus system.

The Cranes was one of the last great acts developed under the Soviet system. A poetic aerial act, it tells of dead Soviet soldiers returning as Cranes. There was beautiful flying and high tech machinery propelled the performers in their flight.   The act had been developed during five years of subsidized preparation. It first toured this country with a Moscow Circus that had been booked by Morris Chalfen who had an exclusive contract with the Soviet government to present its circuses here.   However, after *perestroika*, he no longer had exclusive control of Russian acts and the Cranes returned on their own. They performed in a number of venues, ended up in Reno, and then broke up. There were no subsidized studios in which they could refurbish the act. In addition the act was large.   American circuses, as part of the downsizing they have experienced in the face of rising costs, have come to rely on small acts. Armando Cristiani, a member of the Cristiani bareback family, contends that people here are seldom willing to pay for large acts today.[3] Not only are acts small, performers are expected to present two or three acts-a bizarre echo of the experience of mill girls in this country who were forced to operate more and more looms.

For a while Ringling hired Russian acts or had Youdina create acts with international casts. The contrast with the way in which the Cranes was created is revealing. The state could subsidize the development of an act for years. Youdina, operating under a capitalist budget, was given three or four months. However, she managed to create outstanding acts only to find them compromised as they were fit into a three ring format. Ringling director Phillip McKinley sliced and diced acts to fit into a montage-like spectacle. The goal was not the presentation of acts so much as the creation of effects. As in Cirque du Soleil, McKinley's shows short circuited performers' efforts to connect with an audience as they developed the arc of an act. His frame of reference was MTV and films such as *Moulin Rouge*. Youdina and McKinley had trouble working together, and Youdina found herself out of a job.

Capitalist pressures also affected the work in Russia. Entrepreneurs, some drawn from traditional circus families, created private circuses. The competition between the two private circuses in Moscow is intense. In post-Soviet Russia, circus audiences have changed. Private circuses play to the new moneyed class. Circus is no longer available to the poor or, often, even to the middle class.

---

[2] Youdina interview, September 24, 2000.
[3] Cristiani interview, August 15, 1998.

Life for performers is uncertain. Sometimes they work for state circuses, sometimes for private circuses. Often they do not work at all, and when they do it is on weekends, and they are only paid for the performances they give. Youdina's sister has a mixed animal act. In Soviet times, she had five grooms and all the food the animals needed. Then all support was withdrawn. She took her animals home, fed them as best she could, and found occasional work. For the most part, she is supported by her sister who works in this country. Russian acts today are subject to cannibalization by Western shows who need a replacement for a performer. Performers in Russia are now often capitalist commodities instead of artists.

In the West there was a resurgence of circus, soon labeled the New Circus, in the 1970's as part of the counterculture that developed in response to the Vietnam War. The New Circus featured one ring, focused on the acts, and downplayed spectacle. However, Cirque du Soleil, a New Circus created by street performers, became the largest circus organization in the world with a vast training campus in Montreal and eleven shows. Three tour North America, one tours Mexico, two tour Europe and five are permanent-four in Las Vegas, and one in Orlando, Florida. Cirque du Soleil developed a unique, somewhat surreal, style of presentation that depends heavily on spectacle. As a consequence, Cirque du Soleil, unlike the other New Circuses, turns its performers into something that suggests the interchangeable parts of a machine, or the machinelike choruses in a Busby Berkeley musical, but with a higher degree of skill. Circus may evolve in the way of Ringling and Cirque du Soleil, dehumanizing their performances to build spectacles. Another path is that taken by another New Circus, The Big Apple Circus, that presents acts in a congenial one ring format and, while employing the latest technology, often sets its performances in a nostalgic late nineteenth or early twentieth century setting.

In this country it is no secret that the rich are farther from those who are not rich than they have been since before the New Deal of the 1930's. Big Apple and Cirque du Soleil cater to the affluent. Smaller touring shows, such as Kelly-Miller, maintain low ticket prices and appeal to a different demographic. The three Ringling shows are in the middle where they seem to be experiencing an identity crisis. The Red Unit is a traditional three ring show. The Gold is one ring designed for, although not always playing in, smaller venues; it allows acts more time for coherent presentations than the other two Ringling shows. The new Blue show is ringless, adapted to an arena format. A large television screen substitutes for the intimacy associated with one ring presentations. How audiences will respond is yet to be known.

All circuses with animals, in this country and Western Europe, suffer harassment from the Animal Rights people. That Cirque du Soleil succeeds without animals adds to the arguments against their use in circuses. The economic impact of the efforts of the Animal Rights people is substantial. More than pickets that turn away customers, many malls now refuse to book circuses with animals in response to pressure from the activists. The Animal Rights fringe is active and effective in local and state legislatures. In England, Parliament is considering a ban on animals in touring circuses. If it goes through, many animals will have to be destroyed. Just as the radical right in politics endangers democratic institutions, the Animal Rights people endanger traditional circuses. Relying on ideology rather than research, Animal Rights people refuse to acknowledge that circus animals are well cared for and live longer than animals in the so-called wild which is, itself, disappearing. Ringling is picketed almost everywhere its shows go although Ringling has an exemplary animal care program, and an elephant conservation reserve where more than fifteen baby elephants have been born. Just as Lenin's ideas encouraged circus, the ideas of the Animal Rights people endanger circus. In the face of these pressures, Big Apple dropped the elephant act it had presented for 17 years. Cole Bros gave up its elephants one year and its tigers the next, but negative public response led it to bring back elephants and other animals and find places to perform outside the malls.

Circuses function in the same economy as other businesses. They face rising costs and limitations on how much they can offset them by raising prices. A major factor for circuses is the rising cost of gas. Circus in this country is beset by a radical right, and by economic conditions that are difficult. In addition, circus like any live performance, by definition is expensive because it is hand labor. It cannot be mass produced.

In Russia, the Circus buildings stand on land that is now more valuable than they are and the future of the buildings is uncertain. Circus is not doing well under capitalism in Russia, and circus is embattled under the economic conditions that prevail here.

But like its cousin, theatre, circus hangs on. New permutations of circus are developing. As a result of the new circus schools, performers with skills are working not only in circuses but in the New Vaudeville, the New Burlesque, in new kinds of variety shows and in dance companies. They staff youth circus programs that have found favor with soccer moms as non-competitive activities that teach their children cooperation and the satisfactions of hard work while enhancing their sense of self. Small family circuses like Zoppé and Walker offer promise. Circuses geared to specific audiences–Universoul for African American audiences, Circus Vasquez and several others for Hispanic American audiences-are thriving. Sideshow skills have been combined with circus skills in the *New* New circuses like the Bindlestiff Family Cirkus and Circus Amok. Everywhere, skill levels are high. Graduates of the Moscow Circus School still place well in international competitions. Just as there is reason to despair, there is reason to hope. But as always, economics and politics are fundamental in explaining the ways in which circuses operate.

Bibliography

Albrecht, Ernest. *The New American Circus.* Gainesville, FL: University Press of Florida, 1995.

Cristiani, Armando. Interview, August 15, 1998.

Sugarman, Robert. *Circus for Everyone: Circus Learning Around the World.* Shaftsbury, Vermont: Mountainside Press, 2001.

Youdina, Alla. Interview, Setpember 24, 2000.

Youdina, Alla, and Robert Sugarman. "The Russian Circus Today: Struggling but Hopeful." *Spectacle: A Quarterly Journal of the Circus Arts,* Winter 2006.

Chapter Twenty

The Trickster as Academic Comfort Food: Jesters, Dan Rice, and the Alleged Hero-Fool

David Carlyon

The past few decades have witnessed an academic love affair with the trickster, the clown who challenges power. Though "trickster" originally described a cultural type identified by anthropologists in certain indigenous cultures, that neutral description eventually morphed into praise, especially in the anti-establishment Sixties. Anyone who looked cross-eyed at authority became a hero-trickster. I know the appeal myself. During my undergrad days in those rebellious Sixties, I learned in anthro classes about Native American tricksters, reveling at the implications of telling truth to power. As a circus clown with Ringling Brothers and Barnum & Bailey Circus, I enjoyed the glow of being thought a trickster myself, especially when I snuck in small doses of political satire. Then when I was in grad school, peers and professors who learned I'd been a clown would adopt a knowing air and say, "Ah. A trickster."

However, the cherished model of trickster has significant problems. As "trickster" strays from its origins in ancient cultures, it becomes hopelessly vague. It is also implausible, defying credibility when closely examined. Beyond the shaky foundation of imprecision and implausibility, the trickster-like jester stumbles on the evidence, which turns out to be more anecdotal than solid, with a strong whiff of writerly wish fulfillment. Perhaps the worst problem of the model is that rather than telling truth to power, the trickster as easily lapses into the conservative nature of comedy to reinforce power.

Imprecision is inherent in the scholarly model as it ventures beyond anthropology and its study of ancient cultures. Anthropologists identified the trickster in the details of specific behavior in particular cultures. John Towsen lays out some of those details in his book, *Clowns*, a seminal survey of clowning. He examines clown behavior among the Hopi and the Navajo, and looks at "contraries," members of Plains Indian tribes who were sanctioned to act contrary to tribe norms, such as riding backwards, shooting their arrows over their shoulders, and dressing in rags.[1] Yet the specific behaviors investigated by anthropologists, using the scientific tools of their profession, have too often inflated into a generalized ideal, with little specificity remaining. As a result, any action that seems contrary to authority fits this hazy model. Joke about the President of the United States? You're a trickster. Tease the chair of the English department? Trickster. Mock a motor vehicle office clerk or a giant corporation? Trickster. Such a baggy (pants?) concept offers little analytical effectiveness.

The vague generality of the comic truth-teller fades into a second problem, its implausibility. Consider the jester, an ancestor cliché of the trickster model. Historical actuality morphed into this earlier literary fancy of the truth-telling comic figure as the nineteenth century began to create romantic images of the medieval period, a cultural fashion book-ended by Sir Walter Scott's 1819 *Ivanhoe* and Mark Twain's less idealized, 1889 *Connecticut Yankee in King Arthur's Court*. Comic sidekick in this medieval mania, the jester was imagined saying to the king what no one else dared say. Here was the embodiment of truth armed only with wit and insight taking on the ultimate authority of a medieval monarch. An early articulation of this trickster variation appears in the 1870 autobiography of England's leading circus clown, William F. Wallett. Calling himself the Queen's Jester, he adopted this emerging ideal for himself as he wrote that the mere fool of the past differed from the jester, which was an honorable position "filled by an educated gentleman," with a license to speak truth.[2] "Like the wearers of other professional costumes, legal and clerical, jesters are privileged to say and do many things which would not be kindly received from laymen".[3] And the notion flourished. A century later, Towsen devoted space in his book on clowns to what he labels the "daring political jester."

But is the model plausible? Has any autocrat in the world we inhabit accepted criticism simply because it came from a clown? Try to imagine Stalin or Hitler honoring a person who attacked him with jokes. On a less horrific scale, have leaders tolerated members of their staff who mock them? Did either Bush White House hire someone to taunt either president about his mangled English, or did the Clinton staff include an assistant in charge of ridiculing his roving eye? (The King of Togo gave the title of "court jester" to

---

[1] Towsen, *Clowns,* 6-16.

[2] Ibid., 153-4,

[3] Ibid., viii-ix.

his investment advisor, responsible for $37,000,0000, but as the *New York Times* reported,[4] "The Money Is All Gone in Togo, And the Jester's Role Was No Joke.") In the academic world, would any department chair chuckle complacently if a professor applied a big, red nose and ran into a faculty meeting to make fun of the way the department is run? Clearly the idea is barely conceivable in our time, calling into serious question the persistent belief that autocratic power in centuries past would allow mockery simply because clothed in a motley costume.

Stumbling between imprecision and implausibility, the trickster model trips on faulty evidence. Apparent instances turn out to be more asserted than established. Wallett's autobiography gave three alleged historical examples of the truth-telling jester, William the Conqueror's "joculator," Henry VIII's jester, and the court fool of James I, but Wallett did not relate any of the "truths" each supposedly told his respective monarch.[5] Veneration for the truth-telling iconoclast increased in the nineteenth-century as society industrialized and the countervailing Romantic ideal of the solitary hero mushroomed. In earlier ages, physically or mentally impaired people—some employed as jesters—had been called "naturals" because they were ill-adapted to function in society. Nature was at that time considered a lower state of being. Then, as the Romantic movement propelled the notion that the regimentation of industrialization made society itself ill adapted, "natural" came to mean an inner, freer, theoretically more real self. Along the way, the jester became symbolic as more "real" himself, a "natural" force against a stale, unthinking, regimented life. Charles Dickens employed a variation of this model in his novel, *Hard Times*, as he contrasted a joyous, spirit-enhancing circus against the mind-numbing forces of industrialization. Academia and writers picked up the cue, in the form of the trickster. Despite a paucity of documented instances, this alleged truth-teller survives in stories and an apparent cultural need to believe in them.

One example straddles nineteenth-century history and twentieth-century historiography. America's great clown, Dan Rice (1823-1900),[6] figures powerfully in idealization of the trickster. A famous talking clown, he strode through the raucous, adult world of circus, into the broader world of "the show business," and then public prominence. He expanded his "hits on the times" into political commentary that led to (legitimate) campaigns for public office from the circus ring, as a Peace Democrat in the 1860s. That included a brief, but genuine run for President of the United States. More influentially, he suited the tastes of the emerging middle class, presenting himself as no

---

[4] *New York Times*, Oct 7, 2001, A 22.
[5] Wallett, *The Public Life of W.F. Wallett, the Queen's Jester,* viii.
[6] See Carlyon, *Dan Rice The Most Famous Man You've Never Heard Of.*

rude clown but a gentlemanly "American Humorist" (a generation before that label was adopted by Mark Twain, who saw Rice's circus in Hannibal), and his enterprise as no vulgar circus, but the artistic "Dan Rice's Great Show" (a generation before his ex-publicity agent expanded the title for Barnum & Bailey into "The Greatest Show on Earth," and a century before Big Apple Circus and Cirque du Soleil touted themselves as artistic alternatives to the implicit vulgarity of three-ring spectacle). Occasionally doffing the motley to appear in tailcoat and top hat in the ring, Rice announced repeatedly that he was a gentleman who "aspired to higher things." His aspirational project perfectly matched and furthered the middle class's desire, then as now, to see itself with elevated sensitivity. In performance terms, "aspiration" increasingly meant a quiet, controlled audience and a subdued performance style, labeled "natural" by its proponents. As one result, Rice's rowdy, interactive approach with a participatory audience came to be deemed vulgar, and his career faded. People remembered his Civil War politics, which didn't help as he simultaneously tried to defend his wartime Southern sympathies and claim he had been a special friend and adviser to Abraham Lincoln. (Later writers relied on this Lincoln fiction in Rice biographies.)

A century later Rice was deemed a trickster. Earlier, while he still lived, scattered attempts to retrieve his audience and the continuing power of his name could not overcome the increasing sentimentalization of clowns as figures of fun for children. So raucous, rowdy, adult favorite Rice lived to see himself sentimentalized as "Old Uncle Dan," the youngster's bauble, and then died in relative obscurity in 1900. Few but circus fans remembered him, and then mostly in publicity fictions. Meanwhile historians of performance, when they noticed him at all, confused him with the earlier blackface star, T. D. "Jump Jim Crow" Rice. (Contributing to that confusion was Dan Rice's early career, when he also performed in blackface, at a time minstrelsy was emerging significantly from circus.) The late-twentieth century saw the new addition to accreted images of Rice, fitting newer cultural currents. Once the sentimentalized clown, he began to emerge as the great American trickster. Ron Jenkins characterized Rice as an anti-establishment trickster, a truth-teller who "invited" audiences to challenge authority. In particular, Jenkins depicted Rice fighting to free the slaves.[7]

But Dan Rice had built his phenomenal success by matching the conventional wisdom of his time, not by standing against it, and certainly not by attempting to subvert it. Rice did mock politicians, but that fits the generic joke about politicians used by Americans, including politicians, who score political points by jeering at other politicians for being political. Whatever Rice's general jests, he aligned himself with power. An 1849 publicity

---

[7] Jenkins, "Dan Rice," 86-92.

biography, *Sketches from the Life of Dan Rice*, presented him as the jovial companion of members of the Pennsylvania Legislature, and carousing with leading Mobile politicians (31, 48-56). The January 19, 1856 *Spirit of the Times* alerted its readers that Rice would arrive in Washington, where he would address the politicians "now in wise counsel assembled," and he himself regularly used the same tones of flattery. Throughout his career, he claimed to be friends with mayors, Senators, governors and U.S. Presidents. He was no trickster-outsider. That was particularly true when he pushed his political opposition into campaigns for public office. He could claim to be an underdog, and he did use that hackneyed political device of criticizing partisanship, but he had no intention of subverting the system—only of joining it.

As for the idea that Rice sought to free the slaves, that is simply wrong. He did not advocate abolition, but joined the great majority of his fellow Americans in opposing it, using his towering comic powers to ridicule the idea. (He did ultimately support abolition, but only as it was becoming accomplished fact.) When Rice joked about abolitionists as crackpots trying to destroy the country, he spoke the opinion of most of his fellow citizens. Racism, America's original sin, was a major part of that majority opinion, but it should be noted that there was principle too, based on the Constitution's acceptance of slavery—and on anxiety over the extremists who burned the Constitution in public gatherings, declaring they'd accept the destruction of the country. Even attacking Lincoln and the Republicans, Rice found agreement among huge numbers of his fellow citizens. Rice's was no trickster-like challenge to power, but a politician's attempt to get power for himself.

Historians have invoked the model of the trickster on the same shaky foundation. John Towsen's wonderful book, though a source and model for writing about clowns, falters with the others. Many of the claimed truth-telling instances he cites are apocryphal, based on nothing more specific than a tale of what some jester supposedly said to his lord. The author does refer to an "appreciation of the jester's keen sense of psychology," but the example comes from fiction, out of Shakespeare's *Twelfth Night*, rather than from any historical figure. Other examples are vaguely supported anecdotes; moreover they depict a jester protected as he mocks those *out* of favor. This is not speaking truth to power, but on behalf of power.[8]

The invocation of *Twelfth Night* serves as a reminder that Shakespeare's fictional universe still helps create our own. Among other things, he provided prototypes for our romance of the truth-telling clown. *As You Like It* offers Touchstone, and *King Lear* offers the Fool, the quintessential image of a

---

[8] Towsen, 26-30.

jester saying—and getting away with saying—what an arrogant ruler does not want to hear. Shakespeare also supplied a creed, in *As You Like It*, as the melancholy Jacques expresses his ambition to become court fool: "Invest me in my motley. Give me leave to speak my mind and I will through and through cleanse the foul body of the infected world." But Shakespeare did not stop there. He gave the Duke an immediate retort, that Jacques embodies the evils he would criticize (II.viii.64-69). Shakespeare naturally employed the cultural belief in a truth-telling jester, but his fools and their words served his dramatic purpose, they did not record history.

Mikhail Bakhtin's identification of the "carnivalesque" as a literary invitation to inversion, from his book *Rabelais and His World*, has had a significant influence, but a questionable one. Two salient aspects routinely get lost as his work is magnified into a celebration of transgression. First, he was writing more about the carnivalesque in literature than in life, literary analysis rather than rigorous history.[9] Second, Bakhtin did not limit himself to transgression. He explicitly declared his subject to be the demotic laughter that was both a challenge *and* an affirmation, for it "asserts and denies, it buries and revives."[10] Invoking Bakhtin to support notions of subversion easily skips past that nuance. When Peter Stallybrass and Allen White, in *The Politics and Poetics of Transgression*, describe the carnivalesque as "potent, populist, critical inversion of all official words and hierarchies,"[11] they show their debt to Bakhtin, who referred to suspending "all hierarchical rank, privileges, norms, and prohibitions," but they also inflate the subtlety of his insight into a universalized concept of hierarchical subversion. He explicitly denied subversion applied here, for the modern "satirist whose laughter is negative places himself above the object of his mockery," and does not share in the ambivalent laughter of carnival. Bakhtin deplored the tendency Stallybrass and White ironically exhibit, distorting this folk humor to fit it "within the framework of bourgeois modern culture and aesthetics," in this case the Romantic construct of the special soul in the advance ranks/avant garde of society. Bakhtin explicitly regretted that the carnival ambivalence he identified, which includes self-mockery, was "usually ignored" in the past.[12] Explorations of tricksters continue to ignore it.

The Trickster model becomes explicitly political in Joel Schecter, *Durov's Pig: Clowns, Politics and Theatre*. Schecter organizes his book around the image of Vladimir Durov challenging German authority by naming his pig "Wilhelm" as a way to mock the Kaiser. However, Schecter

---

[9] Wise, "Marginalizing Drama: Bakhtin's Theory of Genre," 15-22.

[10] Ibid., 11, 12.

[11] Stallybrass and White, *The Politics and Poetics of Transgression*, 7.

[12] Bakhtin, *Rabelais and his World*, 10, 4, 12.

acknowledges in a footnote that the incident may be inaccurate. Vladimir Durov's brother, Anatoly, also told the tale, but put himself into it as the hero, the one with the pig and its defiant name. More troubling, the alleged incident may not have happened at all. There is no clear record other than these contradictory accounts by the Durov brothers. Moreover, each of them related the tale to make himself look good, always a warning flag to historians.[13] (Moreover, the joke is an old one: A leading nineteenth-century circus proprietor, W. C. Coup, told of immigrant Germans in the Midwest taking offense at a circus pig called "Bismarck"[14]) This is not to criticize Schecter for inaccuracy; the embellishments may have been based on an actual event, and scholars who spend years wading through primary sources can sympathize with his attempt to wrestle his material into a thesis. Nevertheless, it is illustrative of the trickster problem that Schecter's primary example, the central image of his title, is laced with uncertainty, and may even be fiction.

The same process of antic aggrandizement can be observed in a five-decade shift of translation. Ivan Turgenev's 1841 play, *Nakhlebnik*, anticipating Chekhov, took a wry look at the wasted lives of the landed Russian aristocracy by focusing on a poor gentleman who lives on the charity of wealthier connections. In 1951 an English translation appeared under the straightforward title *A Poor Gentleman*. The title character is described a few times as a "clown" or "fool," and that point is embodied when he dozes off drunk at lunch and his companions put a clown's peaked hat on his head.[15] The same play in a new adaptation by Mike Poulton appeared on Broadway in 2002 as *Fortune's Fool*, with a very different emphasis, signaled by the new title. The "poor gentleman" of the 1951 version has become "Fortune's Fool." That label symbolically aligns him with Touchstone, the truth-telling clown at court in *As You Like It*, especially in his emblematic line, "Call me not fool till heaven hath sent me fortune" (II.vii.19-20). The text elaborates that shift in the play's emphasis. Now, instead of a simple buffoon, the title character is labeled a "jester," and described as if he were at court, making him in effect a court fool, dishonored in the story so he can appear more honorable to the presumptively wiser audience. While both versions depict the character as pitiable, the newer adaptation reflects the shift in cultural trends by making him a hero in the now fashionable jester mode: Mocked, he speaks truth to power. The twenty-first century version of the play, with the New York production given the cultural imprimatur of a Tony Award nomination,

---

[13] Schecter, *Durov's Pig: Clowns, Politics and Theatre,* 1-3, 213-14.

[14] Coup, *Sawdust and Spangles,* 243.

[15] Turgenev, *A Poor Gentleman*, trans. Constance Garnett, 187, 200-05, 229.

inflates Turgenev's poor gentleman from a mere object of mockery to heroic stature as a truth-telling jester.[16]

Perhaps the most profound problem of the trickster model is that it obscures the often conservative nature of comedy. Attempting to mold comic figures into subversive tricksters challenging power belies the repeated use of comedy to reinforce power. Despite the occasional pinpricks of satire, comedy upholds authority more often than it subverts it. Comedy thrives on difference, and the powerless sport the most obvious differences, making the most obvious targets. That is why Towsen's examples include jesters who derided people out of favor at court. That is why Americans have historically tossed around so many jokes about people of color, women, and immigrants, and made "men who like musical comedy" a punch line rather than a description. Consider the popular culture icon David Letterman. Despite his reputation as a provocateur, his jokes essentially uphold the status quo, mocking those that his college-educated audience enjoy seeing mocked. His steadiest comic targets are his corporate bosses, the same people paying him millions of dollars. Moreover, his power rivals or exceeds the power of those he mocks.

Popular culture embraces a sentimental image of the clown. Writers reproduce that sentimentality in the jester, and academics in the Trickster, as seen in generalized jesters, the lingering Dan Rice images, and the fictional Poor Gentleman of theater. While it may be satisfying to conjure fool-heroes that represent our fondest ideals, the attempt falters as analysis. Cut loose from anthropologically-specific cultures, this symbol of subversion becomes ahistorical, more polemical argument than carefully analyzed instance. The notion of the trickster can aid understandings of performance, but to apply it indiscriminately mingles the overtly political and the generally comic, diminishing the former and bloating the latter. The trickster, symbol of challenge, flips upside down to become a cliché, serving up comforting fiction.

Acknowledgements

This is a revised vision of an article under the same title in the *Journal of American Culture*, 25.1-2 (Spring/ Summer 2002): 15-19, based on "The Clown as Trickster?: 19th-Century Circus & 21st-Century Myth," a paper delivered at the Popular Culture Association/American Culture Association conference in Toronto on March 14, 2002. The author would like to express his gratitude to

---

[16] A translation from 1924, *The Family Charge*, shows the same shift, 149, 164-70, 197.

Robert Sugarman and Rodney Huey, members of the panel, for their helpful perspective.

Bibliography

Bakhtin, Mikhail. *Rabelais and His World*. 1940, 1965. Trans. Helene Iswolsky. Cambridge, Mass.: M. I. T. Press, 1968.

Carlyon, David. *Dan Rice: The Most Famous Man You've Never Heard Of*. New York: Public Affairs, 2001.

Coup, W. C. *Sawdust and Spangles*, Chicago: Stone, 1901.

Jenkins, Ron. "Dan Rice." *Theater* 14.2 (Spring 1983.

"The Money Is All Gone in Tonga, And the Jester's Role Was No Joke." *New York Times,* 7 Oct. 2001.

Schecter, Joel. *Durov's Pig: Clowns, Politics and Theatre*. New York: Theatre Communication Group, 1985.

Stallybrass, Peter and Allan White. *The Politics and Poetics of Transgression*. Ithaca: Cornell University Press, 1986.

Towsen, John. *Clowns*. New York, Hawthorn Books, 1976.

Turgenev, Ivan. *The Family Charge*. 1841. Trans. M. S. Mandell. *The Plays of Ivan S. Turgenev*. New York: Macmillan, 1924.

—. *Fortune's Fool*. 1841. Adapt. Mike Poulton. London: Samuel French, 2002. New York production, Dir. Arthur Penn. The Music Box Theatre. New York. 30 Apr. 2002.

—. *A Poor Gentleman*. 1841. Trans. Constance Garnett. 1934. *Three Famous Plays*. London: Gerald Duckworth & Co., and New York: Charles Scribner's Sons, 1951.

[Van Orden, Wessel T. B.] *Sketches from the Life of Dan Rice, the Shakspearean* (sic) *Jester and Original Clown.* Albany, NY, 1849.

Wallett, William F. *The Public Life of W. F. Wallett, the Queen's Jester: An Autobiography.* London, 1870.

Wise, Jennifer. "Marginalizing Drama: Bakhtin's Theory of Genre." *Essays in Theatre* 8.1 (Nov. 1989).

CHAPTER TWENTY ONE

TOWARDS AND AESTHETIC OF CIRCUS

ROBERT SUGARMAN

The often heard response to the fantastic costumes and makeup, the exotic music, and the vaguely portentous stories of Cirque du Soleil performances is that they are "artistic." It is the contention of this paper that the art of circus performance is far more inclusive, and that there are aesthetic ways to consider all circuses.

Circus is an art because it does what art does–it takes material from life and gives it shape. Life *happens*, but art is purposeful even if in intuitive rather than rational ways. Art presents the range of human possibility. In Golden Age Greece the heroes and heroines of tragedy and of sculpture were like the Greeks who viewed them, but greater than them in their ability to transcend the limitations of day to day existence. But functioning so far beyond the norms is dangerous. Extreme effort places one in jeopardy. Where better do we see this enacted than in circus?

I have seen this when watching people perform the seven person pyramid on the high wire. Seven people balance heavy poles that move differently as each person strives to maintain balance in a way that will sustain the group. Four walk on the wire. A shoulder harness holds a bar between the first and the second person, another harness holds a bar between the third and the fourth. On the next level, two stand on the bars wearing harnesses that support a bar between them. On the third level, a seventh person–usually a lighter woman– stands carrying a chair along with her balancing pole. As the person at the rear of the first level calls commands, the four on the wire take a step. At the next command they step again, and continue until they reach the center of the wire and stop. As the seven poles wave to maintain balance, the top mounter places her chair on the bar and sits in it. Then she sits on the back of the chair with her feet on its seat, leans forward and finally rises and stands straight on the seat of the chair. As the Ringmaster used to say when the Great Wallendas did this, "No Princess was ever carried with greater care."

Art is not only about the sublime, but the ridiculous. A great clown like the late Grock, whose work I only know through a video, was earthbound, physical. His costume was too big, his make up broad. He wanted to play a piano, but had trouble because his chair was too far from it. He solved the problem by leaving the chair, going behind the piano, and pushing it closer to the chair, and was delighted with his achievement. Ready to begin, he sat in the chair and fell through it. After he extricated himself and tried again, the chair folded up on him and became a mechanical monster he had to tame. But when he played the piano, or the clarinet, or various sized violins-the smallest carried in a case large enough for a cello-this buffoonish character, beset by all possible physical adversity, with none of the physical appearance of an acrobat although all of the skill, triumphed by making exquisite music. Grock's clown persona was of a naïve child in an adult body.

Just as Grock was a musical clown, Bello Nock—now starring on the Red Unit of Ringling Brothers and Barnum & Bailey—is an acrobatic clown. His persona is that of the class cut-up. Youthful and vigorous, he wears minimal makeup. Goofy, eager, always smiling, he has a fantastic time finding comic twists to acrobatic feats on the high wire, on trampolines, on a sway pole and any other piece of acrobatic equipment. David Larible, formerly the star clown on Ringling's Blue Unit, is a musical clown with a joyous persona. He does not walk, he dances in his large clown shoes. Without the naiveté of Grock, or the adolescent bounce of Bello, he is a joyous adult. Unlike Bello who can fill all three rings with his dynamism, Larible's gentler work was most effective in the one ring setting of Ringling's short lived *Kaleidoscape*. Barry Lubin's feisty Grandma is an elder with an edge. Grandma has performed in three ring shows, but is most effective in the one ring setting of the Big Apple Circus. Clowns are caricatures of us as we are. They face daunting problems, and solve them in idiosyncratic ways.

Some clowns flourish better in small settings, some in large which brings us to the question of scale and spectacle in circus. None is larger than the Ringling Brothers and Barnum & Bailey Red and Blue Units which tour the larger indoor arenas in this country for two years, sometimes venturing into Canada and Mexico. We will look at two recent Ringling Red Unit shows that had quite different aesthetic impact. This may tell us something about the nature of circus itself—large and small.

The stars of the 131st edition of the show were Bello Nock, the elephant Bo, and the singing, dancing ringmaster, Johnathan Lee Iverson. Other performers included Mark Oliver Gebel presenting tigers and elephants; European Sacha Houcke, who joined the circus to present zebras; and there were a number of aerial and acrobatic acts and specs that filled the three rings and the track around them. Bello had four acts in the first half of the show. During each there were interchanges with Johnathan that, thanks to wireless microphones and new technology, had the intimacy of a clown-ringmaster exchange depicted by Toulouse-Lautrec at the one ring Cirque Medrano in the Belle Epoque in Paris. In his fourth act in the first half of the performance, it was Bo, Bello and Johnathan. The specs, animal and aerial acts looked even grander when contrasted to the intimacy provided by the three stars whom the audience got to know well.

By contrast, in the 133rd edition, Johnathan and Bello had much less opportunity to interact with each other and with the audience. Bo was gone. Bello appeared throughout the show, and was featured on the highwire, and with the elephants, but neither he nor Johnathan were the personalities they had been in the previous show. Their relationship was downplayed. The show's director, choreographer Philip McKinley, was, according to the show's publicity, influenced by the film *Moulin Rouge* and focused on nonstop action and spectacle. McKinley had shown the influence of film earlier in the 128th "Sideshow" edition when he interrupted acts with blackouts to shift focus to other acts, and then had the acts resume as if he were editing a film. His aim has been to choreograph the entire arena and, consequently, he has at times diminished the effectiveness of individual acts. Both his work and that of Cirque du Soleil recall the impersonal geometric dance numbers staged by Busby Berkeley in thirties Hollywood movies, but those movies also contained the romantic personal stories enacted by Dick Powell and Ruby Keeler and others. My experience as a spectator is that spectacle, when not complemented by human scale interactions, distances audiences from the performance. Spectacle impresses, it does not engage.

Another traditional aesthetic consideration is unity. The New Circus movement, exemplified by Big Apple, Cirque du Soleil, and Circus Flora, has attempted to achieve this by assigning themes to each edition of their shows. In the 2002-2003 Big Apple "Dreams of a City," the first act began with an introduction of the company as immigrants arriving in New York. Throughout the show costumes and music evoked New York City at the beginning of the twentieth century with the theme appended to existing acts. For example, the first half ended at the Mercantile Exchange, although after the Exchange was established, the display was devoted to juggler Claudius Specht doing the act he had honed elsewhere. Cirque du Soleil does go further. There is an exotic ambience that permeates the acts—if only through costuming, makeup and music.

Since a circus is made up of different kinds of acts, how much unity can there be? How does one unify a trapeze act with an equestrian act unless, as with Sylvia Zerbini in the Ringing 132nd edition and again in the 134th edition, a trapeze artist descends to the ring to take charge of her horses. But even here, there are two different acts presented by the same person. The unity of themes is often superficial, a marketing tool to allow a show to return to the same venue in successive years with a different title, different looks and some new specialty acts. What unifies a circus is physicality. The largely non-verbal performance is rooted in different kinds of human and animal skill.

In considering size, there is the question of three rings versus one. Is one configuration more aesthetically satisfying than the other? The first thing to note is that the distinction is not as great as it once was. The Ringling shows and three ring tent shows like Cole Brothers most often use lighting to focus on one ring and then another. All three rings are only employed when there are matched acts and, due to increasing economic restraints, this seldom happens. There is the question of intimacy. In a one ring show the audience can see performers as individuals. On the other hand, a three ring show makes possible aerial acts like those created by Vilen Govenko in the 131st and 133rd Ringling shows performed over all three rings in a layout that extended 150 feet. The three ring show can, as with the Bo and Bello edition, alternate the intimate with specs and spectacular presentations not possible in the one ring format. Bello Nock, who successfully starred in Big Apple shows, is even more effective in the three ring format due to the dynamic nature of his daredevil activity. In fact, he seems more at home in the larger space.

Moving from the whole circus to individual acts, what are the criteria that makes one act better than another? Alla Youdina, formerly Creative Director New Circus Acts for Ringling and a product of the Soviet circus system, wrote a dissertation in the Soviet Union setting forth the idea that what distinguishes an artistic acrobatic act from a gymnastic demonstration is the use of imagery.[1] Her Spider Web act in the 126th Ariana edition of the Ringling show combined acrobatics and a number of aerial disciplines into a tale of a butterfly ensnared by spiders in their web. Another example of such imagery is the Russian aerial act The Cranes in which dead Soviet soldiers transform into birds.

Imagery is one way to achieve something that goes beyond skill and approaches artistry, but I am not sure it is the only way. A juggler like Kris Kremo is never more than a juggler, but he executes incredible feats with such elan and humor that his act becomes more than juggling—it is a transcendence of juggling. Molly Saudek on the low wire dances with such grace, abandon and joy, that her act is about going beyond expected limitations. Dancing on a wire! So there can be artistry in individual acts when they are done with such elegance that they are not about difficulties, but about going beyond difficulties. Here we are back to demonstrating the possibilities of human achievement. Is not that what characterizes tragedy? Not that it ends in death, but that it has shown the possibilities of life.

---

[1] Youdina. Phone interview, October 26, 2003.

A word must be said about the basic structural element of the modern circus –the 42 foot circus ring reputed to have been invented by English equestrian Phillip Astley in the eighteenth century as the smallest space in which a horse could gallop. The ring made possible circus buildings and touring circus performances. Early circuses were built around horse acts which brings us to the much debated question of the use of animals in circus. The most basic aesthetic principle is contrast and the contrast between humans and animals in size, shape and manner of movement as they work together is fascinating. Throughout history people and animals, working with mutual respect, have demonstrated what such a communion can achieve. We can only hope that the so-called "Animal Rights" activists do not destroy this essential component of circus.

Like theatre, circus has the immediacy of life being lived as the performance is being created. Film director Federico Fellini said to the circus director Raffaele De Ritis, "You are lucky, I am not. You direct circus. I direct movies. In movies, I lie. But in circus you tell the truth."[2] Or as Bello Nock said, "There are no take twos, no stunt doubles, no generated graphics. We show people how to stretch imaginations. There's magic here."[3] Circus is fun. Circus is fascinating. Enjoy it. Some critical understanding based on traditional aesthetic criteria can only make it more pleasurable.

Bibliography

Collins, Glenn. "Creating the Spirit of Carnivale in a Tent," *New York Times,* 28 October, 2003.

'Daredevils Game with Bello," *Akron Beacon Journal.* Reprinted on circuvern@aol.com, 23 October, 2003.

Youdina, Alla. Telephone interview, 26 October, 2003.

---

[2] Collins, "Creating the Spirit of Carnivale in a Tent," B4.
[3] "Daredevils Game with Bello," Circusvern@aol.com 23 October, 2003.

Chapter Twenty Two

Sacred Play:
A Seeker's Guide to the Circus

David Joseph Tetrault

The circus is a sacred celebration in which one can be brought close to something divine without ever realizing it. The circus is more than diversion; it is an opportunity to witness a wonderfully subversive public ritual that redefines what it means to be human, what it means to be in relationship with others, including animals, as well as with gravity, and to attend a huge spectacle in which there are only winners. There is no competition in the circus ring. The challenge is not defeating an opponent, but finding one's own perfection. We need only be available to be astonished. If we are too jaded to be surprised, we need to stay home. When we watch the circus, we see the action and also see others with the same sense of wonder that we have.

I have spent my life absorbed in the study of religion and spirituality. I was ordained as an Episcopal priest in 1973 and served in two of Virginia's premier parishes. Since 1994, I have been one of two chaplains who serve the three traveling units of Ringling Bros. and Barnum & Bailey. We are the ritual makers and listeners who visit the companies on the road and help hold the circus culture together.

When I retired early from Bruton Parish Church in Colonial Williamsburg, Virginia, I felt I had accomplished all I could in parish ministry. I wanted to seek faith, not religion, but I needed a transition so I auditioned for a keyboard position at the local Busch Gardens and worked there eight years. I had a wonderful time learning to be an entertainer. Gradually, my supervisors pushed me to become a strolling accordionist and leave the safety of the stage and the music stand. Our motto was: Any tune at any time in any key. I learned to relax and trust my own talent. I loved what I was doing and learned the sacredness of performance which I had not understood before. I like to talk about this with the older clowns and musicians. Staying present is all there is.

To leave the now is to miss the fun and the potential.

Circus people have immense intelligence, but it is not like mine. Their intelligence is in their ability to do things with their bodies. Bello Nock, *TIME* magazine's best clown in America, is one of the brightest people I ever met. He knows several languages and he's articulate, but his raw physical wisdom is what makes him so fascinating. He can do things with his body that bypass his emotional and intellectual systems. He is out there holding up a mirror to the audience as if to say, "The reason you can laugh at me is because you recognize what I'm doing within yourself." His work is precise, but always has an edge of spontaneity and freedom. It may look nearly the same each time, but for Bello, there is always something new.

The show moves. So must we. I learned that at the first circus I ever went to in 1946. Clyde Beatty-Cole Bros on the rail in Kankakee, Illinois. Dad wanted to go to this incredible thing I had never seen. I watched it unload from the train—all those amazing animals. We went to the show and I was overwhelmed by it. I wanted to go back the next day, but Dad said it was gone.

When I was doing my doctoral work, I was interested in parables—stories, myths and fables. What part of the human spirit do they reflect? I am also interested in the notion of play, something adults have largely forgotten how to do. The circus helps us remember how play looks and feels.

I guess it's tough to think about playing when we are all engaged in the struggle for meaning. We crave stability, something that takes our existence just the way it is, and affirms it. Often these moments come when we reach the place in life where we can no longer use language to describe our experience. Wisdom literature in many traditions points to these moments as opportunities for some greater insight. The daily reality that's going on all around and inside us invites us to raise questions and open spaces in our lives that we have never had to do before. It asks us to let go of the things that don't work anymore; to lighten our load so that play might be a possibility again in this very moment.

The circus is a model of what it means to fall forward into play and not backward into fearful holding on. For the length of the performance, we share a unique social ritual. The circus is where we view mystery in a way that we cannot in any other setting. Somebody like Bello is aware that he allows us to view an altered universe in which he is working/playing. We identify with what he's up to and are invited to see a dimension of human life in which we are bigger than we see ourselves.

At the circus we have an experience in real time in which real people do things that are overwhelming. I can sit through a show hundreds of times and still be astonished. There are times I go on the show when I am tired and I really don't want to be there, but I am and I give myself to it and let it expand my view of myself and the universe. I am reminded again that challenges, met with imagination and courage, are what life is all about.

Long before I ever imagined I would be sharing my life with the Greatest Show in Earth, I went to see the Clyde Beatty-Cole Bros Circus under the big top in Richmond, Virginia.   I hadn't been to a circus in years, but I watched it and felt I was at an incredible church service. Jimmy James, one of the industry's greatest ringmasters, presided like a priest.   There was so much happening he had to give us direction.   "Let all eyes be on". . . whatever it was. We identified with Jimmy who had the only speaking part in the show. He was part of the world of performance, but also part of our world.   He was a bridge to the magic.

The acts are mini-dramas. The parable of the wirewalker challenges the fear of the abyss. The wire walker moves from one point that is safe to another over the great "pit of Sheol" as the Bible says. It is the gaping, fearful hole we feel deep inside over a parent's serious illness or death; over a divorce; over the life of your child that can't figure out what life is about; over waiting for bad news from the oncologist. We know there is a safe place at the other end of this thin strand, but during times of trial all we can do is balance and dare not look down. It is the place of our worst fears where we truly believe we will be carried to extinction. But for the wirewalker, it is just another day in the air. Not only is it a place of passage, it is a place to show off and do tricks of increasing difficulty. There are brother acts that teach us how important it is to be with others over the pit, especially with people who can feel it with you. It is interesting to me that the first written book of the Bible is about Job, a man who suffers without cause or reason. It is a story of the highwire. When he calls his friends to him, they give him lectures and bad advice, rather than just stand with him as companions. It suggests to me that many of the pat institutional answers on all levels have ceased to work. What good is the free market economy if it has no conscience? Maybe there is another way to be with those over the pit

The juggler, always one of my favorites, is the complete example of the up-and-coming employee in Corporate America. The juggler has to stay poised and centered, and at the same time manipulate many more objects in the air than he has hands to manage them.   To make the thing even more exciting for the audience, instead of doing just, say, clubs or balls, he asks for odd objects. Let's toss in a running chain saw, and maybe a couple of live cats, and see where his limits really are. The juggler's story is that of the consummate multi-tasker. He knows that he has to let go all the time. He pushes against the forces of gravity that will bring the objects back to him, but he has to trust that. There is form and flow and rhythm to it all. The conventional juggling pattern, by the way, is the sideways "8"—the sign of infinity.

Animal acts amaze me. They are about living performers and the relationships among them. Each kind of animal act is unique because animals are as unique as humans. It takes a special ability to be with animals—a 24/7 job when you consider their care as well—and to realize they can be cherished friends and performers. But some of them can kill you because wild animals are wild animals. Nothing can change that. I have been told there is no greater backstage alarm at a circus than the words, "Bear loose!"

I did not understand the liberty act for years. What is so great about watching horses go in a circle? Then Ringling's Sacha Houcke took me aside and explained what happens out there. The ring, the symbolic circle of life, is one of the most sacred of universal symbols. There is motion and order and challenges to overcome in the ring. It begins in chaos and ends in order as horses find their place.   I have watched Sacha work. He is patient and loving and knows his horses' limits. He knows each animal's temperament and particular gifts. Horses are difficult. They don't work well, and a horse trainer knows that if he pushes too hard the animal will not do the behavior. The horses are rewarded for their work, not punished or forced to do things they are not inclined to do in the first place.

I remember watching the late Gunther Gebel-Williams train a horse with carrots. He was taking the horse through a trick. Gunther was only about five feet six and all his animals were huge. Gunther was hanging over the neck of a magnificent white horse. He was wearing great big, thick glasses, his cowboy boots, and carrying a whole bag of carrots to help get the very nervous horse through a trick. Gunther knew what the horse could do. I was maybe 15 feet away. There was no sound audible to me, but I could see Gunther's lips move. The horse did the trick and Gunther rewarded it with praise and carrots. I asked, "How did you do that?" He said, "I spoke French to it." "What difference does that make?" "Horses like to be spoken to in French. All the elephants speak German, did you know that?" So that's how it happens. For that moment, I watched a master in action.

When I came on the show, I did not expect Gunther to live up to his publicity, but he exceeded it. He had retired, but still lived on the show and took care of animals that his son Mark presented. In big markets like Madison Square Garden in New York, he did some performing.   I will never forget the sight of him emerging from the portal onto the front track of the show in his showiest wardrobe standing on the back of Conga, his favorite elephant. The crowd went wild. Gunther appeared huge, absolutely mythic in that moment, and alive and as grand as any human being can be. He worked that moment for all it was worth. Nobody realized that after the show was over and lights were down, he could barely walk because the pain in his hips was so bad. Too many difficult tricks done too many times.

There was no hint of that as he entered the great steel arena and began the hypnotic performance he did with tigers. He smiled, he danced, he cajoled, he encouraged. He played and his huge feline universe responded on cue. Never was there a moment where there wasn't astonishment and wonder. He had created a relationship with forces that could kill him in an instant, and it was a relationship of joy and play. One of my favorite moments was when he got all the cats in a row, stood on his toes, snapped his fingers and got them to roll over. It was the most useless thing in the world to watch. And I loved it.

My first memories of a cat act are of Clyde Beatty. I never liked fighting acts, but his was the most powerful and famous of them. He was the image of the great, white hunter who was in control at all times. He had whips and chairs and guns and a hunter's wardrobe. I remember the music as angry. The act was noisy, and Clyde was serious about his work. And the crowd loved it.

The two men did fundamentally the same thing, but told different stories about how to confront wild beasts. For Clyde Beatty there was no question; great forces are to be met with greater force because the only resolution was conquest. You had to take and keep control. Very similar to the current political climate of our time, and especially pertinent to a kid like me raised in a religious atmosphere that stressed rigorous standards of behavior. Gunther's version was different. Gunther never lost control because he was always in a deep trust relationship with the animals, almost as if he had become one of them. There was never domination, and always there was play.

Those who present animals, especially those with extraordinary skill, remind us that the world of relationships is all around us. The circus highlights the odd and nearly imaginary like Zusha the Hippo, the Living Unicorn of a few years ago, or the exotic bear and seal acts. But Johnny Peers' Muttville Comix is an example of great performing done with animals from shelters. How many kids have gone home to see if Fido or Fluffy might be encouraged to manage a trick? It is just a trick, but also a new insight into the profound connection between human and "beast" and, perhaps, the sacred energy that joins them..

I did not like flying acts at first. There was a literal meaning about what it is to depend on another being there at the right time. But then I stayed late a few evenings and watched the Vargas family working. The real act is all inside where nobody sees it. It is all centered in the lower abdomen where the great energy sources are in ancient systems of healing. The energy is what is at work and the performers—strong and coordinated—seem to be following something greater than themselves. I had read some Quantum Physics and String Theory. I realized that all this is open space like life itself. Everything we see appears to be closed, but it is not. It is all open. A flying act celebrates this interdependent web of life. They go back and forth, back and forth, guided by higher principles. It works because they pay attention to everything both inside and outside. Cirque de Soliel performers have pushed the boundaries as they explore what is possible when we put people in motion in an open space.

Many balancing acts fascinate me. The teeter board invites me to take on all I can because there is an innate desire that I have to balance more than I think I can. And remember, balance is NOT about standing still. Balance is dynamic. The Asian acts are especially good at this. I have seen tricks I was sure were gaffed or rigged, but later found that the performer simply believed he/she could do it. They celebrate motion, balance, beauty, speed, challenge. We love to talk these days about what it means to keep our life in balance in a world that seems to challenge even the possibility.

The contemporary circus clown is a shadow of what the clown once was in the circus. There are a handful of interesting ones who help relieve the audience tension and refocus the energy in the arena, but most function as fillers between acts. They make no cultural statement. The contemporary audience's relationship to the clown and humor is clouded with ambiguity. Most understand him as another corporate shill for hamburgers or some other treat. There are great clowns out there, but few are in the circus

I have seen many thrill acts. The seven Torres Brothers whirl around in the motorcycle globe. I have no idea why they don't crash into one another. But they don't—at least I have never seen it happen. There is the swaypole act that Bello's family may have originated. Then there is a human cannon ball and the strong man. These are serious challenges where the stakes are high if there's a loss of focus or a misstep along the way. Few people attempt them. They are about the uniqueness in each of us that is often left unlived. Culture beats it out of most of us, or we simply give up and follow the herd instead of our bliss.

"Crazy" Wilson Dominguez does something usually called the Wheel of Death. The wheel is two stationary open circles larger than the performer and just wide enough for him to walk inside and out. They are connected by a cross piece attached to a center axle that allows the rig to rotate. It looks like a figure eight. It is maybe 40 or 50 feet off the ground when one of the circles is at the apex of the rotation. Wilson goes to the top of this while it is spinning and does a terrifying forward somersault. Wilson is a warm, gentle, Latino with a great gift of balance and a wonderful way with an audience. "How do you do that? What's going on? Aren't you exhausted?" "I get tired, but I can't afford to get exhausted," he said to me. I asked, "What happens when you get to the top of the wheel and you're ready to do that trick? How do you make it happen?"

"Oh," he tells me. "I don't make anything happen." "Then how does it work?" "I get to the top and the trick is there. I just do it. If I get tense and try to do the trick, I'll fall. I know the trick is there. I can see it. So I just relax and the trick does me." I do not know how he can do it six times every weekend, but I know how many times I have failed to do something because I was forcing an act that was not ready to happen. I wasn't paying attention, relaxing, and waiting for the trick to come to me.

I am a musician so I am always interested in the band. I have sat through rehearsals without the band. All the visual excitement is there along with the clatter of equipment and performers shouting cues to one another. There is a lot of clinking stuff, props being dropped, and the working guys on the floor screaming at each other. The music not only covers all that necessary noise, it creates a marvelous environment where the beauty and wonder can happen and the stories can be told. What most of us don't realize is that the acts control the music. So when you see the elephant working, the elephant is setting the pace, and the band director is following the action.

"Spec," short for spectacle, is that great moment in the show when everything comes out on the great hippodrome track, and you see the most incredible collection of people, animals, and gaudy objects—all in harmony. Diverse races and nationalities are together in one place. The dwarf holds the hand of a beautiful woman from a far land who might be holding onto a giraffe. It is a spectacle because it is all working together and wonderful. When you think there could be no more, out come a dozen elephants and a burst of confetti to add even more motion to it all. So much wonder in such a small space. We are invited to fall forward into mystery, and realize that maybe the circus is showing us things about the web of existence that we can never get just by thinking it or reading about it. This is a living experience of something profound, and large, and perhaps even visionary. It's something about astonishment, and beauty, and wonder and is available nowhere else. It is the circus.

CONTRIBUTORS

Suzanne Rogers Brannan completed her Bachelor of Science Degree in Education at New Mexico State University (1977) where she was a Crimson Scholar. She obtained her Masters Degree in Education at the University of New Mexico (2000) specializing in Organizational Learning and Instructional Technologies. She recently retired as an elementary school teacher after some twenty years, having taught 3rd, 5th, and 6th grades as well as art, music, and band. On more than one occasion, her classes put on a circus program for an audience of parents, teachers, and students. She is the co-author of "Drawing Students and Parents In: Creativity and Community through the Magic of Circus," *Education* (Fall 1990).

An independent scholar, **David Carlyon** wrote *Dan Rice: The Most Famous Man You've Never Heard Of,* featured in the *New York Times* and on C-SPAN's *Booknotes.* He has published in *Theatre Symposium, New England Theatre Journal, Theatre Topics*, and *American Theatre*. After his Ph.D. from Northwestern, he was Assistant Professor at the University of Michigan-Flint. He had a play produced at Theatre Virginia, gives master classes in acting, and has consulted on stage movement, including Goodspeed Opera. Carlyon has been a forest fire fighter, military policeman, law school graduate (Boalt Hall-Berkeley), and Ringling Brothers and Barnum & Bailey Circus clown.

Lucelly Gallegos is a native of Chicago, Illinois. Both her parents are from Durango, Mexico. Although she makes her home in Sarasota, Florida, she has spent many summers in Mexico. In 2005, Lucelly received her Bachelor of Arts degree with a major in Art History from the University of Central Florida. Her future plans are to attend the Art Institute of Chicago.

Mort Gamble has worked in higher education fundraising and public relations for over 23 years. His career has included administrative positions at Hood College, West Virginia Wesleyan College, Fairmont State University in West Virginia, and Waynesburg College in Pennsylvania. At Fairmont, he was also the Executive Director of the Fairmont State Foundation, Inc. He holds undergraduate and graduate degrees from West Virginia University, completing his Doctorate in Higher Education Administration in 2003. He has been a circus enthusiast nearly all his life, and traveled with the all-student Circus Kirk in 1973 and 1974. He is married to the former Mary Elizabeth (M.E.) Yancosek of Washington, PA, whose field is economic development.

María de Jesus González completed her M.A. in art history at Bryn Mawr College in Pennsylvania in 1991. She received her doctoral degree from the University of Texas in Austin where she specialized in 20th century Latin American art. She has carried out research in Mexico and the Caribbean. Her publications include articles on the Mexican painter María Izquierdo, the Mexican photographer Mariana Yampolsky, Chicana artists Santa Barraza and Amalia Mesa-Bains, Puerto Rican artist Myrna Baez, and the Mexican collector Lydia Sada de Gonzalez, to name a few. She is currently conducting research for two books: *Latin American Women Painters Living and Working in Florida* and *Women Collectors and Patrons of Monterrey*.

Mary M. Griep received a B.A. with honors from Macalester College and an M.A.L.S. from Hamline University. Her work has been shown in exhibitions throughout this country and in Thailand, Finland and the Dominican Republic. She has been on the faculty of St. Olaf College since 1988 specializing in drawing and painting, and has taught courses in Women's Studies and Contemporary Art. She is currently Associate Professor of Art.

John Haddad is Assistant Professor of American Studies and Literature at Penn State, Harrisburg. He received his A.B. in English from Harvard College in 1991, his M.A. in English from Yale University in 1996, and his Ph.D. in American Studies from the University of Texas at Austin in 2002. He has taught at the University of Central Oklahoma, the University of Texas, and Nankai University in the People's Republic of China. It was during this latter experience that he first developed his interest in representations of China in U.S. culture, an interest that recently culminated in the publication of his e-book, *The Romance of China: Excursions to China in U.S. Culture, 1776-1876* (Columbia University Press, 2007).

After graduating from Ringling Bros. and Barnum & Bailey's Clown College, **Tim Holst** joined the Ringling Blue Unit as a clown in 1972. Since then he has served Ringling as Ringmaster, Assistant Performance Director and Performance Director. Now Vice President for Production and Talent, he tours the world in search of talent for the three Ringling units, and is involved in developing the new editions of the shows and maintaining their quality during their runs.

Rodney Huey earned a B.A. in Radio and Television (1969) and a M.A. in Journalism from the University of Alabama (1971); and a Ph.D. in Cultural Studies from George Mason University (2006). He served as Director of Public Relations for Feld Entertainment, Inc, from 1982-1986. He was named Director of Public Relations for the BHBC Group from 1987-1989; followed by a two-year stint at Read-Poland Associates, Inc. From 1992 through 2002, he returned to Feld Entertainment as Vice President, Public Relations; then was named Vice President for Communications for National Public Radio from 2003-2004. In 2005 he opened RAH PR STRATEGIES, a strategic communications consulting business in Falls Church, Virginia.

Jennifer Lemmer Posey is the Assistant Curator of the Circus Museum at the John and Mable Ringling Museum of Art. She received a B.A. in Art History from New College of Florida and an M.A. in Art History from Florida State University. She worked with Deborah Walk, Curator of the Circus Museum; Museum staff; and circus historian Howard Tibbals to create exhibitions about the history of the circus in America for the Circus Museum's new Tibbals Learning Center.

Jerrilyn McGregory is an Associate Professor of Folklore in the Department of English at Florida State University. She is the author of *Wiregrass Country,* a regional folklife study of the South. Besides this study, she has done fieldwork in Jamaica and the Bahamas. Her essays and criticism have appeared in a variety of books and journals, including *Southern Quarterly.* She has presented papers in America and Europe. She is currently working on publications related to African American folklore, African Diaspora Studies, and onomastics.

Michael H. Means has a Ph.D. in English from the University of Florida. At the University of Dayton, his research has, since about 1975, focused mostly on medieval English drama. Exploring the tensions in that drama between its ostensible purpose of inculcating doctrine, and the obvious delight it brought spectators, led to a search for analogous works. American circus specs circa 1890-1920 proved excitingly useful. Officially re-creating historical events or folk tales of Western civilization, specs "really" served to enlist cultural values in praise and validation of the circus performance.

Marcy W. Murray lives in Sarasota, Florida with her husband, Joe and their children, Christopher and Emerson. She became interested in the connection between circus and popular culture while working with such circus historians as Deborah Walk, Judge Dale and Evelyn Riker, and Jennifer Lemmer Posey at the Circus Museum in the Ringling Museum of Art complex. She credits Janet

Davis (author of *The Circus Age: Culture and Society Under the American Big Top*) and Dolly Jacobs (performer and co-owner of *Circus Sarasota*) with inspiring her to examine the beauty and strength that the circus and its audience demands.

Caroline Nobile is an Associate Professor of English in the Department of English and Theatre Arts at Edinboro University of Pennsylvania, where she has been teaching since 1990. She holds a Ph.D. in English from The Pennsylvania State University, University Park, PA, and an M.A. in English from North Carolina State University, Raleigh. Her specializations are British Literature and Creative Nonfiction Literature, but she also regularly teaches courses in women's literature, American fiction, and freshman composition and research.

Joseph W. Rogers received his Bachelors degree (1949) from San Diego State College, his Masters (1959) and Ph.D. (1965) from the University of Washington. He is an Emeritus Professor of Sociology at New Mexico State University where he taught a course on *The American Circus* in their Honors Program. He is the author of *Why Are You NOT a Criminal?* (1977), and the senior author of *Juvenile Delinquency and Juvenile Justice* (1989), as well as numerous articles in various professional journals. Four of his short monographs, written for the Circus Fans Association of America Education Committee, have been reprinted on the CFA's website.

Robert Sugarman is the author of *Circus for Everyone: Circus Learning Around the World,* about child and adult, amateur and professional circus training; and *Performing Shakespeare: A Way to Learn* about youth Shakespeare programs. He is President of the Vermont Tent of the Circus Fans Association, a member of the Circus Historical Society and a contributing editor of *Spectacle,* the circus arts quarterly. He is a playwright and co-owner, with his wife Sally, of Mountainside Press which specializes in Popular Culture and the Performing Arts.

Peta Tait is Professor of Theatre and Drama at La Trobe University, Australia, and publishes on bodies in circus performance, and on cultural languages of emotion. She has written books on gender and Australian performance, and she is a playwright. Her most recent books are: *Circus Bodies: Cultural Identity in Aerial Performance* (Routledge 2005); *Performing Emotions: Gender, Bodies, Spaces* (Ashgate 2002); and the edited volume, *Body Show/s: Australian Viewings of Live Performance* (Rodopi 2002).

Since 1996, **David Joseph Tetrault** has been one of the two official chaplains to Ringling Bros. and Barnum & Bailey which has three touring units whose home, for all practical purposes, is the road. The chaplains are trusted adults who serve as the community's ritual makers and listeners. Dr. Tetrault, ordained in 1973, is a retired Episcopal priest whose ministry was mainly in Williamsburg, VA, at historic Bruton Parish Church. He is a professional musician, writer and college teacher. He and his wife Ann, a pediatrician, have two grown daughters.

INDEX